Understanding the Life Course

This book is dedicated to the memory of my mother,
Hazel May Green (1923–2001) and to the memory of my friend,
Theo Weaver (1964–2008).

Understanding the Life Course

Sociological and Psychological Perspectives

Lorraine Green

polity

First published in 2010 by Polity Press

Reprinted 2011

Polity Press
65 Bridge Street
Cambridge CB2 1UR, UK

Polity Press
350 Main Street
Malden, MA 02148, USA

ISBN-13: 978-0-7456-4015-0
ISBN-13: 978-0-7456-4016-7(pb)

A catalogue record for this book is available from the British Library.

Typeset in 10.5 on 13 pt Swift
by Servis Filmsetting Ltd, Stockport, Cheshire
Printed and bound by MPG Books Group

For further information on Polity, visit our website: www.politybooks.com

Contents

Acknowledgments

I would like to express my thanks to a number of people whose encouragement, support and contributions both directly and indirectly not only led to the fruition of this book but also enhanced its overall quality. I would like to acknowedge my father, who although never undergoing a university education, passed on to me his voracious thirst for knowledge of all kinds. I would like to thank my very first Social Policy lecturers from Cardiff University in the early 1980s, Maria Brenton and John Lambert, for teaching me the importance of social justice, and my MA Social Work lecturer in the mid 1980s from Birmingham University, Ann Davis, who further extended my belief in its importance. The knowledge and associated support of my Ph.D. supervisors, Wendy Parkin and Colin Robson from Huddersfield University, in the mid-1990s, and the professor I currently work with, Alys Young, also indirectly contributed to the ideas and understandings in this book. My colleague and academic counterpart at Manchester University, John Hopton, has also been a brilliant team player and a supportive colleague in all respects and deserves acknowledgment and thanks.

More directly, I would like to thank the editors I worked with at Polity, Jonathan Skerrett and Emma Longstaff, who not only encouraged me to write this book but have additionally been patient and supportive throughout. Leigh Mueller, the copy editor who works for Polity, also deserves a mention for her excellent work. The comments made by the anonymous reviewers were, furthermore, both constructive and incisive. My gratitude is also extended to Val Aspin and Sue Ferris who had no prior social science knowledge but voluntarily acted as intelligent lay readers for the book. Some of the BA and MA Social Work students at Manchester University read and commented on earlier versions of selected chapters, and Serena Bufton, Nigel Parton and Sue White were also kind enough to read and subsequently act as endorsers for this book.

Introduction

This is a book about people's lifelong experiences from birth to death and how they change, adapt, develop and decline throughout life, although not necessarily in a linear, predictable or progressive manner. Influences on our subsequent life courses include biology, geography and the environment, psychological processes, the socio-historical context, and the national and international political and economic climate. This book is primarily concerned with how sociology and psychology perceive, research and theorize the life course. Understanding these disciplines enables students to think outside of their own parochial experiences, dispelling common misperceptions around people's behaviour and our society. These misperceptions include the belief that biology and chronological ageing have an overwhelming influence on what we become and how we live our lives, or alternatively that problems or achievements certain groups of people experience disproportionately, are due more to their inherent individual failings or merits than to societal influences. These can result in the adoption of inaccurate stereotypes, many of which centre on age categories/features (sometimes cross cut by discriminatory race/ethnicity, gender or class assumptions). These include the pervading images of the innocent child; the delinquent youth; the virulent, predatory young black man; the unattractive middle-aged spinster; and the infirm, confused older person.

Within everyday conversations, subjective comments about people are frequently expressed as fact. These might include the belief women are 'naturally' less technological than men, or more emotional, or that black people are lazy or less intelligent than whites, or even that criminals or drug addicts were born bad or are evil. These are uncritical resorts to (i) biology and (ii) individual/group pathologization. It is therefore important to look at what evidence corroborates or rejects these 'common sense' assumptions, what counts as valid evidence and what ideas underlay such assumptions.

Many facets of individuals are the culmination of multiple influences, rendering it difficult to ascertain, for example, to what extent one's intelligence (in itself a problematic concept) is linked to genes or the environment, or represents an interaction between the two. Complex intersections between the wider structures of society (structure) and the individual's autonomous behaviour (broadly equating to *agency* in sociology and *planful competence* in psychology), and between nature (biology/genetics) and nurture (society/environment/culture), are important. It is, however, difficult to quantitatively assess their respective contributions.

This book focuses on the United Kingdom (UK), but also has relevance to a Westernized Euro-American or Australasian audience, despite political, social, educational and economic differences between countries – some significant, others relatively unimportant. Although UK research is preferentially drawn upon in this book, where little research is available on a particular aspect or where the key texts are not British, research from similar Western countries substitutes or is used in addition to British literature. Many comparative examples are also drawn on purposively. These emanate from different historical time periods, cultures and countries. They demonstrate how diverse people's life courses can be across geography, history and culture, detracting from isolated biological or national understandings. Issues of social class, sex and gender, disability, sexual orientation and race/ethnicity will also be analysed in terms of their impact on people's lives. These differences are often socially exaggerated or distorted and used to create or reinforce significant inequalities. These inequalities may be unseen, unacknowledged, actively denied or even defended (as in the previous examples). Assumed individual weaknesses and strengths and biological explanations are consequently drawn upon as a way of ignoring or supporting injustices that appear to have strong social causes.

The term 'life course' is considered by most sociologists and many life course behavioural and social science academics to be more flexible than other prevalent terms often used by psychologists and biologists. These include 'life span development' and 'the life cycle'. Life course is the preferred term here because there are not always clear, linear, chronological trajectories through one's life which replicate themselves with each generation. 'Life courses' may even be a more appropriate term than 'the life course' in our modern societies, where we 'appear' faced with endless choices about our identities and lifestyles. In post-industrial societies, people from similar backgrounds, sometimes born only a few years apart, can experience fundamentally different lives due to rapidly changing social, economic or political situations which have a lifelong impact. In small tribal societies one's life and identity are already largely ascribed and mapped out, changing little with the generations unless disrupted by Western interference.

Why combine sociology and psychology?

Many books deal with the entire life course from a single disciplinary angle, such as sociology (e.g. S. Hunt, 2005) or life span psychology (Bee, 1994; Hendry and Kloep, 2002; K. Berger, 2005; Santrock, 2009). Alternatively, particular stages of the life course, such as childhood or old age, are analysed from a single disciplinary or multi-disciplinary perspective. Other literature approaches the life course according to a particular aspect, such as disability (Priestly, 2003) or identity (Hockey and James, 2003). Some recent texts deal with human development either from a particular vocational or a combined multi-vocational angle (e.g. C. Beckett, 2002; Crawford and Walker, 2007; Sudberry, 2009). However, because these are often short books, contain many practice exemplars and frequently are more attuned to psychology than sociology, they understandably offer a less theoretical, in-depth and life course orientated viewpoint than this text. No UK books currently available, with this exception, address the entire life course, combining both sociological and psychological perspectives in a comprehensive and theoretical but, nevertheless, accessible manner.

Although this book draws from many disciplines, including demography, anthropology, social policy, biology, history, law and politics, the two primary disciplines are sociology and psychology. This is because they are most useful for understanding human behaviour across the life course with specific reference to the UK and the intended readership of the book. Biological perspectives are important, but need to be located within their relationship to particular societies and not deployed deterministically or in a reductionist manner. Similarly, anthropological or historical perspectives are useful, particularly in a comparative sense, as they help to dispel notions of the 'universally natural' or 'unnatural' in relation to behaviour and customs across different societies. That said, these disciplines are not key explicators of contemporary UK life courses, in the way that psychology and sociology are.

Who this book is for and why it will be useful

This book was written principally for undergraduate and postgraduate students on vocational qualifying programmes, such as students in social and community work, occupational therapy, nursing, medicine, counselling and teaching/education. It offers students access to detailed core sociological and psychological theory and research relating to the life course. This knowledge will act as a foundation from which to understand and relate to people and can positively influence professional decisions and form an underpinning for practice. Although not all students will work with people of all ages or emanating from many different societies, some will. Others may work with one specific group, such as primary school teachers working with young children, or nurses working with older people. However, one rarely works with a certain group or age category in isolation. Understanding kinship ties with family and friends, and how their issues and life stage impact upon their relationships with the children, are important for primary school teachers. Similarly, understanding the significance of historical and social events such as wars and rapid technological advances for older people, as well as assessing the impact of how society treats older people (as wise and useful citizens or as weak and a drain on resources?), are imperative. Many older people previously had to pay for medical care before the NHS and an understanding of the impact this had on poor families would be useful for health professionals, whose elderly patients are reluctant to consult them until any medical condition has deteriorated substantially.

This book will be particularly useful to vocational degree students because, although they have less time than pure single honours degree students to study a particular theoretical area or pure discipline in depth, they will often work in and across multi-professional teams or organizations. Therefore understanding trans-disciplinary social science perspectives will be a distinct advantage. The degree benchmarks for some professional degrees, such as social work, furthermore, require students to acquire an ecological and eclectic understanding of human behaviour. This book is also suitable for students undertaking applied or mixed social science degrees, which include sociology and psychology, highlighting similarities, differences, complementarity and contestations in how these disciplines perceive and theorize life trajectories, stages or transitions. It can be read chronologically through successive chapters but can also be used as an occasional resource or reference text since chapters can also be understood standing alone.

This book examines childhood, adolescence, early adulthood, etc., as chronological age/stage markers whilst simultaneously scrutinizing and problematizing them as such, critically analysing common sense assumptions and stereotypes. So, although the chapters are structured fairly traditionally for ease of reading and reference, no

assumptions are made about the inevitability, accuracy or meanings of any of these age categories. They indicate some chronological
similarities but also increasingly marked differences and shifts, and
historical changes are often evident. Some categories are also relatively new. Adolescence only emerged in the mid twentieth century
and, with growing longevity, old age is now often subdivided into a
perceived third age of good health and comfort and a more dependent
and less healthy fourth age. The book also aims to be strong on empirical examples, constantly interlinking theoretical conceptualizations
with research findings and evidence. Interesting examples and pertinent statistics or quotations, furthermore, are used to support or
extend arguments.

Summary of the chapters: brief contents

Chapter 1

The first chapter will introduce students to the different theoretical
concepts surrounding the life course, stressing linearity and multi-
directionality as well as continuity and discontinuity. The importance
of adopting a multi-disciplinary perspective and understanding the
often indivisible interplay between nature and nurture or genetics
and culture throughout the life course will also be covered. As part
of presenting an integrated perspective, it will be necessary to define
and discuss the different elements and methods of key disciplines
such as sociology and psychology, their subdivisions of life span psychology and life course sociology and in what ways they diverge or
possess common viewpoints. The importance of critically examining
lay viewpoints will be stressed and it will be shown why they are so
problematic and need to be questioned and frequently rejected.

Chapter 2

Chapter 2 illustrates how infancy and childhood are perceived and theorized through the lens of developmental psychology, which explains
how children progressively develop physically, cognitively and psychosocially. Pioneering theorists such as Erikson, Freud, Bowlby and
Piaget are introduced and key research studies are explained to show
how some of their theories originated, alongside an analysis of their
contemporary validity and relevance. Traditional developmental psychology sees growth as an inherently linear, maturational process
and reaching certain psychological or physical milestones or stages,
at definite predefined ages, as indicative of normal development. The

inability to attain those markers at the required time is often seen as indicating abnormal development. Although more recent developmental psychology takes the social context into account, it pays far less attention to this and structural factors than sociology does.

Chapter 3

Chapter 3 both critiques and represents a challenge to traditional developmental child psychology and traditional sociology approaches, drawing on literature from the new critical developmentalists and the 'new sociology of childhood' theorists. Developmental psychology is initially criticized for its apolitical conservative stance; its representation of the child as a 'naturally' developing being, relatively unaffected by external influences; its overemphasis on measurement; its biological determinism; its relative ignorance of cross-cultural differences and its view of the child as unequivocally deficient. The 'new social studies of childhood' conversely illuminates the multiple cultural and historical constructions of children and childhood and shows how children today are far more competent and able to be autonomous than we frequently allow them to be or give them credit for. The new sociology of childhood confirms childhood is a subordinated social status where protectionist, paternalist decisions are frequently made on behalf of children, who are rarely asked their opinions or seriously involved in important decisions about their lives. It also highlights the ways in which children are often both exploited and overprotected today and how social divisions like gender and social class profoundly affect how they are treated and their subsequent life course trajectories.

Chapter 4

Chapter 4 examines the early teenage years from the beginning of puberty to early adulthood. Psychologists use the term 'adolescence', whilst sociologists disproportionately refer to the term 'youth' in preference, although youth refers to a more extended period. Early psychological developmental theory placed great emphasis on biological changes and assumed these caused emotional changes during puberty, although contemporary psychologists are much more cautious about forging causal links. Physical and intellectual development as well as identity, personality and independence are additionally important issues for psychologists of adolescence and therefore will be examined. Sociological themes pertinent to youth covered here include the longitudinal demonization of young people and associated 'unnecessary' moral panics; changes in youth unemployment and higher education; young people's changing values and political beliefs; their consumption-driven behaviour; the impact of new technology and how social inequalities such as those related to social class, race/ethnicity and gender impact on all of these issues.

Chapter 5

This chapter examines young adulthood, extending from about 18 up to 40 years. Psychology concentrates here on physical, cognitive, moral and psychosocial changes and development. Psychological claims of a new developmental period, 'emergent adulthood', are evaluated from both psychological and sociological vantage points. The key socio-logical topics analysed are the transitions into and markers associated with contemporary adult status; the role work plays for young adults and their dissonant expectations and subsequent experience of work; the importance and function of leisure, sport and new technology and how family, friendship and relationship structures and practices have fundamentally changed. These have become more heterogene-ous and flexible due to significant technological, attitudinal, legal and social changes. How social inequalities and divisions impact on all of these is also examined and analysed.

Chapter 6

In this chapter middle adulthood is examined, despite its relative contemporary and historical neglect by both disciplines. Physical, cognitive and psychosocial changes are scrutinized with an empha-sis on whether or not concepts once popular in psychology, such as the 'empty nest syndrome' or 'the midlife crisis', are universally applicable experiences. Assumptions about inevitable physical and intellectual decline are investigated and found to be deficient and overly simplistic. There is moderate physical senescence in middle age, alongside some intellectual decline, although it does not have a significant impact and gains can still be made in some cogni-tive areas. In the section on sociology, ageing, self-perception and body image during midlife are revealed as very important, particu-larly for women. The significance of and various changes in leisure pursuits and physical activity are analysed as are various lifestyle changes relating to travel, food and eating. Negative and positive media representations of middle-aged people, depicting them both as an inspiration and as selfish and an impending drain on societal resources, are examined. The demands and stress work places on mid-lifers, who often have other onerous caring family responsibilities, are also analysed, with both gender and social class being shown to be important mediators. The impact of the new reproductive technology and attitudes towards it are evaluated with respect to later motherhood, as are different kinship and living arrangements, such as gay and lesbian relationships, long-distance partnerships and single person households.

Chapter 7

In this chapter the concept of old age, potentially the longest life stage, extending from 60 years to a possible 120 years, the known upper limits of our life span, is analysed. Old age is, however, a movable feast and seems more associated with institutional markers such as compulsory retirement and pension ages than any objective or strictly chronological factors. In other societies old age may not be judged by chronological age but by family hierarchy or ranking, or characteristics such as vitality or wisdom. In the section on psychology, various explanatory theories of ageing are examined alongside physical, cognitive and psychosocial changes. The societal negativity surrounding old age and previous assumptions about dramatic physical and mental decline are evaluated and found to be greatly overstated. Psychological studies confirm older people have greater compensatory and adaptive facilities than previously thought, most being very independent. Within sociology, a key theme is that of ageism which can pertain to any age but has been particularly detrimental to how older people are represented and treated. Various theories drawn on to explain the negative treatment of the elderly such as 'structured dependency theory' and 'the civilizing process' are also evaluated. How one's specific cohort, generation and associated prior life experiences impact on how one experiences old age is also reviewed, as is the impact of social inequalities which have a cumulative affect throughout life. These can confer either significant advantage or disadvantage in terms of health and longevity, income, housing and lifestyle. Depictions of older people as a demographic time bomb in terms of extensive future care needs are also critically evaluated.

Chapter 8

This chapter is devoted to grief and loss and death and dying. Traditional psychology mostly develops individualistic theories to explain the emotional stages people go through when they know they are dying or when they have been bereaved. However, newer psychological theories appear less dogmatic and less stage orientated.

They are more cautious about labelling different forms of grieving as pathological or problematic and are more aware of the social context than earlier psychologists, but are still not sufficiently attentive to its impact. Sociologists tend to pay little attention to individuals' emotional states and feelings, being more concerned with the different social contexts death and dying take place within and how these impact upon our attitudes and how we confront and respond to death. Sociologists show how the progressive medicalization and bureaucratization of death in modern societies have led to us having less acquaintance with it. We therefore have become increasingly fearful about how to respond when we are dying or someone close to us dies or is diagnosed with a terminal illness. Sociologists also illustrate how social inequalities affect significantly how and when we will die and what we will die from, following the cumulative advantage or disadvantage argument previously presented. Despite this, sociologists rarely engage with the significant emotions death and dying engender both in us as individuals and in societal responses.

This introductory section has therefore explained why possessing a multi-disciplinary understanding of the life course is important for students on many vocational degree courses and for those studying mixed social science degrees, illustrating how a deficit of such knowledge can leave students resorting to inaccurate, culturally or historically specific and discriminatory lay and anecdotal viewpoints. It has also summarized the contents of the individual chapters and justified why a chronological perspective of the life course, albeit a critical one, is being utilized in this particular text. The following chapter lays the conceptual and theoretical foundations for the subsequent chapters. It explains key aspects of psychology and sociology and their specific orientations to the life course, clarifies key terminology and finally analyses the current state of play in relation to interdisciplinary life course research.

CHAPTER
01

Understanding the Life Course

Introduction

This chapter will introduce you to the concept of the life course and to the disciplines of sociology and psychology through which the life course will principally be investigated. Initially key changes in UK society impacting on people's lives since the early 1970s will be outlined and summarized, many being discussed further in later chapters. Following this, there will be a consideration of why reality television and lay theories of human behaviour are flawed. The key tenets of psychology and sociology will then be explained, and their relationship to life span psychology, sociology of the life course and general social science research methods will be clarified, with key terms delineated and explained. Finally, the current state of the field of life course studies in relation to multi-disciplinarity and its future potential will be explored, alongside some classic illustrative examples of life course research.

You may find this chapter dense and theoretical in places, in comparison with the other chapters which may appear easier to navigate and understand. This is because this chapter offers a grounding or underpinning for the following chapters and does not presuppose readers have any prior knowledge of social science. The other chapters can be read without this one but understanding this chapter will enrich and deepen the reader's experience of the rest of the book. It is also a chapter that can be continually revisited to verify meanings and terms used throughout the text.

Changes affecting the contemporary life course in the UK

Changes in Work, the Family, Lifestyle and Education

Any understanding of the life course, as well as being embedded within historical and cultural influences, needs to take into account societal, technological and political changes. Irwin (2005) cautions that life course analysis frequently fails to engage sufficiently with the enormity of change in most domains of social life in the late twentieth century. These changes include the re-organization of the family (and living arrangements) and expected roles and practices, with particular reference to gender; and the demise of class-based solidarities, whereby families and communities inter-generationally were traditionally allied to political parties and key institutions associated with them, but no longer are, and the associated rise of individualization as opposed to collectivization. This occurs when individuals are more concerned about themselves and their small kinship or friendship groups than the whole society's wellbeing and feel, often wrongly, that a multitude of life choices are open to them and that age-related life stages are increasingly less relevant.

Rapid technological change is also important (S. Hunt, 2005) and has many social repercussions. Today's young adults have grown up with computers, the internet and mobile phones. People in their forties upwards, many of whom did not personally encounter computers until their twenties or thirties, will be much less au fait with some aspects of the 'new' technology. The recent UK television series *Life on Mars* and its sequel *Ashes to Ashes* provide an excellent fictional illustration. A detective is 'apparently' involuntarily transported from contemporary society back to the 1970s. He finds 1970s society completely alien and he is frustrated and initially immobilized by the lack of technological resources at his disposal, no longer being able to use mobile phones, the internet and DNA markers as key work or lifestyle tools.

A transition has also occurred from being a factory-based producing, industrial society to a service-orientated, consumerist society. This, alongside various financial crises, heralded initially by the 1973 OPEC oil crisis, has impacted on the availability of employment and the types of work now obtainable and our lifestyles and attitudes towards purchasing goods. Many jobs today are part-time and temporary, offering comparatively less security, lower pay and poorer conditions than prior to the 1980s – a process known as *casualization* of the labour force. Furthermore, in the UK we have the longest working hours of any country in Europe.

Klein (2000) documents the transition in the late twentieth century from generic goods to branded designer goods, whereby shopping becomes a source of meaning and desire – hence the colloquial term 'retail therapy'. Many people affiliate to and derive their self-perceived status from possession of the newest offerings from these brands (for example, 'having to have' the latest PlayStation console, Apple iPhone or Nike trainers). The rise of consumerism, clearly evident since the

1970s (Garnett, 2007), and associated designer labels also places pressures on poorer families to compare themselves to others, aspiring to ever more expensive goods and services. When poorer families are comparatively worse off than sectors of society they compare themselves to, precluding them from buying items and partaking in activities which would be considered normal for their group, this is known as 'relative poverty'. In some other countries income may be far lower, but because people compare themselves favourably to others in similar situations, they may experience fewer negative psychological symptoms.

Although few in the UK die today of 'absolute poverty' in terms of starvation or lack of shelter, some old people still die of hypothermia nearly every winter because they cannot afford heating and some communities are dispossessed and alienated, ravaged by poverty, crime and violence. Education has also changed and, despite political rhetoric surrounding lifelong education, this has never been incentivized and older people do not have access to higher education loans. The demise of means-tested 'liveable' grants may also have deterred many potential working-class and mature students from going to university. Nevertheless, more and more young adults are encouraged to enter higher education or, alternatively, to engage with post-18 vocational training.

Demographic Changes

Life expectancy has increased phenomenally as the birth rate has (until recently) steadily declined, leading to families becoming smaller and a rapidly ageing 'greying' population, in which older people are living longer and growing proportionally larger compared to other ages in the population. This links with many other changes, such as the death of a parent in middle age now becoming a life course marker. Life expectancy rose because of vastly improved environmental conditions and diet, alongside major advances in medical knowledge and technology. The birth rate initially declined for a number of reasons. The advent of successful contraception, such as 'the Pill' in the 1950s, the increasing social and economic independence of women alongside sex equality laws, long working hours and the steady decrease in full-time housewives have all contributed. However, both birth rates and life expectancy vary according to age, gender, race and ethnicity, disability and social class and interactions between these. One reason for recent increases in the birth rate is immigration, alongside, more marginally, many women bearing children at much later ages than previously. The number of people living in Britain in 2009 exceeded 61 million. There were 408,000 more people living in Britain in 2008 than in 2007, the biggest increase in the population in one year since 1962. In 2008, Britain's birth rate was also at its highest for fifteen years, with 19,000 extra births in that one year, compared to the previous year (Savage, 2009). Although 24 per cent of all births in 2008 were to women born outside the UK, 56 per cent of the additional 19,000 births in 2008 were to those immigrant females, with the largest number emanating from Pakistan, closely followed by Poland (Savage, 2009; Bosely and Saner, 2009). Interestingly, both countries are very pro-family and patriarchal. In Poland, Catholicism is the dominant religion and forbids contraception, although it is not illegal. In Pakistan, 97 per cent of the population are Muslim and, although Islam's teachings mostly permit contraception, there is significant resistance.

Globalization

Globalization is a contested, complex concept but challenges the view that nation states such as England and France are self-enclosed, self-governing territories with 'native' citizens and clear national behaviour and cultural attributes. It puts forward the viewpoint that the globe is becoming more interconnected as people increase their knowledge of other parts of the world and have greater access to and communication with them. National boundaries, practices and identities are therefore becoming weaker and loosening. *Economic globalization* is related to the expansion of capitalism through international trade and economic imperialism forged by multinational corporations. *Political globalization* focuses on transnational governance, for example the United Nations or the European Union. *Cultural globalization* describes the interconnectivity between the global and the local in terms of social practices and customs.

The 'global village' metaphor referring to the whole world becoming smaller (Robertson, 1992) holds true in relation to the potential that new technology, including computers, telecommunications and air travel, holds for instant/rapid communication and fast access to previously difficult-to-reach places of the globe (Urry, 2000). However, some people have more opportunities and access than others. A girl in India who puts together computer components for a Western company may have a negligible chance of being able to purchase or even use a computer and even less possibility of ever being able to travel outside her country. Some theorists consequently see globalization as entrenched Western imperialism of the globe, whilst others view the whole process as being 'up for grabs' once it has been set in motion, and Western countries are increasingly concerned about the potential power of nations like China (Jordan, 2006).

Temporary and permanent immigration in the UK have increased, particularly with the influx of new countries into the European Community and unrestricted movement within it. This augments previous immigration from the New and Old Commonwealth countries, significant from the 1940s onwards. Alongside recent emigration from the UK and refugees and asylum seekers, these changes suggest the UK is now a country of many different ethnicities and 'colours'. The number of mixed-heritage people, furthermore, tripled since the turn of the century (Song, 2007). According to the 2001 census, 1.2 per cent of the population self-identified as being of mixed heritage (many being under the age of 16), rendering it the UK's biggest ethnic minority group.

A key feature of globalization is hybridity, in which different cultural tastes, pastimes and goods are fused. The term 'Asian fusion cuisine' is now becoming mainstream in the UK. Curry has replaced the traditional Sunday roast as the favourite meal and is a strong competitor with the traditional fish and chip takeaway. Musical styles such as rock and Asian music – Bhangra – and Celtic and African music are mixed to create their own distinct forms. Globalization may therefore result in very different mosaics of people living together in the same urban agglomerations, with some having very little understanding of each other or mutual interaction. Using an example to relate this to age and the life course, an elderly white, outgoing British female may never meet her neighbour, a first-generation elderly Asian female immigrant. Her neighbour perhaps never worked outside the home or learnt English fluently and, since the death of her husband, is lonely and isolated as her children live elsewhere and she fears travelling much farther than the corner shop. In contrast, another second- or third-generation West Indian teenager may embrace some characteristics associated with her West Indian heritage and other characteristics associated with mainstream British behaviour and pastimes.

Unreality TV, people's perceptions of human 'nature' and lay theorizing

Unreality TV

Until around the turn of the century in 1999–2000, few media programmes dealt with understanding 'real' people's actions, motivations and lives. We, or at least the TV and radio channels, seemed to think it was more important to understand the minutiae of plant or animal life or interior design than to understand ourselves. Now an endless amorphous, cheap-to-produce mass of reality TV is appearing. This appears to 'aim' to help people to control their 'difficult' children (*SuperNanny*), 'unruly' teenagers (*Boot Camp*) and 'antisocial' dogs (*It's Me or the Dog, The Dog Whisperer*); to understand why and how they relate to their relatives (*Wife Swap*); to attract a partner through grooming them both in behaviour and dress sense (*Trinny and Susannah*); to eat properly (*You Are What You Eat*); or to keep their apparently health-endangering abodes sanitary (*How Clean Is Your House?*).

What distinguishes all these programmes from genuine social science and the natural sciences is that they are made solely for entertainment value. They are featuring people who will inevitably be behaving unusually and probably differently from how they might customarily behave in their everyday lives, and who will not be representative of the 'ordinary' person because they have selectively volunteered, have been chosen for their interest value and know they are being filmed. Can you, for example, imagine collecting your faeces and giving them to an expert who will evaluate your bowel health in front of millions of viewers in any real-life situation (*You Are What You Eat*)? Similarly, when/if you clean your kitchen, do you routinely place dirt under a microscope to examine bacteria (*How Clean Is Your House?*)? If you view confessional chat shows, such as those hosted by Jeremy Kyle and Jerry Springer, would you volunteer to go on if you had a personal issue? Most probably you would not, but these programmes still attract prurient and voyeuristic curiosity in their many viewers, arguably through exploiting those already marginalized and disadvantaged. Some viewers potentially may also take the messages they convey seriously or believe they are helpful in understanding human beings and their life courses.

These programmes frequently draw on simplistic and repeated formulae, often based on behavioural (reward and punishment) psychology and modelling (copying). They therefore tend to focus on the individual and individual change in a superficial manner. For example, in both *Wife Swap* and *Supernanny*, some men leave all housework and childrearing to their wives. Although the programmes may encourage them as individuals to change their behaviour, if it is adversely affecting the family, how society encourages both males and females to behave very differently, but 'naturally', is never considered. The founding modern reality TV programme, *Big Brother*, features an analysis of group interaction and individuals' personalities and motivations by psychologists. However, the individuals in *Big Brother* are distinguished more by their immense vanity and exhibitionism than any randomly selected group might be. They are also placed in a very artificial short-term environment, where only certain aspects of their behaviour are screened and analysed, again dependent upon their evaluated entertainment value. If we shift attention momentarily from social to natural science and take Ben Goldacre's justified and humorous criticisms of the self-styled nutritionist and entrepreneur, Gillian McKeith, who researched and authoritatively presented *You Are What You Eat*, we discover not only that she purchased her 'fake' Ph.D. off the internet, but also that many of the scientific claims she propounds in her programmes and books are quite simply wrong and 'bad science'.

Therefore, although we might think we are learning a lot about people or science from these 'reality TV' programmes, we should be guarded about taking them too seriously, as we should also be when reading isolated journalistic accounts of particular groups of people. In relation to age-based assumptions and stereotyping, unless we look to talent shows such as *The X Factor* and *Pop Idol*, it is notable that most reality TV shows featuring older children and teenagers represent them as problematic and troublesome, reinforcing prejudiced beliefs – which will be critiqued later – based on or influenced by the repeated and historically enduring demonization of young people in media and public representations.

Lay Theories and Human 'Nature'

This book should help you to understand people throughout the life course and relieve you of any belief that these TV programmes approximate reality or are scientific. Sociology is concerned with the impact society and its institutions have on our behaviour and understandings, with particular reference to power structures and relationships between individuals, groups and the wider society. Psychology is more concerned with the individual per se: their physical, cognitive, moral, social and personality development; individual differences and how people learn and become motivated – although social psychology focuses more on group processes. Sociology and psychology are academic disciplines which take human behaviour seriously, studying it rigorously through scientific research techniques, although much ongoing debate about what constitutes valid science, useful research or transferable knowledge exists within both disciplines.

The general public place great faith in numbers and statistics, but they are mostly unaware that these can be manipulated or that the studies they are based on may have been conducted incompetently, or the results deliberately or inadvertently misinterpreted. Similarly, what may be regarded as fact and the truth for hundreds of years may be revised or discredited at any time, so no theory or results from a research study can ever be shown to be unequivocally and timelessly the eternal truth (Magee, 1973). Nonetheless, a theory becomes more credible and stronger the older it is and the more researchers have tested it in different areas and repeatedly confirmed it. The general public also tend to associate research methods with either natural science laboratory experiments or questionnaire surveys. Most are unaware that many different, often competing, research methods, designs and frameworks of understanding reality exist or they dismiss them without understanding them.

There are key differences between lay and good social science theories, and whilst some lay theories may be correct (even if the reasoning behind them may be flawed), many others are counter-intuitive (Furnham, 1989). Perhaps because people tend to think they are experts on human 'nature', they consequently draw on simple 'common sense' explanations and their own parochial experience of reality to explain complex and multi-faceted phenomena. The main problem with lay theories is therefore that they are often derived from people's small pool of personal experience or hearsay; contain unacknowledged assumptions or contradictory premises people are either unaware of or do not see as problematic; frequently confuse cause and association and cause and effect; rarely look for disconfirming examples and are often resistant to modification in the light of changing evidence (Furnham, 1989).

If we take masculinity and femininity as examples, these comprise of certain behavioural or personality characteristics people often associate unequivocally with being male or female. Most social scientists today (with the exception of some evolutionary psychologists) would accept, on the basis of many years of research and theory that gender is a socially constructed phenomenon. Many lay people, however, often assume gender is a biological, sex-based inevitability. For example someone could put forward the theory men are 'naturally' better managers because they are more in control of their emotions than women. It may later be asserted by the same person that rape or male violence should be condoned because men are 'naturally' 'sexu-ally incontinent' or are aggressive, without the lay person discerning the contradiction inherent in the two statements. If pressed further, behaviour may be attributed to biology, with lay people talking vaguely about hormones or evolution but being unable to offer any deeper analysis.

In contrast, social science theory and research will be well specified and will follow logical principles and procedures. Social scientists therefore will not assume, if two events seem related to one another, or occur together, or one follows the other (sometimes known as *correlation* or *association*), that one necessarily causes the other (*causation*). For example, if I start taking a particular medication and begin feeling tired, I may assume it is the side effect of the medica-tion, which it could be, but it may equally be something very different such as an emerging underactive thyroid problem. Lay theories also almost always resort to the individual or their biology, and rarely are social factors considered. People most often object to sociological or social science findings because they claim they state the obvious (Giddens, 1987). They therefore need not be rigorously researched, many claim, as 'common sense' offers a cheaper and quicker alternative. Conversely, if findings run counter to common sense, the general public often reject and ridicule them ('of course that can't be the case because everybody knows otherwise, or that wasn't my or my Aunty Nelly's experience, so of course it's wrong . . .'). This is particularly the case if research findings challenge widely held, emotionally important beliefs of individuals or problematize political agendas. One notable example is the recent dismissal in 2009 by the government of one of their key scientific advisors on illicit drugs, Professor David Nutt, for suggesting government policy ran counter to the scientific evidence on the effects of drugs. Although, admittedly, far less conclusive evidence exists on illicit drugs, compared to legal drugs such as tobacco and alcohol, because of the obvious difficulties in gaining ethical clearance to conduct experimental studies, the evidence available suggests alcohol and tobacco cause far more damage than Ecstasy. Nutt was prepared to state this openly, humorously revealing fewer deaths occur from Ecstasy than from horse riding or eating peanuts (Wolff, 2009), and, although he has been criticized for this, his intention was to locate the problem of Ecstasy in a realistic and less sensationalist context.

Social science findings are, furthermore, frequently contrasted unfavourably with the unrealistic perception that natural science conclusively finds out certain facts which can be instantly applied to improve all our everyday lives. Yet there is as much dispute about and modification to natural science results as there is to social science findings, and often years of research are needed before the few successfully transferable findings can be applied. Another criticism is of the incomprehensible nature of social science jargon, but every discipline uses some terminology as a form of insider's shorthand. The findings of natural laboratory scientists in white coats who use incomprehensible jargon and impressive technology are frequently revered and seldom challenged (Sapolsky, 2000), but their findings are rarely interpreted as emotionally threatening in the way social science findings may be. What the lay person also generally fails to realize is that the more successful social science concepts and findings are, the more invisible they become. They tend to be absorbed generally into our everyday understandings, for example, the concepts of *in-groups*, *stigma*, *charisma* and *institutionalization*, and, despite politicians often debunking social science, they enthusiastically – though somewhat hypocritically – apply research which might benefit them, such as that identifying the features which promote interest and applause during public speeches (J. Platt, 1989).

To sum up, lay theories are problematic because they are generally based upon anecdotes or an individual's own narrow experience or understandings, which are accepted without question, and most lay critics of social science do not have an awareness of the logical premises and research methodology social science is based upon. The general public also tend to experience social science research they disagree with as emotionally threatening and therefore reject it, or they alternatively dismiss it as unnecessary because it confirms what they thought they already definitively knew in terms of their 'common sense'. However, although some of this 'common sense' could originally have emanated from social science but then slowly and unconsciously become embedded in their everyday understandings of social situations.

Sociology and psychology

Sociology

Sociology is a nurture discipline based around understanding the significant influence society has on us at different levels. These range from the micro context of friends, family and small groups to the mid or meso level of organizations or similar-sized structures. The macro level of political and social norms, major economic and other institutions, attitudes and legislation and the interconnections between all levels and the individual are also important. Consequently our peer group (acquaintances and friends of similar age, often with similar backgrounds and interests) may have a profound influence on how we behave and our likes and dislikes. However, they are in turn also influenced by the family they live in (micro context), the schools they have attended and the neighbourhood environs they reside in (meso context), contemporary and past educational structures, media attitudes about young people, legislation, and prevailing wider political and social attitudes (the macro context). Therefore, other than 'its empirical grounding in careful observation and description of facts, sociology as a discipline is characterized by its rigorous search for interconnections among different domains of society and its systematic use of comparisons' (Beteille, 1996: 2361)

Thinking sociologically

C. Wright Mills (1959) claimed sociology is about understanding the relationship between society within its wider historical context and our own biographies and inner worlds, thus comprehending where we and others are located and why. If, for example, one person suffers long-term unemployment, then this is a personal issue with many potential causes or solutions. When thousands of people endure long-term unemployment, then this becomes a social or political problem which cannot be blamed on the individual, individual solutions being largely ineffectual. P. Berger (1963) sees grasping sociology as progressing from being in a puppet show where we are unaware others are pulling our strings to having a wider awareness of how the society we live in works and influences us, and therefore to perhaps resisting societal pressures and norms and, through this process, thereby changing ourselves or others. Bauman (1990) describes sociology as the sharpening up of our critical social thinking, whereby we continually examine and scrutinize everything we have accepted as normal, natural and inevitable or preordained up until now. Abercrombie (2004) believes sociology's main moral enterprise is to investigate basic, often 'common sense', assumptions about social life, however personally upsetting they may be for us. Bruce (1999) contends sociology is more complex than the so-called 'hard' natural sciences because it deals with human goals, motivations, beliefs and values in the context of complex societies. A common theme threading these viewpoints together is one of complexity, critical thought, coherence and consistency and not taking anything for granted about society and one's place within it.

Socialization

For many years sociologists used the term *socialization* to refer to the potentially lifelong process of individuals learning and acquiring the *norms* (expected ways of behaving and thinking) and values of their societies. These were seen as being endowed via both individuals and institutions such as school, work, the media and families. Lately there has been much criticism that socialization has been represented as an over-psychologized one-way process (from society hypodermically into the individual, e.g. Stanley and Wise, 2000) and should be viewed as much more dynamic, diverse and multi-directional. Behavioural approaches within psychology, such as Bandura's social learning theory, also explain socialization through learning via copying and modelling, and reward and punishment. There are also many competing and complementary perspectives within sociology. These involve continual debates as to how far the society (*social structure*) shapes and moulds the individual versus the extent to which the individual is able to effectively exercise 'objective', autonomous choices over their lives (*individual agency*) and whether our society is generally a fair and democratic place or grossly corrupt and massively unequal.

Structural consensus and conflict theories

Some sociological perspectives are macro structural in that they focus largely on how society determines individuals' lives. *Functionalist (consensus/order)* theories often draw on organic metaphors, such as the body. Society is presented as comprised of interrelating parts functioning harmoniously together for the benefit of everyone, and values are shared. Functionalists deny the existence of extensive societal conflict and unjust power inequalities, presenting society as a meritocracy where those with the highest status, most interesting and best-paid jobs procure them wholly through their own merit, intelligence, diligence and application.

Conflict theories on the other hand perceive society as characterized by persistent conflict and inequality, the best-known theory being Marxism, but many theories relating to feminism and racism are also structural conflict theories. A Marxist perspective construes capitalism as thriving where the sole purpose of economic activity is maximizing profit. Economic instruments of production (i.e. capital – money or financially valuable assets) are privately owned and labour is provided by exploited and estranged workers (*the proletariat*). They are paid the lowest possible wages to produce commodities or services. The profits from these are appropriated by the owners of capital (*the bourgeoisie*) who expand their businesses and accrue ever-increasing personal wealth. Although Marx may have been over-confident about capitalism's demise, he did envisage its global appropriation as the leading capitalist imperial nation-states (and now multinational corporations) secure ever-expanding territories as sources of raw materials and labour to exploit and profit from (Hughes, Martin and Sharrock, 1999: 70; Klein, 2000).

Micro theories and postmodernism

Both Marxism and functionalism are macro structural theories, but micro (social action) theories also exist within sociology, of which *symbolic interactionism* is the most prominent. This theory assumes that human beings are able to think, unlike animals, and reflect upon their lives and their and others' actions. This occurs through the interpretation and deployment of symbols, such as the symbols within language (Mead, 1927/1934). For example, driving a Rolls Royce is a symbol of affluence and shaking your head in our culture symbolic of disagreement or disbelief. The concept of self is important within symbolic interactionism. Cooley (1902) introduced the concept of the 'looking glass self' whereby individuals are able to reflect on how they appear to others and how others might judge them. There are therefore many ongoing debates about agency and structure and about conflict and consensus between different perspectives.

A new contested perspective in sociology, which has gained ground since the early 1970s, is known as *postmodernism*. This perspective repudiates the grand narratives of Marxism and functionalism, claiming our lives are much less predictable, ordered and coherent than has been assumed. Postmodernism proposes we live in a fragmented uncertain 'risk' society where neither science nor modernist sociology are able to predict or solve our contemporary issues and problems (U. Beck, 1992). Lyon (2000), however, argues postmodernism does not assume the disappearance of modernism. It assumes a kind of intermediate situation where capitalism is undergoing radical restructuring and some characteristics of modernism are very apparent, while others are difficult to define or are very inflated. Some theorists therefore talk about *high modernity* or *late modernity* rather than *postmodernity*.

Psychology

At its simplest, psychology has been described as 'what goes on in people's minds' (C. Beckett, 2002: 2), or the study of the mind and of behaviour relating to both humans and animals (Hayes, 1994: 1). However, there appears to be no generally accepted definition of what psychology is as an academic discipline (Furnham, 1989), although it is far more focused on the individual than sociology is. McGhee (2001: 6) asserts 'there is no *single* best way or thinking about behaviour and experience, no *single* perfect model for creating psychological knowledge, no *single* solution to the puzzles of mental life. Rather we should take the view that psychology is multifaceted and requires many different perspectives on knowledge.'

Different psychological schools of thought

Psychology is therefore perhaps better subdivided into specific areas. These include *cognitive psychology*, which deals with thoughts and mental processes such as perception, representation, memory and language; *individual differences*, i.e. how one individual differs from another, in, for example, intelligence or personality; *physiological psychology*, which focuses on the brain and the nervous system – for example, how conditions such as stress impact on these; *social psychology*, which examines how people interact with each other and includes studying attitudes, prejudice and group behaviour; *occupational psychology*, which deals with work, focusing on areas such as satisfaction and motivation; and *developmental* and *life span psychology* which are concerned with one's whole life. Psychology generally, as a discipline, seems profoundly influenced by Darwinian evolutionary theory, which is based on the precepts of survival of the fittest and natural selection. These centre on the notion that those species who survive over many generations have physically and mentally adapted most effectively, their features or characteristics slowly evolving in tandem with the changing environment to enable them to have an optimum chance of survival.

Changes within developmental psychology

Developmental psychology concerns itself with human development from infancy to old age and involves a number of different theories. It also draws upon other branches of psychology such as social psychology to understand group behaviour and attitudes and individual differences psychology to comprehend the nature and measurement of intelligence. For much of the twentieth century, developmental psychology concentrated on childhood. For example, in Erikson's first conceptualization of the six stages of man, only one stage dealt with adulthood. In his revised list, three out of eight stages now deal with ages 16–25 and over. Recent life span psychology, however, recognizes that people change and develop throughout the life span in adulthood as well as in childhood. Although contemporary life span psychology now takes the social context into account, this is often done in a very politically conservative and narrow manner (Settersen, 2009). Terms often utilized in psychology, such as 'biopsychosocial' and 'psychosocial', by virtue of the order of words, suggest the significance of the social is minimal. Furnham also subdivides psychology into two specific cultures, 'scientific' and 'humanist'. The scientific culture takes its cue from the methods of hard natural scientists and its underlying assumptions are that you can predict, understand and control and measure all human behaviour (1989: 48). The humanist culture believes the opposite: that human behaviour cannot be studied for causal links and is often unpredictable and immeasurable. Similar epistemological debates exist within sociology, although the scientific or positivist culture in psychology has much greater influence than in sociology.

Life course sociology and life span psychology

Life course sociology and life span psychology are both subdivisions of, but draw widely from, different aspects of their parent disciplines. They are relatively new subdisciplines, having only emerged in the last thirty to forty years. The USA and Germany also appear to be the forerunners of these perspectives, with the UK lagging significantly behind. Most life span books are therefore undergraduate psychology texts from North America. Much self-identified life course or life span longitudinal research (research that takes place over a number of years, identifying changes and connections over those years) emanates from either North America or Germany. One established journal on the life course exists, *Advances in Life Course Research*, which transitioned from an annual book-series-type journal to a quarterly journal in 2009, with another journal emerging in the same year entitled *Longitudinal and Life Course Studies*, but again generally the key contributors are German or North American. In the UK, although one recent introductory text on life course sociology exists (S. Hunt, 2005), others examine particular aspects of the life course such as social relations (Allan and Jones, 2000) or identity (Hockey and James, 2003). Texts examining the life course at different stages or ages are also largely American and psychological (for example Schaie and Willis, 2002, on middle age), although a number of British books examine childhood and old age but not necessarily from a life course perspective. That said, research or theorizing does not necessarily have to be conducted or thought out from a life course perspective to be useful for understanding the life course.

Life course sociology

Prior to the 1980s in British sociology, the term 'life cycle' was drawn on more frequently than 'life course', or the two terms were used interchangeably (Bryman et al.,1987), but the area in general was neglected. The 'life course' is now viewed as a more appropriate term than the 'life cycle' because of its emphasis on historical and broad, blurred and ragged transitional periods rather than clear-cut ages and stages. Although there has been some British interest in recent years (e.g. Hockey and James, 1993, 2003; Hunt, 2005; Allan and Jones, 2000; Irwin, 2005), life course research and theorizing still remains limited. Some UK sociologists, however, do stress the necessity of developing a sociology of age which considers the interconnections between the social and the biological, the individual and society, and history and the present (e.g. Finch, 1986).

Key terminology explained

Two common terms in sociology relevant to the life course are that of *cohort* and *generation*. 'Cohort' generally refers to a group of people sharing a common characteristic, such as going to school or being born within only a few years of each other or experiencing a significant event, such as a war, at the same time. The word 'generation' on the other hand tends to indicate kinship lineage, such as parent generation or child generation. However, 'generation' has been used synonymously with the word 'cohort' to describe a political genera-tion or a generation that self-identifies in terms of its differences from other generations and uniqueness, and becomes politically active in this respect (Braungart and Braungart, 1986). An example of this could be the generation that lived through the Great Depression in the 1930s in America or England. Extreme economic recession fol-lowed the collapse of the stock (financial) market, accompanied by mass unemployment and stark 'absolute' poverty, affecting many and lasting almost a decade. In the 1960s many young people also cam-paigned for causes such as CND (Campaign for Nuclear Disarmament), women's, black and gay people's rights, and against wars they saw as unnecessary and cruel such as the war America waged against Vietnam, and research has shown their political views/activism had endured twenty years later (McAdam, 1989).

Pilcher (1994a) acknowledges that a group could be both a cohort and a generation simultaneously but suggests that the term *generation* be used when referring to generation in the kinship sense, and *social generation* used to signify generation in the cohort sense. Mannheim (1952), in his seminal article on the sociology of generations, argues that the historical is important socially and individually. This is because, in their youth, individuals attain a generational conscious-ness, which is formed out of their experiences and the socio-political climate, affecting their whole lives. Much research substantiates this but, as Denzin (1989) cogently points out, retrospectively we may demarcate particular turning points in our lives as significant – such as developing a serious illness in young adulthood – which do not in any way coincide with particular ages, stages or social or political experiences.

Other important descriptors include *transitions* and *trajectories*. 'Transitions' refers to changes in status and role which are generally known about and prepared for – such as from being single to being married, or from student to full-time worker – whereas 'trajectories' are long-term, such as trajectories of schooling, work and parent-hood, and may include a number of transitions within them. Some transitions may become compressed or conversely dispersed over time, such as the transition from education to first full-time work becoming decompressed with the expansion of higher education (George, 1993). Others become less common and predictable than before, such as marriage and parenthood in young adulthood, or the death of a young child, which in the USA dropped from a 62 per cent probability in 1900 to a 4 per cent possibility in 1980 (Uhlenberg, 1980).

Age and stage persistence

Ages and stages are, despite the above, still important because we expect certain age-related behaviour and role positioning from ourselves and others. We frequently stereotype age, seeing children and the elderly as more vulnerable, dependent and less purposive than young and middle-aged adults and still draw on outdated concepts such as white-haired grandmothers who sit in rocking chairs knitting (Pahl, 2000). In 1997 Sufiah Yusof made headlines when, at the age of 12, she was accepted by Oxford University, but retrospectively her life reveals a succession of tragic events. These range from her inability to finish college, to her disclosure of years of physical and emotional abuse from her father which led to her being placed in foster care at 15, an unsuccessful, short-lived marriage at 19 and recent tabloid claims, in 2008, that she was working as an escort. However, in this case it is unclear to what extent Sufiah's problems were the result of being coerced to participate in activities she may have been intellectually but not emotionally ready for, of the prolonged parental abuse she endured and/or of how others treated her in relation to how they perceived the potential disjunctions between her chronological age, intellectual abilities and social interactions.

We also recognize how our bodies change over time and their increasing limitations with the advancement of age, although we may not be aware of this day by day. Therefore, age identity might not be as rigid as it was, but it is still there nevertheless. Winning a significant amount on the lottery when one is eighty and getting around the house is an effort is a very different experience from if one was twenty (Hockey and James, 2003). Holstein (1990) also gives the example of how a psychiatrist regarded a man of 55–60 to be a prime candidate for involuntary hospitalization and incarceration on the ground of mental illness because he was obsessed with having sex and bragging about his numerous female sexual partners, behaviour the psychiatrist saw as only appropriate for teenage males!

Key mechanisms for exploring the life course

A sociology of the life course focuses on patterns, trends and change through individuals' lives and how historical, societal and political norms, situations and transformations impact upon them. Mayer (2003) views life course sociology as being about how individual lives become embedded within social structures through a socio-historic multilevel process, with a particular focus on social positions and roles. Mayer contends sociologists search for three mechanisms to account for the shape and form life courses take. The first mechanism revolves around how institutions shape people's lives. For example, in the UK, education from the age of 5 to 16 is compulsory, defining and regulating educational careers. It is scheduled at particular times, involves particular tasks and activities at different ages, often streams students according to ability and results ideally in qualifications and certificates. Another example might be employment law which defines who is gainfully in work or unemployed, regulates minimum conditions, hours worked and wages paid, and stipulates a compulsory retirement age. Family law defines who is regarded as married, divorced, single or in an otherwise acceptable union and who is the legal guardian or carer of a child.

The second mechanism focuses on trajectories and transitions. It ascertains whether certain transitions – for example, from education into first employment or from being single to being married – are made at certain ages or within a certain time span, and whether certain precedents earlier in individuals' biographies – for example, single parenthood – shape the timing or even the possibility of achieving certain outcomes.

The third mechanism is associated with the fact that individuals are divided into cohorts and affected by both preceding and succeeding cohorts, which influence individual opportunities (according to some academics) far more than individual or situational conditions (e.g. Macunevic, 1999). For example, one's likelihood of finding a partner may vary over time depending on the numbers, behaviour, desires and communication networks of those searching at the same time. A recent, somewhat sensationalist and rather sexist article in an Australian newspaper, 'Cougars Ready to Pounce', although depicting older women as predatory sexual animals, nevertheless illustrates the latter point graphically. Demographic analyses cited showed far fewer men in their forties and fifties were single when compared with their female same-age counterparts, who were much more likely to be single at that same age. These midlife women were consequently initiating relationships with single, much younger men, whom they often met in bars, including men in their twenties, of whom there was a surplus because their female same-age counterparts had often opted for relationships with men in their thirties (Ganska, 2010). Life courses within sociology are therefore not just about individual biographies but about 'patterned dynamic expressions of social structure [applied] to populations or subsets of populations . . . governed intentionally or unintentionally by institutions and [also] are the intentional or unintentional outcomes of the behaviour of actors' (Mayer, 2003: 5).

Constructionism and de-traditionalization

A constructionist perspective that takes interpretations into account is also very important both to counter rigid age and stage typologies and to explore their meanings for people (Holstein and Gubrium, 2007). In two separate studies of older people, for example, neither group categorized themselves in terms of age but in terms of everyday interactions and other conceptualizations (Matthews, 1979; Kaufman, 1986), but this could have been because of the negative connotations and stereotypes which surround old age. Recent commentators, furthermore, argue that we have transitioned from a standardized, Western life course where roles, stages and expectations at different ages were relatively coherent and predictable to a postmodern view of a de-standardized or de-traditionalized life course (e.g. Macmillan, 2005) where life stages have little contemporary relevance. Individuals are now presented as being confronted with numerous life choices alongside much uncertainty and instability. Significant social role overlap also now occurs, particularly in relation to roles such as parenthood or independent living that were previously viewed as demarcating particular life stages. There is, however, tremendous debate about whether various facets of ageing, social inequalities, and the way institutions and careers are often centred on chronological age may mean our choices are much more limited than has been suggested.

Psychology and the Life Span

Life span psychology has been described as 'the study of individual development (ontogenesis) – a lifelong adaptive process of acquisition, maintenance, transformation and attrition in psychological structures and functions' (Baltes et al, 1999: 472). Nature and nurture are combined but much attention is focused on individual differences relating to ability and personality. These are seen to have a biological basis and genetic foundation which cause age-related variations across the life span. In life span psychology, child and adult development are explained through a number of different theories. Some of these complement each other, others seem in direct conflict.

Life span theories

Bee (1994) subdivides these theories into three kinds. Firstly, there are stage theories assuming development has a goal or endpoint, according to age, whether that relates to thought processes, integration of the personality or moral reasoning (see Freud and Piaget introduced in chapter 2 for examples). Secondly, there are stage theories, mostly related to adult development, which are not goal-orientated but document the different stages and changes individuals go through (see Levinson, 1978: ch. 5). Thirdly, other theories argue that development has goals and proceeds in a direction, but they are not stage theories.

Maslow (1943), for example, argued we operate according to a hierar-chical pyramid of needs, whereby one lower-level category must be satisfied before others can be met. At the base are our (i) *physiological needs* such as food and shelter, followed by the next tier, (ii) *safety needs* which centre around predictability and security, and then (iii) *social needs* relating to friendship and intimacy, and (iv) *esteem needs* such as self-respect, recognition, status and self-esteem. Maslow felt these four 'deficiency' needs had to be met before we could aspire to (v) *self-actualization*, which was about living creatively and reaching one's peak. He later added another category – (vi) *self-transcendence*, the ability to rise above one's own sense of ego and be altruistic and wise – but research generally does not tend to substantiate such hier-archical ordering of needs. Finally, there are learning theories which see behaviour as neither stage-like nor qualitative but determined by rewards, punishments and modelling (see Skinner and Pavlov in chapter 2).

Non-chronological variables

Although the focus is very much on age-related stage development in life span psychology, non-chronological age variables are also recognized. These include one's *subjective age*, which may be older or younger than your chronological age ('you're as old as you feel'); or how others perceive you: *other-perceived age*; *social age*, the extent a person's roles and behaviour parallel social expectations regard-ing someone their age; *functional age* which is comparative and is a judgement about whether someone's bodily systems, such as heart and lungs, intellectuality or dexterity, compare to similar-aged peers; and *biological age* which relates to potential life span. Therefore, a fit 55-year-old may have a lower biological age than an unfit and unhealthy 40-year-old. Cross-cultural research has shown chrono-logical age has the greatest salience in modern Western societies, but questions about age make little sense to respondents in the most rural and least-developed societies (Keith, 1990)

Different developmental dimensions

Most life span and developmental psychologists also differentiate between different developmental dimensions. They focus on: (i) *physi-cal or biosocial development*, which includes physical growth throughout the body, including changes in motor development, our senses and bodily systems; (ii) *cognitive development* – thought processes and their deployment in relation to how we learn, remember, communicate and deal with problems; (iii) *personal development*, focusing on the developing self, including theories of attachment and affection, our emotions and feelings more generally, and personality traits; and

(iv) *social development*, centring on interpersonal relationships such as those between friends, family members and peers (Sugarman, 2001). Life span psychologists also tend to concur that development is multi-dimensional and multi-directional, although it is often, conversely, treated as rather unidirectional, with the biology dimension being over-privileged in many textbooks. Baltes (1987), who is more histori-cally and socially orientated than many life span theorists, sees the life span involving both growth and loss at every stage. Even when loss occurs, Baltes argues we possess *plasticity*, the ability to stretch or retain our abilities through compensatory mechanisms. These might include glasses for someone short-sighted in middle age, or using various cues to aid failing memory. Baltes also acknowledges the interactiveness, multi-disciplinary nature and historical and cultural embeddedness of the life span.

Social science research methods

Positivism and Intepretivism

Sociology and psychology now use similar research methods although epistemological and philosophical disputes about what constitutes valid science and knowledge proliferate. Consequently, debates abound surrounding which research designs or methods are the most scientific or effective to use. However, psychology and sociology also emanate from different historical origins. Psychology originally modelled itself on the 'hard' natural sciences, seeing the laboratory experiment as the key research design and issues of observable behav-iour, measurement and quantification as imperative. Psychology also initially posited the researcher as a detached, formal investigator or conduit with no impact on the research process. Traditional psychol-ogy therefore adopted a positivistic stance, assuming the existence of objective facts and truths, which spoke for themselves and did not require interpretation or contextualization.

Sociology, however, comes from more varied origins, influenced by both positivist and interpretive traditions. Durkheim (1897/2002), for example, studied suicide through an analysis of coroners' report-ing of the causes, accepting coroners' reports as objective fact, then trying to discern whether societal factors such as religious beliefs and social integration impacted upon suicide. Durkheim therefore conformed to some positivist traits. More interpretive sociologists, however, later pointed out that the coroners worked on their own evaluations of what constituted a suicide and criticized Durkheim for only looking at possible social meanings, not the individual meaning that could have been attributed to the act by the person. Therefore some deaths categorized as suicide may not have been, and others which did not conform to coroners' expectations of suicides may have been suicides but were not labelled as such. For example, a death of a climber who fell from the top of a mountain, left no suicide note and was not known to have been unhappy or have had mental health problems is unlikely to be categorized as a suicide, although it could have been. Coroners could also have been strongly influenced by relatives' interpretations of events, if they did not want the death categorized as a suicide (Baechler, 1979). Therefore, coroners' labelling of certain deaths as suicides cannot, for the above reasons, be accepted as making that suicide an objective fact.

Quantitative and Qualitative Research

Quantitative studies involve large amounts of people and focus on measurement, quantification and statistical analysis. They are normally associated with a positivistic stance, whereas qualitative studies which focus on smaller numbers of people but research them in much greater depth are often linked to interpretivism. However, this is not always the case as one can have a positivist qualitative study and an interpretivist quantitative study. Some studies and research projects also employ both quantitative and qualitative research methods and analysis. Quantitative studies enable a small amount of information to be gathered about a great many people or objects and therefore possible connections can be drawn between variables and reasonable claims made about the results being generalizable or representative. Qualitative studies are more concerned with understanding and exploring the experience of a small amount of people in great depth, but are difficult to generalize from because of their specificity and small numbers.

Key Research Designs and Methods

A design is a framework for the collection of data. Our design choice is informed by whether we are interested in cause and effect, generalizing from smaller to larger groups, understanding the meaning of behaviour in specific situations, or comprehending the interconnections between different social phenomena and change over time (Bryman, 2004). The experiment is the only design where cause and effect can be inferred or observed. In classic experiments, two comparable groups are studied under the same conditions but one factor or variable is manipulated in one group, so any changes noted can be attributed to that factor which has a causal effect. Real life experiments which occur 'naturalistically' can also be studied but it is much more difficult to standardize conditions. However, the main problem with the laboratory experiment in relation to human beings is that the results may not be transferable outside the artificial confines of the laboratory as people know they are being studied and they may therefore behave very differently in their real life contexts.

Another key design is cross-sectional design, sometimes termed survey research, which principally deploys research methods such as written questionnaires and structured interviews but may draw on additional sources and methods such as official statistics and diaries. This design may involve collection of both qualitative and quantitative data, and collects data about many cases at one point in time. The data are then used to detect and analyse patterns.

A third design, longitudinal design, is little used because of its cost. It is often an extension of survey research, using questionnaires and interview data, but data are collected on various occasions over an extended period of time, not just once. There are two main types of longitudinal research, one being the panel design in which information is collected from different types of cases such as people, households, schools, etc. One example is the British Household Panel Survey (BHPS) (see chapters 4 and 5). This began with a nationally representative sample of approximately 10,000 individuals, who are interviewed annually about issues such as health, housing, income, work, values and household organization to ascertain social change. The other type is the cohort study, which selects an entire cohort or a random selection of a cohort for study. The National Child Development Study (NCDS) is a cohort study in which 17,000 children born in one week in March 1958 were followed-up at ages 7, 11, 16, 23 and 33 in respect of health, family, parenting, income and occupation, housing and environment.

A fourth design is the case study which involves collecting intensive and graphic details about a single case. A case could be a study of a single event, perhaps a disaster such as the bombing of the World Trade Organization, or a study of a single family, school classroom, hospital ward or an entire organization, such as Social Services. Some researchers, for example Denscombe (1998), also view ethnography as a research design, whereby a group or a culture of some kind is studied intensively by the researcher who lives or spends extended periods of time, possibly years, with them, with the aim of really understanding and being able to describe their 'lived experience'.

Various research methods are deployed within different research designs, although some methods are more commonly suitable for or found within particular research designs. The main research methods used within social science generally are questionnaires (a written series of questions with mostly fixed multiple choice answers which must be filled in by the respondent or the interviewer), various types of interviews (guided conversations with a research purpose), structured and unstructured observation, diaries and the analysis of documents. Research questions and studies may test out a theory framed in a hypothesis (*the hypothetico deductive approach*) or the theory or hypothesis may emerge from the data themselves (*the inductive deductive approach*), although the two approaches are often harder to subdivide clearly than one might assume. Most research methods and designs can contribute to an understanding of the life course in some shape or form. Longitudinal studies are very useful for discerning 'objective' events, transitions and trajectories, and changes over time, but other research methods often need to be employed to understand meaning and influences.

Life span psychology, life course sociology and multi-disciplinarity

Although life course and life span theorizing, after three decades, is still in its infancy, there were tremendous hopes and expectations for collaborative work between the different disciplines at the onset which unfortunately have mostly not been realized (Mayer, 2003; Levy et al., 2005; Settersen, 2009). This section examines the extent to which interdisciplinary cooperation or understanding has been achieved and delineates the problems sociology and psychology (and the natural sciences) encounter in relation to working together. The aim of this book is much more modest than integrating multi-disciplinary research and – given that there is little of it available, particularly in relation to the UK – what it attempts to do is to give the reader a flavour of both the psychology of the life span and the sociology of the life course. They are set alongside each other with respect to variously roughly drawn age categories, and their key points, strengths, weaknesses, complementarity and contestations are highlighted and discussed.

Seminal Interdisciplinary Life Course Research

Although recent theorists, as above, lament the general lack of inter-disciplinary cooperation with respect to the life course, when the work of two of the first pioneers of life course research is examined, their understanding and incorporation of different disciplines is evident, particularly in their later work. Elder, whose work on the US Great Depression is now regarded as groundbreaking, refers to 'sociological social psychology' (1994: 12) and places himself within that category as well as using the term 'life course' rather than 'life span'. Although publishing mostly in psychology journals, his discussion of sociology and key sociological theorists and his stressing of the importance of four central themes to the life course paradigm – [i] 'the interplay of human lives and historical times, [ii] the timing of lives, [iii] linked or interdependent lives, and [iv] human agency in choice making' (1994, 1998) – would evidence his trans-disciplinary bridging. Similarly, Baltes, another founding 'life course' psychologist, stresses the importance of multi-directionality and multi-disciplinarity and the importance of history in his later work.

Elder's (1974) work on the Great Depression is fascinating and informative in this respect. He found very clear links between family hardship and negative child outcomes. Economic pressures caused by debt, unstable work and income loss led to individual and marital stress, followed by ineffective parenting which then undermined children's academic performance, self-esteem and peer acceptance. Elder stresses the importance of timing in that it is not just what happens to an individual which is important, but the event's historical, social and personal antecedents, as well as relationships and issues loosely connected with developmental stage and capabilities. For example, children from Berkeley, born 1928–9, who experienced their most vulnerable childhood years during the worst of the Great Depression and entered adolescence when their parents worked 'sunup to sundown' in essential industries during World War II, fared much worse than children from Oakland. The Oakland children were born into more stable and prosperous childhoods in the early 1920s, only experiencing the economic collapse during adolescence. Elder (1986), nevertheless, found military service in young adulthood was a great equalizer of past disadvantage, offering a structured environment, responsibility and new opportunities for those with previously disrupted or even disruptive and unstable lives. However, later military mobilization in one's thirties, which lifts people out of families and adult roles, is more likely to disrupt and disadvantage.

In the 1980s in African American families in Los Angeles, giving birth in early adolescence often had long-term negative consequences relating to terminated schooling and limited employment opportunities thereafter, the teenage mothers expecting their mother to help care for the child but this rarely occurring because their mothers felt too young to be grandmothers (Burton and Bengston, 1985). In another study of African American young mothers in Baltimore, USA, those who received maternal support and were able to stay in school, or who married the father, counteracted many of the possible long-term disadvantages of early parenthood (Furstenberg et al., 1987).

Barriers to Interdisciplinarity?

What are the barriers to interdisciplinary collaboration and how might they be overcome? It has been suggested that 'the desire of the participants to work together, their acknowledgement of the importance of mutual learning rather than competition, even less the pursuit of disciplinary hegemony, and a fundamental working knowledge allowing understanding and an appreciation of the conceptual and methodological panoply of neighbouring disciplines' are imperative but by no means easy to achieve (Levy and the Pavie Team, 2005: 7). Difficulties include problems with vocabulary – some terms used by both sociology and psychology have completely different meanings. 'Norm' in sociology refers to cultural expectations regarding behaviour, but relates mostly to statistical prevalence within psychology. At other times different terms are used for the same or similar phenomena, but still there are nearly always differences. For example Baltes et al. (2006) introduce the term 'biocultural co-constructivism' to describe life-long human 'development', whereas Settersen (2009) refers to 'agency within structures'. Although both seminal life course experts would acknowledge the life course is a dynamic interplay between biology, society and history and involves psychological, sociological, institutional and demographic factors, it is notable that the psychologist, Baltes, flags up biology as paramount and uses the term 'culture', which does not necessarily acknowledge the political context. In contrast, biology is absent from Settersen's 'sociological' terminology.

The different disciplines also historically had different frames of reference. Traditionally, developmental psychology focused on the young and occasionally the very old, whereas most sociological work, until recently, focused on the adult years. Social psychology does not seem to be very 'age'-specific but, particularly in the USA, most of its empirical work has been conducted in artificial experimental situations with easily accessible college students, unrepresentative, by virtue not only of youth but also of their social status and stratification. While psychology has a close affiliation with biology, sociology for the most part has retained a wary distance. This particular issue will be examined in depth below because – although comprehensible conversation between neighbouring social science disciplines may be fraught with difficulty but potentially achievable – profound differences paradigmatically, as well as in knowledge and technique, may render understanding and collaboration even more complicated between the natural and social sciences.

One of the key criticisms of sociology (from psychologists) has been that it tries to understand the social by the social, paying little if any consideration to the biological and psychological (Mayer, 2003). However, although this could be seen as one of its shortcomings, it is also its most valuable aspect, because biological reductionism and individual pathologization are so prevalent (Settersen, 2009). The implications of biology and ageing are, furthermore, far more readily drawn upon in theories justifying the status quo, particularly in relation to areas where there are significant inequalities, rather than by those seeking to criticize and change the status quo (Pilcher, 1994b). One example of this is Thornhill and Palmer's (2000) infamous evolutionary biology theory which claims men are biologically predestined to rape females, a claim which could be used to excuse males raping females (see also the sociobiological and evolutionary psychology arguments on 'race' and intelligence in chapter 3).

Many sociologists, however, do acknowledge the importance of the body. Adam (1990) in her social analysis of time, argues sociologists need to concede that humans are organic matter that declines and degrades. The very fact we physiologically respond to light and dark and need to eat and sleep at certain times means these factors permeate the social, rather than being totally constituted by the social, although such activities are not unresponsive to change in relation to cultural demands. Similarly, the new sociology of the body theorists stress firmly that we cannot elide the body out of existence but must analyse our embodied states, and cannot separate mind and body but must study them as conjoined and interdependent. This is not a claim that our bodies control and define us, merely that our bodies and minds together constitute us as human beings and the physical materiality of the body inevitably entails constraints. For example, we may be able to have gender reassignment surgery and take hormones to make us look physically similar to the sex opposite to that we were born into (transsexuality), but we can never become genetically or reproductively a member of the opposite sex or replay our earlier childhood gender socialization as male or female. Additionally, finances permitting, we are able to have plastic surgery to remove lines and generate a younger appearance, but this will not necessarily enhance our longevity or prevent us suffering from age-related illnesses and diseases.

Newton urges caution in relation to sociology embracing a biological perspective. In his examination of sociologists of medicine and the body who attempt to incorporate a biological perspective, he argues there has been '(i) insufficient questioning of supposed links between the social and the body, such as that between emotions, "stress" and ill health, (ii) too easy an acceptance of arguments that derive from research grounded in naturalistic and desocialized contexts, and (iii) insufficient interrogations of existing psychosocial concepts, such as that of "stress"' (2003: 24). One good example Newton provides is that researchers often accept uncritically the claim that there is a relationship between stress and illness without thoroughly scrutinizing the evidence, one large statistical study failing to identify a clear link between various work stressors and particular physical illnesses (Karasek et al.,1987). Temporary psychosomatic experiences do not always have long-term impacts on health, and at times there is evidence of decoupling of biological and psychological factors rather than convergence. Therefore, although one's body may register physiological signs 'normally' associated with stress, if the individual neither shows behaviourally, nor admits, any psychological stress, the 'truth' is not necessarily inherent in or revealed through the body, as we are interrogating the interaction of multi-faceted, complex processes.

Recent research, including mapping the human genome, also casts serious doubts on genetic primacy. In a study of thousands of patients utilizing comprehensive genome-wide scans and multiple genetic markers, genes were unable to explain why some children had Attention Deficit Hyperactivity Disorder (ADHD) and others did not (Sonuga-Barke, 2010). However, although ADHD may not be a good example, given concerns that it may be a manufactured, socially constructed illness (Coppock, 2005), diagnosis and treatment arguably benefitting pharmaceutical companies more than the individuals themselves (Breggin, 2001). Even the weaker biological claim that genes create vulnerabilities which environments may possibly cause to be expressed is being increasingly challenged. Some previous studies appeared to show a particular gene variant meant individuals were more likely to become depressed if also maltreated when children. Despite this, a recent meta-analysis of 14,250 people with mapped DNA from fourteen studies confusingly showed that the variant did not render those with it at greater risk of depression than those without it, even when the variant coincided with childhood maltreatment (Risch et al., 2009).

Other theorists writing in both psychological and sociological journals chide sociology and some psychological approaches for their 'biophobia' or biological hostility, arguing that sociological and biological approaches can be complementary and coexist (Cacioppo et al., 2000; Freese et al., 2003). These latter articles examine how both the social and biology are interdependent and mutually influence each other at a number of different levels. Both articles also overtly and inadvertently demonstrate that we have a long way to go before natural scientists, sociologists and social psychologists are really able to understand, trust and work productively with each other. Natural scientists seem to view social scientists more as 'arty' cultural interpreters than as 'real' scientists. Conversely, social scientists often see natural scientists as 'hard-headed' but short-sighted positivists who reject the view that their personalities, opinions and politics can have any effect on how research is conducted, what results are seen as relevant and how they are analysed and then disseminated. Both frequently see the other as possessing unacceptable political agendas. Whereas sociologists tend to view biological scientists as deterministic, conservative and upholding an inequitable status quo, natural scientists are prone to typecasting sociologists as left-wing, 'bleeding heart' liberals who do not want to believe human beings may be 'naturally', for example, sexist or promiscuous. The situation is not helped by many evolutionary biologists/psychologists devoting considerable energy to trying to prove innate evolved sex differences which posit men as naturally violent, promiscuous or selfish (e.g. Buss, 1999). Most social and natural scientists also find it difficult to understand each other because academics are rarely grounded in or traverse fundamentally different disciplines, the exceptions often being those who, interestingly, criticize rather than corroborate the determinism of most evolutionary psychology approaches (e.g. Fausto Sterling, 2000; Rose, Rose (and Jencks), 2000).

Biological dimensions of development are therefore described in this book in accordance with life span psychology's stress upon them and its adherence to both nature and nurture as key influences on and predictors of our lives. Some sociologists' and natural scientists' criticisms that sociology has mostly ignored biology and the body but can no longer afford to do so are also accepted as valid points, and it is conceded that much more collaborative research needs to be conducted by natural and social scientists in the future. However, in accordance with the conclusions that may be drawn from the preceding discussion, wherever biology may be potentially over-privileged or strongly emphasized in explanations for behaviour and emotion in this book, those claims and evidence will be examined rigorously and critically.

To sum up, this chapter has introduced the reader with no prior social science knowledge to the key tenets of psychology and sociology and their respective life span and life course subdivisions, alongside an understanding of some of their most important research methods, terminology and concepts. It has also demonstrated how significant demographic, global, social, economic and political changes since the early 1970s have profoundly changed how we live in the UK in far-reaching ways. These have different impacts for the life courses of those of different ages and with different prior experiences. The misleading influence of lay theories and 'unreality' TV was also exposed, as were the problems associated with integrally and equally embracing the viewpoints and concepts of both sociology and psychology in life course research and theorizing, although this was seen as a desirable future goal.

Reflection and discussion questions

To what extent and in what ways is your life up until now different from your parents' and grandparents' earlier lives? (It may be necessary to discuss with relatives and to select key areas to talk about such as education, consumption, employment, and new technology.)

Have you or others ever resorted to anecdotal or lay theorizing? Ascertain, using Furnham's work, the flaws inherent in your or others' thinking for at least two examples.

What are the similarities and differences between life span psychology and life course sociology?

Recommended reading

For further information on social science research methods, Bryman's (2004) text is an excellent introductory but in-depth text. A shorter and less complex, but still highly informative book in terms of key points is Denscombe's (1998) book on conducting small-scale research projects. Settersen's (2009) article on the collaboration between sociology and psychology in respect of life course research and theory is also a key reference work, and any recent articles which review, analyse and synthesize previous research and theorizing on the life course in the journal *Advances in Life Course Research* are worth consulting.

CHAPTER
02
Traditional Psychological Approaches to Children

There are many different approaches to and understandings of children and childhood, even when only considering psychology and sociology. Prevalent, populist contemporary views about children, however, are often drawn exclusively and uncritically from traditional developmental psychology. These shape many people's beliefs about a 'good' childhood and what constitutes a 'normal' or an 'abnormal' child. The wide-ranging influence of traditional psychology is evident in the many child-rearing books written for parents and professionals and in media and 'common sense' depictions of children as 'naturally' developing through various emotional, social, cognitive and physical stages. Children are therefore seen as implicitly deficient – 'mini adults' in the making, who possess little knowledge and few skills and are compromised in their ability to make good decisions. According to traditional sociological socialization approaches, it is social structures and institutions – such as the political and educational institutions – and learning through others – such as the family, television and peers – which mould the child. The child has little active part to play in what they are and who they become. Conversely, traditional psychological approaches tend to see biology as the greatest influence. These two quite paternalistic perspectives position the child as overwhelmingly and unidirectionally created by either society (socialization) or biological maturation and genetics (developmental psychology) or both, although socialization recognizes constraints on development linked to socially constructed inequalities rather than to inborn differences.

This chapter focuses predominantly on developmental child psychology, a subdiscipline which tries to discern clear principles that provide a coherent framework for understanding children's growth. After examining general physical growth and memory in children up to adolescence, key developmental and learning theories will be analysed. Freud focuses on the unconscious, psychosexual development and how defence mechanisms may impede this. Erikson, following on from Freud, sees development proceeding through psychosocial stages but does not view sexual development as primary. Bowlby takes into account some of Freud's notions of the unconscious mind and Erikson's notion of the collaboration between the psychological and the social to understand how children become attached to significant others. Piaget concentrates on cognitive development, claiming that, as children proceed through discontinuous qualitative stages (one stage must be reached before the child can go on to another distinctly different stage), their thinking chronologically becomes more sophisticated, logical and abstract. The behaviourist psychologists stress learning via modelling (copying others) and reward and punishment, but they do not link learning with stages, age or maturity, so are not strictly developmental. After describing and evaluating these various theories and the research they are based upon, children's acquisition of language will be examined as an exemplar to show how a variety of different theories may need to be integrated to understand particular areas. Criticisms of traditional psychological theories and recent developments will also be analysed, and overall strengths and weaknesses evaluated.

Physical development and memory

Physical Growth

At birth the average child weighs approximately 7.5 pounds and measures about 20 inches (50 cm) in height. Infants typically double their birth weight by the fourth month, and by the end of the first year it triples. Growth slows in the second year but at 24 months children weigh approximately 30 pounds (13 kilograms) and are 32–36 inches tall (K. Berger, 2005). The significant weight gain in the first year is due to fat laid down to provide insulation for warmth and to store nourishment, in case teething or illness interfere with eating. The baby's height and weight are normally measured statistically by percentiles, which relate to averages in the population. An average child is said to be at the fiftieth percentile and 49 per cent of children will be above this and 49 per cent below. What psychologists think is more important generally than initial percentile measurement, because of differences in the social context and genetic divergence, is a rapid drop in the percentile. Reductions in weight are often the first signs of poor nutrition, followed by reduction in percentiles of height and finally of head growth. If nutrition is insufficient the brain carries on growing but the body does not, a phenomenon known as *head sparing*.

New-born babies spend most of their time eating and sleeping, sleeping approximately seventeen hours per day. Regular ample sleep equates with positive health if no adverse factors impede it, and growth hormones tend to be released during sleep (K. Berger, 2005). New-born babies often wake at variable intervals during the night and sleep during the day, although 80 per cent of 1-year-olds sleep through the night. By the age of 2, the brain weighs 75 per cent of its adult weight, and the body 20 per cent. In the first two years, the numbers of dendrites, the branch-like extensions of neurons in the brain, which electrically conduct messages between the neurons, expand exponentially up to fivefold, a process known as *transient exuberance*. After this, many neurons wither because of lack of use. Therefore, what the brain experiences in the early years shapes it greatly. Proliferation and pruning occur particularly related to sight and hearing in the first few months, suggesting if an infant has a rectifiable sight or hearing problem, it should be identified as soon as possible. The sense of hearing is acute at birth and certain noises can startle, soothe or interest new-borns. Vision is much less developed and new-borns focus on objects 4–30 inches away, often staring fixedly. By 6 weeks, they look more intently and actively and smile at human faces. At about 14 weeks, *binocular vision* appears – the ability to coordinate the two eyes together to see one image.

New-borns also exhibit a number of reflexes, including the stepping and breathing reflexes, as well as reflexes to maintain constant body temperature, such as crying or shivering when cold or tucking their legs in towards their bodies. In terms of *gross motor skills* – those involving large body movements – if new-borns are on their stomachs they wiggle and attempt to told their heads up and move their limbs as if swimming. They slowly gain muscle strength and between 8 and 12 months most infants can crawl well, progressing to climbing up and over objects. Walking progresses similarly from very stilted steps to smooth, coordinated walking. The average child can walk holding hands at 9 months but starts to walk competently and autonomously from 12 months onwards. *Fine motor skills* start with reflexive grasping and sucking motions, and by 6 months babies are able to reach for, grab and move any object that their hand can accommodate. They can also transfer objects hand to hand, point at things and know what another person is pointing at.

Between ages 1 and 7, children lose their baby fat and slim out, and their lower body increases in length, although overall growth slows, from 3 until adolescence, to an increase of 2–3 inches in height and 5–7 pounds in weight per year. By age 6, children's brains reach 90 per cent of adult weight, and body proportions and bodily movements are similar to an adult's, although motor skills and general coordination improve continuously through young and middle child-hood. Cultural patterns (such as feeding boys more than girls in some Asian nations), diet and environmental conditions interact with genetic predispositions, so, in countries or areas where children may become malnourished or physical activity is curtailed, growth may be less or become stunted (Green and Taylor, 2010). There is also, ironi-cally, major concern in the UK and the USA about childhood obesity, which can cause significant short- and long-term health problems such as developing type 2 diabetes. Cole et al. (2005) note that young girls are more agile than boys, who in turn are better at dribbling, catching and kicking balls. Furthermore, in middle childhood, gender differences in motor ability – such as boys being better at gross motor skills, often requiring force and power, and girls excelling in fine motor skills tasks such as drawing and gross motor skills such as skip-ping, which require coordination and balance – increase. Cole et al. claim not only maturation but prior practice leads to increased motor skills. However, they neglect to explain further that successful gender role socialization will almost inevitably result in boys overall being more proficient at male gender stereotyped activities and girls in female-labelled activities. The different sexes are encouraged to par-ticipate in and practise activities which are seen as more appropriate for one sex than the other, and often discouraged from engaging with gender-atypical activities.

Memory

Infants find it difficult to process and remember things during their first year, and most adults will be able to recall little before their third year. However, an experiment was conducted in which 3-month-old infants were encouraged to move a mobile by kicking their legs. After one week, some of these infants given the same apparatus mostly kicked vigorously, immediately indicating memory. When other infants from the original tests, who were not tested a week afterwards, were tested two weeks later, again with the same appara-tus, they only began with random kicks. This suggested no previous memory, although some memory was later reactivated by prompts. By 9 months, babies' memories improve substantially and a baby watch-ing someone play with a doll can memorize and copy this the next day – *deferred imitation*. By the end of their second year, infants remember complex sequences such as how to put teddy to bed or set the table, performing these after simple prompts and after doing the activity only once (Bauer and Dow, 1994). Memory and cognition are thought to develop simultaneously. There are also two types of memory. *Active short-term (working) memory* involves information only remaining in the brain for a few seconds if it is unattended to, unprocessed and unlinked with previous experiences. It is therefore easily forgotten. *Long-term memory* is about storage and retrieval and our brains can retain vast amounts of information for potentially limitless amounts of time. Young children have difficulty with memory because of poorer attention spans, limited knowledge which affects understanding, and slower registration. Unlike older children, they have not yet attained a repertoire of strategies for holding information for longer periods in working memory. These include (i) repetition and rehearsal; (ii) organizing information to be remembered into easy-to-recall categories; and (iii) elaboration – making connections between different things they have to remember (Cole et al., 2005).

Psychoanalytic development

Sigmund Freud was the first important child development theorist, those succeeding him either emulating the way he divided development into clear-cut stages or challenging this, with others disputing his claim that development is primarily sexual or that the unconscious is important. Notwithstanding many problems with Freud's theories and interpretations, he is still a 'founding father', being a pioneer who took child development seriously and tried to explain it, completely without the benefit of previous in-depth knowledge.

Personality Development

Underpinning all Freud's work is the assertion that the unconscious mind (frequently represented as an iceberg, with our conscious mind being the smaller, visible tip and the unconscious mind the larger, invisible and inaccessible mass beneath the water) influences most of our behaviour (Davenport, 1994). Freud (1856–1939) posited three components to our personality, which are in constant tension and competition: the *id*, the *ego* and the *super ego*. The id represents our raw impulses, unmediated by comprehension of others or our environment, and is driven by the *pleasure principle* (Strachey, 1940/1969). The id is the newly born baby screaming because it is hungry, and it is dominant for the first twelve months. The ego, sometimes called the *reality principle*, mediates between our desires and needs and what reality dictates. So we may be hungry, but know no food is available or that it is socially acceptable to eat at a certain time. The super ego represents our conscience and notions of right and wrong and begins to operate from the age of 3 or 4 when we start to apply the *morality principle*. We may therefore be ravenous but so may our siblings and we may have only a small amount of food to share. Our super ego therefore might internally instruct us to share the food equally, not devour it instantly and leave none for others. Freud argued that the infant initially starts with the id, our basic and unprocessed instinctual drives, then begins to assimilate and develop the ego in terms of reality's constraints, and later the super ego becomes incorporated into our personality. This is initially what the voices of more powerful people, such as parents say about right and wrong, which then becomes internalized as our conscience. However, change often occurs at adolescence when we begin to separate from our parents and question the 'rightness' or 'morality' of others' opinions. Freud argues that personality problems can occur later in life if the ego is insufficiently strong to mediate between the id and the super ego.

Freud argued that development occurs through stages and is ruled by libidinal drives, and with each stage pleasure is linked to a particular body area the child is preoccupied with. Up to 1 year, the mouth is claimed to be the key body part and Freud called this the *oral stage*. Food is the main source of gratification and the infant gains as much emotional nourishment from sucking as he/she does nutritional nourishment from food. Freud cautions that excessive or insufficient oral stimulation at this stage can manifest itself later in difficult relationships and in problematic drinking, eating and smoking. In early childhood, between 1 and 3 years, the focus becomes the anus (the *anal stage*). The child's pleasure is therefore centred around defecation, but conflicts occur as the child is trained to use a potty and thus to control immediate toileting urges. Freud argues that fixation at this stage can lead to either an *anal expulsive* (untidy and over-generous) or *anal retentive* (excessively ordered and over-possessive) personality later. In the preschool years (ages 4–6) the *phallic stage* occurs, during which the penis is the focus of sensual interest and the child develops sexual feelings for their opposite-sex parent. After this a period of *latency* follows during which the child is not particularly interested in any body part and energy is channelled into conventional activities like sports and school work. At adolescence, Freud claims that the *genital stage* begins and lasts throughout life. This is when an opposite-sex partner is sought to compensate for distance from the opposite-sex parent.

Freud drew many of his theories from his middle-class, often psychologically troubled, female patients. Therefore one could plausibly argue he was dealing not with normal but with potentially abnormal development. Many of Freud's female patients also disclosed their fathers had sexually assaulted them as children. At first Freud believed them, thinking incestuous rape could be the cause of many of their adult difficulties, but he later claimed these were delusional fantasies. In 1981, Jeffery Masson, the projects director of the Freud archives, was dismissed because he claimed Freud had intentionally suppressed these key findings of incestuous child abuse from his earlier work. Masson asserted Freud had been unable to come to terms with the 'truth' of his patients' disclosures, fearing a public outcry and losing his reputation if he publicly revealed his findings (Masson, 1984). To deal with this, Masson argues, Freud reconfigured the claims of sexual abuse as fantasies and devised an elaborate theory to explain them, the Oedipus theory (the Electra theory when it relates to girls). Freud claimed this came into play during the phallic stage between the ages of 4 and 6, when girls and boys apparently have sexual feelings towards their opposite-sex parent and are jealous of and want to displace the same-sex parent. Freud described boys being frightened of castration by their fathers because of concern their hidden desires for their mothers would be discovered, whereas he asserted girls become aware they do not possess a penis and therefore display *penis envy*. According to Freud, these feelings can only be resolved by identification with the same-sex parent, which occurs during the genital stage when adolescents become interested in unrelated opposite-sex partners.

Defence Mechanisms

Freud therefore sees some people as becoming fixated or 'stuck' at certain psychological stages or returning to these during trauma. Although many today ridicule Freud's psychosexual stages, they have permeated into our collective consciousness. We might, therefore, call someone anal if they seem obsessed with power, order and control. Freud also saw people as dealing with problems with what he called *defence mechanisms* (these are coping strategies commonly used to stave off or delay fear and anxiety). Although Freud saw defence mechanisms frequently deployed by children, he expected a mentally healthy adult to resort to them less often. Some are consciously drawn upon, such as *suppression* (pushing to the back of your mind something you don't want to acknowledge or confront). For example, you might have an imminent exam which you should be revising for and feel anxious about it, so you push thoughts of it away. People deploy other strategies, often without being aware of them, such as *repression*. This involves unconsciously burying in our mind something it is difficult for us to deal with, such as child sexual abuse. *Projection* is another defence mechanism involving transposing onto others your unacceptable unconscious. So, if you accuse someone of being greedy it may be that this is your unacknowledged feeling about yourself which you are projecting onto them. Although Freud saw most defence strategies in adulthood as unhealthy or destructive, he viewed *sublimation* – in which people put their repressed energies, for example sadness about rejection by a loved one, into working really hard – as a potentially productive defence mechanism.

Freud's work is controversial not only because it partially grew out of his denial of child sexual abuse and focuses on an empirically untestable unconscious, but also because men are positioned as the norm. Females are represented as deficient and 'other' because they do not possess a penis, although it is likely that penis envy, if it occurs, is symbolic, and relates to men's greater power rather than to women actively desiring the corporeal possession of a penis. Although Freud's theories are contentious and he was obviously strongly influenced by his sex, his middle-class upbringing and the prevalent attitudes of nineteenth-century Vienna, he is still a very important developmental theorist. Freud's most important contribution was to lay the groundwork for greater understanding of personality formation. His theorization of defence mechanisms also still has much resonance today. However, the Oedipus/Electra Complex remains highly problematic, not only in terms of his denial of the reality of child sexual abuse but because family relationships are now much more divergent. There is also currently greater awareness of how gender is socially constructed, and of gender inequality, and arguably greater acceptance of same-sex sexual relationships, which would invalidate the genital and phallic phases. Therefore, certain aspects of Freud's theory seem irrelevant today and his unassailable preoccupation with sex and the penis, and their positioning as key tenets in child development, remain highly problematic.

The psychosocial approach

Erik Erikson was more aware than Freud of how the psychological and social interacted, although positioning the term 'psycho' before 'social' suggests the psychological elements were of greater importance. Unlike Freud, Erikson does not necessarily see one stage as having to be successfully completed before the next stage can be entered, although he presents his stages as a series of challenges the child has to engage and wrestle with. He is also less concerned with sexual aspects of development than Freud was. Initially, Erikson's stages were child-focused and only one stage concerned adult development. However, his later work placed more emphasis on adults.

In the first year, the initial stage Erikson documents is *trust vs mistrust* during which the child needs to develop a sense of security and receive stable care in order to achieve trust, and if this does not occur the child may become suspicious and fearful. In the second and third years, the second stage is *autonomy vs shame and doubt*, when the child is striving to gain some independence from others and takes pride in its abilities. In the fourth and fifth years, the stage of *initiative vs guilt* takes precedence. This involves exploring the environment and initiating and planning new activities but trying not to feel shameful or guilty. From 6 to 11, *industry vs inferiority* is the key stage, in which, ideally, the child starts to feel competent and proud of its achievements, but negative feelings and punitive responses may detract. During adolescence, the experience of *identity vs role confusion* predominates. This stage is about learning to see oneself as a separate (from family and other people), competent (not dependent or not still learning), individual, and ideally having successfully negotiated and consolidated one's identity. The young adulthood stage involves trying to initiate and sustain deep, intimate relationships. Middle adulthood is a time where *generativity vs stagnation* vie for dominance. It involves productivity, setting oneself new challenges and making a contribution to wider society. Late adulthood is about making sense of one's life and ideally seeing one's achievements positively rather than despairing over what was lost or not achieved (see chapters 4 to 7 for greater elaboration on adolescent and adult stages).

Attachment

John Bowlby (1969, 1973, 1980) was the key progenitor of attachment theory. Although his theory did not explain developmental stages, it did try to understand how infants form attachments to their adult carers which can significantly impact upon their future physical and mental health. Bowlby wanted to preserve some of Freud's insights about the impact of early experiences but he subjected them to greater scientific testing and therefore defensibility.

Attachments are affective emotional bonds formed with others, a secure attachment being characterized by intimacy, emotional security and physical safety. Human babies are born almost entirely helpless and remain dependent for a long time (unlike many animals). Bowlby argued they are also born with initial innate reflexes to orient them towards other humans and attract attention and care. Initially – and other research has reinforced these findings – a baby will smile indiscriminately, although from 2 months babies engage in social smiling. Young babies also show a distinct preference for faces or face-like structures. Babies therefore attempt to attract the attention of preferred attachment figures by cooing, engaging carers in eye contact and developing the rudiments of primary inter-subjectivity through reciprocal contact. This is sometimes knows as *proto conversation* and may involve turn taking and eye contact in relation to making noises, facial expressions and bodily movements. Although there is debate about how many individuals a baby can be attached to and at what ages, and what sex the carers should be, Bowlby asserted initially one 'female' mother figure was necessarily the primary carer for an infant (*sexist monotropism*). Later research, however, revealed babies can be attached to a number of familiar people when very young but that, at between 3 and 6 months, they begin to show preferential attachments, although these are as likely to be to children as to adults and attachment to one prime and female carer is neither necessary nor even desirable (Woodhead, 1997).

Bowlby conducted research which he claimed showed that poor attachment to, or separation from, the primary carer can harm infants. He proposed a link between *maternal deprivation* (a term which for him encompassed not only separation of child and mother but also abusive or neglectful parenting) and problems in adolescence and adulthood, including mental ill health and criminal behaviour. Bowlby also looked at the short-term effects on children separated from their mother. He found babies tended to go through a series of stages after separation. These initially involved protests, as enacted through searching, screaming and crying; followed by despair and detachment where all interest in other factors appears to be lost; and thirdly, finally, turning attention to other activities, but in a listless, unenthusiastic manner. If the attachment figure is adequate, Bowlby argues, the child will develop a secure base, trusting in carers and in self, and will explore unknown situations confidently and believe that, if the parental figure disappears, they will return. Drawing from Freud, Bowlby describes a child who has not received secure care as being in a situation of *dissuagement* – a consistent state of unmet need likely to manifest itself in the deployment of defence mechanisms. These coping devices, along with various other strategies, are used simultaneously to diminish anxiety and to attract support and care. Bowlby asserted children's experience with their carers became internalized mentally in an *inner working model* – a template of what is effective in relating to other people, which guides children's future behaviour. Early ideas, including Bowlby's, predicated on observing children separated from prime carers have also been extended into an influential theory of life span socio-emotional development (Howe et al., 1999).

Modern psychoanalytic theories and attachment

Since Freud's pioneering work, a clearer connection has been forged between psychoanalytic and attachment theories, as both focus on early relationships and how we represent and act on them (Steele and Steele, 1998). They both, furthermore, concur with constructions of an internalized working model (a mental state guiding our behaviour) containing ideas about what other people are like and what can be expected from them, what sort of a person we are, and relationship expectations.

Ainsworth et al. (1978) proposed different mother/baby attachment styles from experiments they conducted. In a well-known and now much cited study, they analysed babies' behaviour when separated from their mothers and then confronted with a stranger before she returned – *The Strange Situation*. *Secure attachment* occurs when the main carers(s) are sensitive to babies' needs and communicate with them and inspire confidence. If the carer is separated from the child, there is some distress but after their return reassurance is quickly established. *Anxious/insecure avoidant attachment* occurs when the parent is unable to be responsive to the child's needs or rejects them. This results in the child showing little overt emotion and failing to react when a parent leaves or return. These children rarely seek physical contact but often continually observe the carer in an aloof, wary manner. *Anxious ambivalent attachment* occurs when the carer is inconsistent, at times being warm, affectionate and sensitive, and at other times unavailable or hostile. These children become distressed if separated from their carer(s) but are not reassured on their return. Recent research, furthermore, suggests it is more important for researchers and professionals, particularly those who may come into contact with abused or neglected children, to focus on the child's responses rather than the carer's behaviour, as the latter can be more easily edited during observation (Crittenden and Ainsworth, 1989).

Disorganized attachment occurs when the carer evokes fear or appears frightened herself/himself, but is the only source of potential comfort. The child may therefore behave in ambivalent ways, such as wanting to be picked up and cuddled but then freezing or looking away. The fourth response is of the *non-attached* child, a child who has been fed and clothed but has received little human interaction. This occurs in the most deprived situations, such as the Romanian orphanage children studies (Rutter et al., 1988). However, C. Beckett (2002) suggests it can also transpire if there is only one carer and they are permanently and profoundly mentally ill. Rutter (1995) later modified Bowlby's early ideas, taking exception to the term 'maternal deprivation', firstly because it wrongly assumes a necessary female primary carer and also because it fails to differentiate between a lack of emotional attachment and lack of cognitive stimulation, although both could be simultaneously absent. Rutter's Romanian research also found psychological deprivation to be more significant and enduring than nutritional deprivation. Cumulative evidence now suggests women who remembered their mothers as rejecting them were overall more likely than other mothers to spurn their offspring, although those who gave coherent accounts of this rejection were less likely to reject. Adverse early familial experiences combined with poor attachments have also consistently been found to be linked with criminal and antisocial behaviour (Bacon and Richardson, 2001).

Winnicott, a child psychoanalyst, also discussed *object relations* (1953), whereby, if the child finds in its main carer a mirror through which its needs are met, this gives the child a sense of power and security. Conversely, when needs are not mirrored, a denial of the child's own feelings occurs and he/she compulsively watches the carer, trying to pre-empt their reactions. When a child has experienced problematic attachments, they may replay earlier dysfunctional roles with new carers or within intimate adult relationships. For example, if you had a parent who made you feel unworthy of love and attention, frequently abandoning you with inattentive strangers, at adulthood you may anticipate that, and behave as if other people will still abandon you now. Because of this *defensive exclusion*, it is difficult for some people to change their internal working models (C. Beckett, 2002). Painful and unresolved feelings therefore often manifest themselves in primitive and unconscious ways.

Splitting occurs when people simultaneously believe two incompatible ideas, such as that their father loved them very much and that their father was cruel and manipulative to everyone, without being aware of their inherent contradictions. When people are unable to confront past trauma and link it to its effects, splitting often also manifests itself symptomatically, but unconsciously, through depression, aggression, hysteria and psychosis. Splitting also occurs through *dissociation* whereby a coherent and cohesive sense of self fails to form, disrupting developmental processes (McElroy, 1992).

Mothers maltreated by their own mothers as children, who subsequently developed secure attachments with their offspring, differed from other maltreated mothers who did not. They reported having had a parent or substitute parent who had provided love and support, currently had a supportive husband who was involved in childcare and had an awareness of how the care they received as children could impact on their parenting abilities, many having undergone therapy at some point (Morton and Browne, 1998). It therefore appeared that they had been able to change their internal working models.

Cognitive development

The most compelling theory of cognitive development was developed by Jean Piaget (1926, 1964). Piaget, a Swiss academic, noticed, whilst working on standardizing intelligence tests, that children of certain ages consistently gave the wrong answers to specific questions. He therefore hypothesized that children's thinking was qualitatively different from adults' and subsequently studied them extensively to ascertain how learning and intelligence progressed. Piaget viewed children as not being able to progress to certain stages (which he perceived as qualitatively different), until they attained certain ages and had mastered certain areas – *discontinuity*. Because of this he has been seen as a biological maturationist, although he did acknowledge the environment. Piaget argues that the child's development through, and adaptation to, the stages he formulated takes place via two main concepts, those of *assimilation* and *accommodation*. Assimilation refers to how the external world is experienced and integrated into one's mind, so new events and stimuli are fused into one's pre-existing knowledge and understanding. So a 10-month child handling a book with tactile features may initially understand tactile features to be a defining quality of books. The child may later find a book without tactile features and then will have to adjust his understanding to the point that some but not all books have these features. Accommodation concerns how pre-existing structures of knowledge in the mind are extended and modified, which may involve altering pre-conceived notions of understanding, so new experiences can be interpreted and incorporated into one's mental schema.

Piaget divided children's development into four chronological stages.

(i) the *sensori motor* stage (0–2 years) features learning and progression via a combination of motor actions (reaching, grasping, kicking, etc.) and sensory impressions, learned from touch, smell, sight and hearing. Some actions are instinctual reflexes, such as the baby turning to suckle for milk towards a potential breast – *rooting*, the baby initially sucking or grasping anything put in its mouth or hand – or the invocation of reflexes which close the lungs and cause swimming motions if underwater. Many of these instinctual reflexes are extinguished within a few months, but others, such as blinking or recoiling from heat, remain. Babies and infants therefore cannot be seen completely as a *tabula rasa* or a blank slate. Piaget argues that, initially, babies cannot differentiate between themselves and other objects and people, seeing these as extensions of themselves. The understanding that infants are separate from the rest of the world comes as a major revelation for them and has normally occurred by

2 years. Infants also have no idea of *object permanence* – of an object existing any longer than one can see it. In Piaget's experiments, if you cover up a small ball with a blanket, a baby up to approximately 9 months old will no longer grasp or search for it, which Piaget interpreted as the infant believing the object no longer exists.

(ii) During the *pre-operational* stage (2–7), Piaget found children initially are still concerned with very physical and tangible actions such as finding and retrieving objects, but slowly begin to represent objects and events mentally and symbolically. So a 3-year-old girl may, for example, hold up a banana and talk into it, pretending it is a telephone, or may treat a stick as a wand or a gun. However, children are still often misled by superficial appearances and misjudge reality, being unable to conserve number, mass, volume, length and area. The famous conservation test, devised by Piaget, involved pouring an amount of liquid from one glass container into another differently shaped one, and asking children whether there was more or less liquid in the new container. The children thought more liquid was in the taller, thinner glass with a higher level. They were unable to reverse the process mentally and comprehend that the amount of water remained unchanged. Children are also *egocentric* at this age according to Piaget, and unable to perceive the world from different viewpoints.

A lovely experiment, reinforcing Piaget's assertions of superficiality of appearance, was conducted by DeVries (1969) who had a friendly cat, Maynard, which he encouraged the children to get to know. He then put a dog's mask on Maynard's head and put him behind a screen so only the mask and his tail were visible. The children were told the cat was going to look different and have a dog's face before being asked 'what kind of an animal is it now?' Then, to put some doubt into the equation, they were asked whether it was really a dog and whether it could bark. Children aged 3 were entirely guided by external appearance and thought the cat had metamorphosed into a dog, 4- and 5-year-olds were uncertain, but 6-year-olds were not fooled. Children during this stage are also unable to deal with more than one dimension of a problem at a time: *centration*. So 7-year-old children know what dogs are and that they are also part of a bigger class called 'animals'. They can count up how many dogs and how many animals there are when shown a picture of a number of dogs. However, if you ask them if there are more dogs than animals (after you have asked them to count how many dogs there are), they will tend to say more dogs because, according to Piaget, they can only deal with one grouping at a time. Children of this age also exhibit *animism*, attributing life-like qualities to inanimate objects such as dolls or even external forces such as the wind.

(iii) During the *concrete operational* stage (7–12) children begin to demonstrate logic when dealing with problems. They realize objects are still 'real' and exist even if they cannot see them. They demonstrate reversibility and the ability to represent mentally, and compare what went before with what is happening now. They therefore comprehend the core properties of an object are permanent and that superficial changes do not alter these. They clearly understand that changing the shape of a container water is in does not alter the amount of liquid, or that a boy growing his hair long and wearing a dress is not female. They can apply multiple criteria to objects – Daisy is a cow and is an animal and is black and white and belongs to Farmer Jones. They are able to understand hierarchical relationships: that one item comes before another or is more important or ranked higher than another. Operational thinking thus allows children to combine, separate, order and transform objects hierarchically. Piaget also argues that at this stage egocentrism declines and children communicate better. They understand how others may feel about them and can weigh up inconsistencies and ambiguous situations, such as a person behaving in one way and thinking in another. Their mother being polite to someone she really does not like for the sake of social convention might be one example. They also begin to punctuate their games and interactions with rules and to take intentions into account.

(iv) From 12 to adulthood, the *formal operational* stage is seen as the pinnacle of achievement regarding both logical and abstract thought and is characterized by sophisticated systematic thinking. Although Piaget claims some individuals reach this stage at adolescence, others never attain it (see chapter on adolescence for further examination of this stage and a full analysis of moral development in children and adults).

Modern cognitive developmental theory

Although contemporary cognitive theorizing owes an important debt to Piaget, there have been many queries and counter claims surrounding his theories. as well as some additions, further verification and support. Vygotsky, a Russian social scientist – in contrast with Piaget's focus on biology – was more concerned to demonstrate how culture, language and social interaction transmit ideas, influencing development. Vygotsky's most influential theory (1978) was the *zone of proximal development*, representing the difference between what a child can achieve alone and what they can achieve if initially supported and actively guided by another. A parent helping a child ride a bike for the first time without stabilizers may initially instruct the child didactically whilst walking alongside, supporting the bike's full weight and controlling balance. They may let go of the bike at first for just a few seconds but then for increasingly longer periods, accompanying this with encouragement and advice until eventually the child has the confidence and the requisite skills to ride unaided. The adult's skill lies in neither boring the child by helping them with something easy nor subjecting them to failure by presenting them with something too difficult, but in strengthening and extending their capabilities by providing a scaffold.

Gibson challenges Piaget's view that children slowly make sense of their worlds through their senses, and argues babies have an inborn perceptual system which functions from birth. Gibson and Walk (1960) developed a visual cliff, an even platform with a deliberate visual illusion half-way across, suggesting the second half of the platform was much lower and they could potentially fall. Babies were reluctant to crawl across the second half, although, as they were 6 months old, it is debatable whether this showed a learnt experiential fear or some innate perceptual apparatus. Piaget also suggested tactile interaction with objects was necessary to understand them perceptually but habituation tests with babies prior to where they engage physically with objects appear to show they can visually differentiate between shapes. Also studies of Thalidomide children, without hands or feet, showed they developed normal perceptual skills despite their inability to grasp for, hold and touch objects, suggesting infants were well equipped perceptually from the onset (see Affolter and Bischofberger, 2000), although these children did still physically interact with objects with other body parts.

Another criticism challenged Piaget's claims of object impermanence up to 18 months. Research by Bower et al. (1970) showed that children were surprised (measured by heart rate) when an object did not reappear after going behind a screen. Other research has shown babies reach for objects when the light has gone out and they cannot see them (Bower and Wishart, 1972). However, most babies do not manually search before 8 months. Some commentators have shown that the more complex the task is, and the more steps it involves, the less likely babies are to be able to master it. This may be related more to memory than to cognitive object impermanence (Bryant, 1990), suggesting that, although Piaget's conclusion was right, his explanation required modification. So reaching for a toy in the dark is simpler than remembering where a ball was placed under a blanket and then attempting retrieval. Preschool children's illogicality has also been questioned by others (e.g. Donaldson, 1978; Siegal, 1991) who claim children miscomprehend the adults' language or see the set tasks as too complex, irrelevant or nonsensical, which a number of experiments have confirmed (Fishbein et al., 1972; Baillargeon et al., 1985). Nonetheless, there is still significant debate as to whether, or to what extent, preschool children can demonstrate logical thought. Dunn (1988), however, argues that naturalistic studies where children are studied in their 'normal environments' are better indicators of cognitive development than predesigned artificial experiments. In an examination of morality, it was found that some very young children have an understanding of both intentionality and morality. For example, one 2-year-old was upset because her older sibling had pushed her (she knew the action was wrong); and other children did things they knew were forbidden, such as picking their noses or surreptitiously eating stolen food (Dunn, 1988). In relation to Piaget's claim of the transition from the pre-operational to the operational stage, younger children therefore do seem able to perform some transitive tasks but only under special conditions, so whether there is a distinct step from the pre-operational to the operational stage is still debated and Vygotsky's zone of proximal development may partially help to explain the transition.

The main criticisms of Piaget are therefore that: (i) the stage model depicts thinking as more consistent and discontinuous than it is; (ii) children can perform some tasks earlier than Piaget suggested, under special conditions; (iii) he did not take sufficient account of the role of the social; and, finally (iv) he is rather vague about the mechanisms that produce cognitive development, such as assimilation. However, these weaknesses do not invalidate his main theories or undermine the magnitude of his tremendous achievements.

Learning theories

Learning theories are generally unconcerned with the unconscious mind, internal states or developmental stages. Many focus only on the relationship between overt stimuli and resultant observable behaviour, showing how behaviour can be both learnt and unlearnt. Many of the experiments the early learning theorists conducted on humans were cruel and would not be allowed to happen now. Additionally, many experiments were only carried out on animals and then generalized to human behaviour. They are therefore problematic because the extent to which one can extrapolate from a study carried out with animals to humans is a highly contested issue.

Classical conditioning was discovered by a physiologist, Ivan Pavlov (1849–1936). When a bell was sounded immediately before his dogs received food, after a short while the dogs salivated at the sound of the bell. The dogs therefore forged a connection between the bell and food, anticipating they would be fed soon after they heard the sound (Pavlov, 1927). This response, a *conditioned reflex*, could be extinguished fairly rapidly, if the bell stopped being followed by food – *extinction*. However, such conditioning can quickly be reactivated if, for example, the bell is followed by food again after a few months: this is known as *spontaneous recovery*. Animals and humans also forge related connections, so if such a dog hears a similar noise to a bell, they might initially salivate – this is known as *generalization*. Dogs can conversely be trained to differentiate between different stimuli which are quite similar (*differentiation*), for example the differing tones of a bell. As C. Beckett (2002) points out, many pet dogs and cats become attuned to their owner's car engines, appearing at the window or door only when they hear this particular engine.

J. B. Watson coined the term *behaviourism* and thought that conditioning techniques could be used to produce conformity in people, and believed, following on from Locke's notion of the *tabula rasa*, that children could be moulded to become whatever adults wanted them to be:

> Give me a dozen healthy infants, well formed and my own specified world to bring them up in and I'll guarantee to take any one at random and train him to become any type of specialist I might select – doctor, lawyer, artist, merchant-in-chief, and yes even beggar man and thief, regardless of his talents, penchants, tendencies, abilities, vocations and race of his ancestor. (Watson, 1930, cited in Thornton, 2008: 12)

In the 'Little Albert' study, a 'normal' 9-month-old baby, deliberately startled by a loud unpleasant noise every time he was given a docile white rat to play with, rapidly showed intense fear whenever it appeared and attempted to escape (Watson and Rayner, 1920). This fear developed into a full-blown phobia, with the baby generalizing from the rat to all other white furry things, and even fearing men with white beards.

B. F. Skinner (1953) later described another type of learning, *operant* or *instrumental conditioning*. Certain behaviours can be encouraged and others discouraged via clear punishments and rewards. Concepts relevant to classical conditioning, such as extinction, discrimination and generalization, are also applicable to operant conditioning, but classical conditioning is different because it is exclusively about conditioning to respond to new stimuli. Skinner's most well-known experiment was with a rat which he taught to press a lever in order to receive food. Initially, the rat pressed the lever indiscriminately but soon forged a connection between pressing the lever and the appearance of food, pressing it from then on with increasing frequency. This is what Skinner calls *positive reinforcement*. *Negative reinforcement* occurs when, for example, a rat has to keep on pushing a lever to prevent an electric shock. Skinner also investigated different schedules and types of reinforcement, and found reinforcing a specific behaviour sporadically kept the behaviour active for longer than always reinforcing it and then stopping completely. Therefore, if these findings are tenuously extrapolated from animals to humans, if a child is only doing her homework well to receive pocket money, if the reward stops, she is likely to put substantially less effort into her homework. In comparison, if the same child only receives positive reinforcements sometimes after producing good work, she is likely to try diligently to produce it long after rewards have ceased.

Skinner also showed how you could produce very complex behaviour in animals by slowly *shaping* their actions to what was desired with reinforcements. Initially, reinforcement might be given to a pigeon as a reward for doing something very general like pecking a ball, but then it would have to push it forward to get food, with the eventual goal or intention being to shape the pigeon to push a ball, for example, into a net or through a maze. How fast certain behaviours are learned or unlearned depends greatly on *schedules of reinforcement*, but some reinforcers are more powerful than others. With rats, behaviours were extinguished far slower after morphine had been given as an inducement than with other reinforcers. Contemporary research and analysis of learning theory, however, suggests it involves more than learning by association and reinforcement and that other factors, including cognition, have to be taken into account. Even early studies by Skinner showed that rats could find their way round a maze if they had to swim, even if they had only gone by paw last time. Since the muscle movements are different for swimming and walking, so the rats must have produced a mind map to enable them to navigate the maze the second time.

Martin Seligman (1975) compared two groups of animals in an experimental situation in which one group could prevent an electric shock – by, for example, pressing a lever – and the other could not. When tested later, those who had previously been subjected to unavoidable electric shocks failed to try to prevent them. Unlike the control group, they had learned to become defenceless – a phenomenon Seligman called *learned helplessness*. Pavlov also subjected his dogs to a task differentiating between two small and very similar shapes, which they found almost impossible, becoming distressed and disorientated. In another test, Pavlov used an electric shock rather than a bell or buzzer as the precursor for food. He found these experiments impacted negatively upon the animals' capacity for learning for a significant time afterwards. These experiments suggest children who have learnt they have little ability to change unpleasant situations when young may listlessly accept unpleasant but changeable future situations and this may lead to depression. Other psychologists have found animals learn faster through observing other animals complete tasks than through operant conditioning. Bandura (1977), for example, found observational learning was very important in children, who learnt through reading and listening as well as observing and were more likely to copy people they saw as similar to themselves, as having high status, and if they saw the model rewarded. Four preconditions stipulated for effective modelling were: (i) *attention*, which could be affected by sensory capacities, arousal, emotional state, complexity and previous reinforcement; (ii) *retention*, remembering what was seen, symbolic coding, mental images and symbolic rehearsal; (iii) *reproduction* – actually reproducing the behaviour observed; and (iv) *motivation* – having a good reason to copy that behaviour such as previous or promised incentives. Bandura's social learning theory is therefore more complex and multifaceted than earlier learning theories, explaining behaviour as an interaction between cognitive, behavioural and environmental factors. The next section also highlights the importance of flexibility and combining theories.

Language acquisition

This final section will show how various theories combined may help to explain children's language acquisition better than solely relying on one theory alone. Human beings are the only species that develop language, and it is also species-universal in the sense that all infants learn language unless they encounter severe environmental conditions or have significant cognitive or sensory impairments. There appears to be a critical learning period between the age of 5 and adolescence. After this, language acquisition is much more difficult and ultimately often unsuccessful, as shown by studies of feral children and of second language learning.

Much of the speech directed at babies is different from normal conversation and occurs in most cultures, being variously dubbed *parentese* and infant-directed talk (IDT). IDT can be differentiated from normal speech by its emotionally positive tones, greater exaggeration, and switching from high to low tones, as well as slower and clearer speech. Babies, furthermore, seem more receptive to IDT than to normal adult speech. Infants also comprehend language before they speak it, and their speech initially lags significantly behind their understandings. Babies' repertoires of sounds are very limited in the first two months, after which they start pronouncing simple speech sounds like 'ooh' and 'aah'. At 6–10 months they begin to babble, mostly using their native language sounds. Congenitally deaf babies exposed to sign language also start to babble at the same time (Petitto and Marentette, 1991), but for those not exposed to sign language, for whom a communication deficit often occurs, babbling is delayed (Oller and Eilers, 1988).

Infants learn their first words as familiar sounds but rapidly comprehend that words do have meaning. First meaningful words occur at 10–15 months. They comprise mostly of nouns such as toys and people's names and occasionally phrases indicating events, such as 'bye bye', but comprehension is complicated by mispronunciation. They may say 'nana' rather than 'banana' because they are unable to reproduce the 'ba' sound. By 18 months they have acquired roughly fifty words, but after that rapidly expand their vocabulary, learning new words almost every day, and start to combine words into sentences. By the end of their second year, although young children talk to other children, they tend to be egocentric and not very reciprocal. These pseudo-conversations are referred to as *collective monologues* (Piaget, 1926). By 5, children can produce full narratives and refer to the past, which those aged 3 and under are unable to do. The average 5- to 10-year-old can use language as well as adults, although their vocabulary is more limited (Cole et al., 2005).

But how do children learn language? Various views exist, some relating to theorists previously examined, but none singularly provides satisfactory explanations. *Learning theorists* argue that children learn language from copying others and responding to positive reinforcement, which to some extent seems logical. However, a *nativist perspective*, such as that adopted by Chomsky (1988) and Pinker (1994), contends language is too complex to be learnt solely by parrot-like imitation. Additionally, infants and children continually produce words and sentences they have never heard before, for example, 'I hurted' or 'I catched the ball'. The nativists therefore propose we are biologically equipped to learn language through an internal, genetically endowed LAD, or language acquisition device, which equips us with a universal grammatical structure.

The *semantic perspective* contends cognitive and social factors are hugely important. Cognitive development seems to precede language development, and children are impervious to learning grammatical rules before a certain period that may be linked to their developing cognition. This has led some academics to reject Chomsky's nativist views completely (e.g. Donaldson, 1978). Socially, children therefore need to understand and make sense of human situations before they can interact fully in the world, so neither parrot-like learning nor being endowed with an LAD are sufficient for learning language; children need also to endow it with meaning. Children's attachments and internal working models may also profoundly influence the speed at which they learn language, and how and why they communicate. Therefore, many of the main theories examined in this chapter could be used to understand language to some extent, or why in some situations it might be delayed.

Conclusion

This chapter introduced students to the key theorists and the main theories which try to explain children's psychological development, also exploring their strengths and weaknesses. It briefly outlined children's physical growth, then covered psychosocial, psychoanalytic and cognitive development, additionally incorporating more recent revisions to these approaches. Behaviourist and learning approaches were then briefly outlined. The last section demonstrated how a number of different theories may be important in explaining development – taking children's language acquisition as an example. The main critics of traditional psychology are the 'new sociology of childhood' theorists, although critical developmentalists have recently emerged and some cross-cultural theorists also negate developmental psychology's Eurocentric bias. The claims of these three groups will be evaluated in the third chapter. By the end of chapter 3, students will then be aware of the strengths and weaknesses of both childhood psychology and the sociology of childhood and their different theories.

Reflection and discussion questions

Who are the most important child development theorists? Why?

What are stage theories and why are they so prominent in developmental child psychology?

What are the key tenets of attachment theory and why might they be important for health, education and social care practitioners to understand?

Recommended reading

There is a vast range of lengthy but introductory child development texts emanating from North America, the texts by Siegler et al. (2006) and Cole et al. (2005) being both in-depth and accessible. Thornton's shorter (2008) text on human development, which focuses predominantly on children and adolescents, is a shorter but well-set-out and analytical UK example, as is Davenport's (1994) introduction to child development. Journals worth consulting for more up-to-date research include *Human Development*, *Developmental Psychology* and *Child Development*.

The New Social Studies of Childhood

Has [critical psychology] been too afraid of 'throwing out the baby with the bath-water?' . . . the developing baby does indeed have to be thrown out. It is a changeling. The real bath-tub is occupied not by a naturally-developing baby but by a real baby, whose development has to be made through human activity.

(Morss, 1996: xii)

Introduction

Although developmental psychology treats childhood implicitly as a universal, ahistorical period (as one can surmise from the last chapter), it is nevertheless essential to locate childhood within history, ideology and culture and to understand the mutual inter-dependence of adulthood and childhood. For example, if we claim children are innocent and underdeveloped, we simultaneously imply developed and not-so-innocent adults. The UK, in comparison to many developing societies, is, furthermore, an ageing society, where people live longer than ever before and fewer children are born. Children therefore become, for the first time in history, a numerical minority compared to adults. This situation precipitates debates about genera-tional distributive justice and the division of labour between young and old (discussed further in the chapers on middle and old age), and has led to both 'growing up' and 'growing old' extending and becoming more culturally differentiated from each other (Zinnecker, 2001). The generational divisions also include significantly different birth cohorts within them who were profoundly influenced by differ-ent historical events such as war, economic recession, technological advances and the advent of consumerism.

This statistical change has direct effects on children's lives. Adults who care for and teach children become older, and the influence of siblings and cousins decreases as that of grandparent and older generations increases. Adults also have less opportunity than before to interact with children, exacerbated by societal fear of adult–child abuse and traffic accidents, which further restricts informal contact. The worst-case scenario envisaged is that adults and children become strangers and fearful of each other. Interestingly, in a recent UK questionnaire study involving 2,000 primary and secondary school children and 500 adults, only a minority of children felt most adults were friendly towards them. Of the adults, 33 per cent agreed with the statement 'The English love their dogs more than their children', with 25 per cent not being sure and only 42 per cent disagreeing (Madge, 2005). Therefore, in an individualized, ageing society, many adults may reject responsibility for supporting 'other people's' children. This could be linked to increasing child poverty in the UK, which sits contradictorily alongside our cradle-to-grave welfare state and claims that we are now a child-centred society and that children are precious emotional and future economic resources.

Within traditional sociology, the environment and the social have always been fundamental to socialization, overriding the importance of the biological, genetic and physical. The child in earlier sociological depictions was seen as dependent and immature, the 'future generation' in training (e.g. Durkheim, 1961), but far less concern was shown with them in the present. There have also been ongoing arguments about who benefits from socialization. Structural functionalists view socialization as imposed by, and positive overall for, society. Other sociologists argue particular groups benefit more and accrue more material resources and power, status and influence than other groups – some claiming this is largely achieved through *ideological hegemony* (Gramsci, 1971). Marxist sociologists see socialization as inculcating the socio-economically poorer echelons of society into conformity and not challenging the iniquitous social order. Marx claimed this ideological indoctrination was perpetrated, at the time he was writing, through religion being 'the opiate of the masses' and people being persuaded hard work and acceptance of their lowly ascribed position would lead to rewards in an afterlife. Might the mass consumer society and an 'obsessive' preoccupation with gaming and reality TV be the new opiates for the masses? Feminist sociologists claim differential socialization of boys and girls leads to them behaving in different and oppositional ways and to more advantages in terms of influence, status and resources for males.

For traditional developmental psychologists, although the social context is increasingly seen as important, it is less significant than the biological and the genetic and has been imported as an add-on to earlier theories. A politicized awareness of the status of childhood is also generally absent. The emphasis is on how children develop through universal, natural and inevitable chronological stages, alongside support from other humans. The study of various 'wild', 'feral' or 'unsocialized' children has conclusively demonstrated that without integration into a human culture, children do not 'naturally' go through these stages. Case studies of these 'wild' children suggested some were raised by animals or survived alone in 'the wild', or alternatively they were found after extensive cruel treatment from other humans and/or deliberate isolation from human contact. Genie, for example, was locked in a darkened attic tied to a potty chair with minimal human contact until the age of 13 (Rymer, 1994). When found, most of these children understandably could not talk or sometimes even walk, and their behaviour was primitive and animalistic. Even with intensive support, affection and teaching, none, unfortunately, was able to overcome their past and reach normal developmental milestones or integrate into society fully. This suggests there is a critical or sensitive time period for some aspects of development and illuminates the importance of combining both nature and nurture simultaneously.

The preceding chapter outlined how psychology presents child development as a universal, linear, individualized process which biology and genetics dominate, the social context perhaps slightly altering when and how certain people reach certain stages or perform certain actions. Only learning theorists consider the environment highly significant, but in a simplistic, mostly non-cognitive manner, predicated on modelling, reward and punishment. From the 1980s and 1990s onwards, some sociologists, who have subsequently become known as the 'new sociology of childhood' theorists, however, began to challenge both the socialization (old sociology) and developmental psychology paradigms. They therefore proposed more heterogeneous and complex ways of understanding childhood (e.g. Jenks, 1996; Corsaro, 1997; James and Prout, 1997; Gittins, 1998; Lee, 2001; Mayall, 2002; Wyness, 2006).

Critical developmental psychologists simultaneously emerged, who were, to varying degrees and for various reasons, critical of developmental psychology (e.g. Henriques et al., 1984/1998; Stainton Rogers and Stainton Rogers, 1992; Burman, 1994; Morss, 1996). Some cross-cultural psychologists criticized developmental psychology's unacknowledged middle-class, American and Eurocentric bias but many continued to accept developmental psychology's general validity otherwise (e.g., Berry et al., 2002; Robinson, 2007). Since then, childhood studies has forged a more interdisciplinary, social path with sociologists, anthropologists, political scientists, economists and social geographers collaborating productively. However, the ideological hegemony of orthodox psychology and its usefulness as a servant of powerful interests (Dafermos and Marvakis, 2006) means that, thus far, it has remained relatively protected from and impervious to criticisms or new knowledge (Thorne, 2007).

The following examples illustrate how this diminution of the social occurs within psychology and expose the resultant problems. In the sixth edition of Kathleen Berger's US life span psychology text, she recounts that, when her first child was not walking by 14 months, she consequently became anxious as she had memorized the developmental norm that a 'normal' child should be walking by 12 months (K. Berger, 2005: 135–6). She initially thought her daughter walking later was predominantly dictated by her genetic make-up, due to her grandmother coming from France where children walked 'late', also citing ethnic differences as attesting to the power of genes (rather than viewing behaviour as a product of culture or an interaction between culture and biology). Eventually Berger concedes that practice 'at walking', combined with the cultural attitude of a different carer, might have made the difference (i.e. the important factors were social). Although this paragraph may confuse its intended audience, novice psychology undergraduate students, it nonetheless reveals the difficulties associated with subscribing wholesale to developmental psychology and illuminates its biological reductionism.

In the second edition of Siegler et al.'s US child development textbook (2006), the authors claim that a small tribe of hunter gatherers in Brazil, 'the Piraha', perform poorly on 'standard tests of numerical reasoning' because of limited words to describe number. This claim is set in the context of examining language and cognition, but nowhere is it explained that in the Piraha's culture numbers are generally superfluous. Although language and perception are two of developmental psychology's areas of study, it seems immune to their power to convey cultural norms and privilege. A photograph of a black man in a loin cloth, looking bemused by various objects which he is supposed to sort and count, whilst the caption below says he is unable to do so, could be inadvertently interpreted as an iconographic representation of the 'primitive savage'. It could mirror early Western colonialism in which black people were subordinated to white people. Images are also recalled more easily than words and, although constructed for a particular audience, often invoke ambiguous emotions and trigger multiple meanings (Gittins, 2004; Burman, 1994). These problems occur because Western developmental norms are expressed as prima facie standards and the two examples given highlight the difficulties facing nurses, physicians, teachers and social workers, who are often introduced uncritically to traditional psychology and then expected to make important decisions about children. Developmental psychology is also often incorporated into policy and practice instruments such as the 'Framework of Assessment' for social workers (DoH, 2000: 10–11, in Taylor, 2004).

This chapter will initially outline and evaluate criticisms made by the 'new' sociologists, critical developmentalists and cross-cultural theorists about traditional developmental child psychology. It will then evaluate the alternative methods and observations they present for understanding and studying childhood. The final section will contrast and compare traditional developmental psychology with the new social studies of childhood.

Criticisms of developmental psychology

Universality and Technologies of Measurement

Developmental psychology makes sweeping, universal claims about children but fails to locate childhood or itself historically or politically (Burman, 1994). Psychology's origins, however, coincide with the social unrest in Europe in the late nineteenth century when rapid urbanization and industrialization illuminated social problems, including the poor physical state of army recruits. These problems provoked political and upper-class concern about genetic degeneracy, 'feeblemindedness' and the overall 'poor' quality of the nation's 'stock'. This resulted in a furore of testing and measurement, with certain groups, such as working-class children, being seen as potential threats. In conjunction with the rise of other 'psy' professionals in the nineteenth century, such as social workers and psychiatrists, psychology (i.e., through drawing up physical and psychological milestones) contributed to childhood becoming the most 'intensively governed sector of personal existence' (N. Rose, 1991). The clinic and the school became the obvious laboratories of measurement, where children were designated normal or abnormal. Intelligence testing also led to children's mental age being linked to their chronological age and moral and political agendas were disguised underneath this assumed scientific neutrality.

> What is perhaps different about standardized testing, compared to other forms of testing or examination, is that the moral evaluation that underlies the description is rendered invisible and incontrovertible through the apparent impartiality of statistical norms and administration through the power of the institutions that can enforce statistical description as moral political *prescription*. (Burman, 1994: 19 – original italics)

Morss (1996), an anti-developmentalist, following on from his epigraph in the introduction – which is used as a central, critical idea threaded throughout the chapter – argues, furthermore, that assumptions that babies are like X or do Y at a certain age/stage are often inaccurate and do not really help practitioners. Thurtle (2005), a nursing academic, initially argues positively that taxonomies of norms and benchmarks enable child progress to be monitored by early years' practitioners. However, Thurtle then ironically shows that the criteria screening should be judged by – that it is simple, acceptable to most parents, accurate, repeatable, sensitive and specific to what it is testing for – are frequently difficult to fulfil. A distraction test to determine hearing in 8-month-old infants, in which accuracy and repeatability depend on the competence of the testing staff and the test's sensitivity, can lead to false positives, some children being diagnosed with a hearing loss when they can hear well, and false negatives when others are inaccurately judged to have normal hearing. This increases the anxiety of some parents unnecessarily and reassures others wrongly. Even with simple growth monitoring activity, Thurtle concedes there is much debate about normality, when and how regularly children should be weighed and measured, and when/whether concern is justified.

Biological Determinism, Individualisation and Sidelining the Social

Developmental psychology's roots also lie within Darwinian evolutionary theory, in which children were seen as primitive, savage and undeveloped, although recourse to pre-Darwinian notions of genetic heritability was more important than environmental adjustment through variation. Burman (1994) illustrates how, even in areas as diverse as attachment and language, descriptions of 'normative' development quickly elide into 'naturalized prescriptions' linked with biology and evolutionary genetics. Further to Gibson and Walk's experiment, Burman problematizes and expands the debate as to whether an infant's ability to avoid potentially dangerous depth situations is due to learnt behaviour or innate perception, through a study applying face recognition knowledge to the visual cliff experiment (Sorce et al., 1985). As in the original experiment, mothers were at the other side of the platform, but here facial expressions were key for whether infants crossed to the deep side. Most crossed when mothers smiled or looked interested, but few when she looked angry, which might signal restraint. This experiment shows that reducing complex human behaviour to simple unilinear explanations is rarely possible. In this scenario, motivation, attachment and communication must be considered, alongside learnt behaviour and potentially genetically endowed depth perception. In most developmental child psychology books, this experiment is, however, not even mentioned, demonstrating how clearly entrenched the biological and genetic are within psychology, and how subordinated the social is.

Burman (1994) criticizes the tendency to attribute any seemingly social behaviour, such as smiling, to biological pre-programmed responses or a unilateral micro cause, arguing babies also smile when they have control, due to mastering certain tasks or attracting attention, rather than smiling always denoting affection or sociability. Notions of reciprocal responses in infant/mother communication are also often collapsed back into biology in which the mother is very important in shaping the infant's responses. Another criticism Burman has, which relates to previously cited research, is that potentially different interpretations of a change in the babies' heart rates are not being acknowledged. In the habituation tests (previously discussed), when infants were suddenly shown novel shapes, or objects that had disappeared suddenly re-appeared, their heart rate changed. This was interpreted as the infants showing interest and being able to differentiate between different shapes. However, Burman argues, on the basis of other research, that this may represent a fear rather than an interest response. These interpretation debates again indicate the danger of attributing unilateral and universalistic reasons to pre-linguistic infant behaviour.

Burman contextualizes developmental psychology within an uncritical, nineteenth-century patriarchal society, where men viewed themselves as able to study children with scientific detachment whilst representing women as constitutionally incapable of objectivity, therefore requiring surveillance themselves and in terms of *their* childcare. Burman lambasts those espousing contemporary dogma such as 'breast is best' for guilt-mongering women. She also criticizes familial assumptions, often implicitly reflected in psychology texts, which posit the only real acceptable family as a heterosexual nuclear family and any changes from it, such as black female-headed families and lesbian and gay families, as deviations. Burman also chastises psychology for viewing attachment primarily as the mother–child dyad, mothers still being blamed for their children's problems within the clinical literature, from which notions of the 'naughty' or 'dysfunctional' child emerge. She, furthermore, poses some interesting questions when she asks why we focus on individual development not family or societal development, or why development is often considered in isolation from structural influences such as poverty, racism and sexism.

Woodhead (1997) argues ideas about children are constantly revised, but paradoxically still masquerade as 'natural' cross-cultural, universal 'truths'. He shows how children's perceived 'objective' psychological needs, embedded in textbooks and health and welfare workers', teachers', policy makers' and parents' behaviours, problematically reveal latent and unproven assumptions, exposing more about adults' values than about a child's essential requirements. For example, countless commentators agree children have certain *needs* such as 'affection' or a 'full-time mother figure', but the effects of not having those needs fulfilled, their cultural variability or different ways of meeting them are rarely acknowledged. Woodhead, however, unlike Morss, does acknowledge the universal applicability of some needs and actions such as babies protesting vigorously from 7 months if forcibly separated from people they are attached to, and paying attention to the human face to attract proximity and care.

Cross-cultural Differences – Attachment, Cognition and Communication

Most socially orientated theories of childhood generally concur that psychology incorporates cross-cultural differences as an optional add-on to, and as polarized from, biology, thereby marginalizing the social. Psychology's claim of universal stages is flawed because cross-cultural differences for developmental psychology only inform the context of development rather than structurally altering what development is and how it occurs. A 'universalistic' developmental psychology based on experiments conducted on only 19 per cent of the population (Europe constitutes 12 per cent and North America 7 per cent), ignoring 81 per cent of the globe, is consequently highly problematic (Woodhead, 1999).

Cultural differences impact significantly on traditional tests such as the Strange Situation tests (Ainsworth et al., 1978) and on our often Eurocentric understandings of healthy infant/carer attachments. In Western European countries, the 'anxious/avoidant' classification is more common than in Japan and Israel where the 'anxious/resistant' category is more frequent. However, even within Europe, significant differences can be found. In a video-taped Strange Situation experiment in Germany, 49 per cent of the infants could be labelled 'insecure avoidant', more than twice those normally detected in Euro-American samples (Grossman et al., 1981). However, within that specific cultural context, maternal norms encouraged early child emotional and physical independence. In contrast a Japanese mother and child are viewed as inseparable and the child as an extension of the mother (Goodman, 2000). A suicidal Japanese mother will often kill her young children first, a practice known not as child murder but as double suicide, *Oyako Shinju*, because it is thought to occur out of love, motherless children being seen as condemned to incomplete lives.

In China, the use of the 'avoidant' category as an indicator of insecure attachment has also been questioned as mothers encourage early child independence, often relying on grandparent childcare, and in many African cultures multiple carers are the norm. Western parents often put children in their own rooms at an early age, but Asian and African cultures would see this as abandonment or neglectful (Morelli et al., 1992). Also, in Brazil where child mortality is around 70 per cent in shanty towns, maternal indifference and neglect were seen as a rational response to ill or deficient children. Scarce emotional or material resources were reserved for healthy children, thought to have the best chance of survival (Scheper Hughes, 1992). Therefore, how a child might react to being left by their mother, introduced to a stranger and then reunited with her depends on many variables. These include culturally acceptable attachment and child rearing styles, whether their mother was the main carer, whether there were multiple carers, scarcity of resources and whether being left alone or with strangers in an unfamiliar environment was common.

Studies have therefore shown the Strange Situation attachment styles differ considerably. We also cannot assume identical responses across different cultures mean the same or that different responses can be interpreted oppositionally. The emotions felt could be the same in a particular situation but cultural expression may be different, or vice versa. In some cultures, direct eye contact is seen as indicative of trust, in others as evidence of obeisance or even disrespect (Robinson, 2007). Subtle attachment behaviours are difficult even for well-trained observers to discern with children from unfamiliar cultures. Crittenden and Clausen (2000) therefore suggest the terms 'secure' and 'insecure' attachment should be replaced with terms such as 'adaptive' or 'maladaptive' for the particular culture. However, some contexts may always be abusive and negative for children, such as being a child soldier or a child in a concentration camp. The behaviours and attachments necessary to survive in one context, such as in a violent situation, may be adaptive in the short term but counterproductive in relation to long-term survival or success. Therefore two issues seem important: how much attachment behaviour is adaptive to the context, and how abusive or violent the context is – although abuse and violence are also to some extent culturally relative concepts.

In terms of cognitive development, it has been argued Piagetian tests are impossible to apply without Eurocentric bias (Owusu-Bempah and Howitt, 2000). Many societies do not value or understand sophisticated information processing strategies. Consequently, attainment of the 'higher order' abilities seems clearly linked to experiencing Western-style education (Woodhead, 1999). Differences in results, which often involve non-Western children lagging behind Western children, may be invalid and methodologically problematic if children view testing as irrelevant, suspicious and dangerous. Nyiti (1982) found children performed better when tested by indigenous researchers, suggesting elements of trust and familiarity with the culture are important. Similar problems occur with intelligence, and lower IQ scores historically have been manipulated and mobilized to claim certain racial groups are innately less intelligent than others (e.g. Jensen, 1969; Herrnstein and Murray, 1994). Intelligence also appears to be a peculiarly Western concept. In Mandarin, the nearest equivalent, applied to those who try hard and are socially responsible, is 'good brain and talented' (Keats, 1982). In some African tribes, 'intelligence' encompasses intellectual and social skills used to benefit the community (Wober, 1975).

How people communicate also inevitably impacts on studies. In many Asian countries *filial piety* – respecting, honouring and obeying parents – is paramount. Being direct is a Western norm but could be interpreted as rudeness in collective cultures such as Japan where maintaining harmony is so crucial that embedded ambiguity and implicit messages prevent offence. Living by the clock is also the norm in Western countries but being late or measured by time is incomprehensible to other cultures (Brislin and Yoshida, 1994), such as the Australian Aborigines. As 70 per cent of the world lives in collectivist cultures (Triandis, 1995), measuring development and communication or cognition from a Western perspective, in which competitive, capitalistic individualism is revered, would therefore seem problematic.

The Deficient Becoming

The child is conceptualized in both traditional developmental and socialization theories as a human becoming, a work in progress – a deficient inert creature programmed by either society or biology to become the future completed, adult model. According to both critical structuralist sociologists such as Marx and functionalists such as Durkheim and Parsons, the child is overwhelmingly shaped and moulded by the society it inhabits, whether this is to the ultimate advantage of society overall or advantages certain segments of the population more than others. In psychology, the 'normal' child goes through biologically preordained stages in an orderly, linear fashion. The chaotic, multi-directional and less than certain trajectory of growth and development, and the child as an active agent, may be cursorily acknowledged in some texts but are never fully taken on board. Although since the late 1990s an increasing number of books on adult psychological development have appeared, the majority of textbooks are still about child development, giving the impression adulthood is the finished ideal model of humanity. The focus thus remains on children as the main objects of change. Children are therefore, by default, judged as always physically, intellectually and cognitively hierarchically inferior to adults, little attention consequently being paid to their strengths and their abilities.

The 'new sociology of childhood' theorists and other social perspectives

Although many criticisms levelled by the new sociologists and others towards developmental psychology have validity, to have influence they must also present alternatives. In this respect, although the critical developmentalists have incisively critiqued studies and perspectives within their mother discipline, they have somewhat understandably tended to be eclipsed and marginalized by it. Conversely, because sociology has had a historical tradition of challenging the status quo and of epistemological and methodological flexibility and plurality, it has embraced new, more liberatory ways of understanding children's lives.

Social Constructions of Childhood

Probably the most important contribution sociology has brought to the debates around childhood is *social constructionism*. It was, ironically, a historian, Philippe Ariès (1960), who analysed mediaeval paintings and documents, concluding that, at the time, childhood simply did not exist (and therefore was a social creation) because as soon as children could talk and walk they were depicted as mini-adults, engaging in the same activities as adults. There have been many disagreements about Ariès' methodology and interpretations but he was the first scholar to disrupt embedded preconceptions of universal, unchanging childhoods, although his social constructionist/deconstructionist work was not really seriously built upon by sociologists until the 1980s and 1990s. Since then there has been a proliferation of constructionist work, which can be divided into strong/radical and weak social constructionism (Wyness, 2006). An example of strong constructionism is Stainton Rogers, and Stainton Rogers' (1992) work, which completely divests childhood of any biological, tangible substance and sees it as entirely comprised of stories and discourses – ideas about what is true, natural and right, embodied in our social practices, legislation and belief systems. Childhood in this interpretation is, therefore, what we create and validate as childhood. Woodhead (1997) ackowledges that much of what we believe to be natural about childhood is socially produced but he conversely still acknowledges some universal, global child-hood needs and behaviours, so his version of social constructionism is weaker.

Kitzinger (1997) explains how our socially constructed and senti-mentalized views about children's innocence, passivity and asexuality are a doubled-edged sword in the fight against child sexual abuse. These stigmatize the abused child and the non-abused sexual child and justify adults depriving children of any potentially protective sexual education. Thus childhood is represented not as a dynamic interactive experience but as a series of qualities, in opposition to adult qualities, which generally we adults glorify and attempt to pre-serve (but are we referring to the mystical or mythical walled Garden of Eden or the prison of childhood?). Therefore, the abused child is no longer a child; s/he has been robbed of childhood. Ironically, these adult-idealized qualities, such as innocence and purity, are those fetishized and manipulated by those who sexually abuse chil-dren. Yet at the same time children's smaller size and lesser life experience, less developed cognition and poorer knowledge must also render them more susceptible to abuse, although it is adult ideas about, and treatment of, children which exacerbate this situ-ation. So a weaker social constructionism in which developmental stages and embodiment are both considered, alongside the effect of social constructions and discourse, seems more logical, but sociolo-gists still justifiably fear biologism being misused for discriminatory political purposes.

What is therefore problematic in many sociological accounts of children is either a silence about or total dismissal of development or the awkward use of alternative terms such as 'supplementation' (Lee, 2001) and 'development through dependency' (Jenks, 1996: 41). Some social scientists argue that many contemporary psychologists are attuned to the social, and diversity and difference (Fawcett et al., 2004); that psychological concepts such as attachment, although flawed, are highly useful in understanding how children approach relationships; and that, within some psychological areas, the child in interaction is highly significant (Dunn and Deater-Deckard, 2001; Smart et al., 2001). Hobbs (2002), a psychologist, also contests socio-logical claims that theorists such as Freud and Piaget deny agency, accusing sociology of 'writing off' psychology before giving it a fair hearing or providing a valid alternative.

Historical Constructions

Like developmental psychology, sociology is a relatively new discipline, approximately a century old, although philosophers, scientists and social reformers were interested in children long before. There is no doubt that childhood is both culturally and historically a highly movable feast and that historical evolution does not always indicate ongoing 'progressive' treatment of children. Although the age of criminal responsibility was 12 in the Middle Ages, in the eighteenth century a 7-year-old girl was hanged for stealing a petticoat (Pinchbeck and Hewitt, 1973). In 1968, when an 11-year-old girl, Mary Bell, was put on trial for strangling two younger boys, media reportage was restrained, focusing on rehabilitation and her disrupted, abusive family upbringing (H. Cunningham, 2006). Conversely, twenty-five years later in 1993, when two 10-year-old boys, at the youngest age of criminal responsibility in the UK, were found guilty of killing 2-year-old Jamie Bulger, press reports and the judge's pronouncements were vindictive. The boys were depicted as 'evil fiends' and the police had to restrain hordes of angry, baying adults outside the court (Franklin and Horwath, 1996), suggesting a significant shift in attitude. Mary Bell's later attempt in the 1990s to write a book explaining her childhood experiences was similarly met with outrage, although books written by adult serial killers such as the Kray twins were conversely rapturously received and gratuitously read. At a similar time to the Bulger case, a comparable child murder occurred in Norway, but the emphasis there was on rehabilitating the children back into the community rapidly, albeit with intensive psychological and psychiatric input. The responses from both the public and the murdered child's mother were non-condemnatory, unlike reponses to the Jamie Bulger killing, and the children who killed were seen as victims as well as the child who was killed (Hattenstone, 2000).

To understand these dissonant responses, historical and cultural representations of childhood therefore need to be located within specific material and social circumstances and ideologies. In the UK, the Judaeo-Christian belief that, since the fall of Adam and Eve, all children are marked with the stain of Original Sin has a long history. Ideas of children's 'wickedness' hardened with the creation of the Protestant Church in the sixteenth century, reinforced by philosophers such as Hobbes (1588–1679) who viewed all humankind as intrinsically amoral. The Puritans believed 'evil' children could be redeemed by education and strong discipline, exemplified in Victorian England by phrases such as 'spare the rod, spoil the child' and 'children should be seen and not heard'. John Locke, an English philosopher (1632–1704), in contrast, perceived a child's mind as a blank slate (*tabula rasa*) which culture and society inscribed upon. Although accepting that children could genetically have different abilities and temperaments, Locke felt the environment had an over-riding influence, the finished adult primarily being the result of childhood teaching and instruction.

Jean Jacques Rousseau, a French philosopher (1712–78), was also influential, asserting children were innately good and pure, qualities nurtured through positive education and upbringing, or conversely corrupted by unsuitable rearing. Rousseau introduced the concept of children going through adult-supported 'natural' stages of develop-ment, a viewpoint still discernable within developmental psychology. Both Locke and Rousseau also helped to form the concept of socializa-tion. The Romantic poets such as Coleridge concurred with Rousseau but argued children possessed additional qualities of wisdom, aes-thetic sensitivity and profound morality (Heywood, 2001) and should be worshipped as the embodiment of hope.

However, regarding disabled children (and adults) across all histori-cal periods, exploitation and violence are linked with fear and hatred (Waxman, 1991). This is because associations made between disability and lack of control, and others finding disabled people's appearance or behaviour alarming or unpleasant, subsequently lead to their 'oth-ering' and dehumanization. Therefore, historically, disabled children in the UK were more likely than other 'children' to be seen as evil. Many, alongside disabled adults, were incarcerated and segregated from the eighteenth century onwards until as late as between the 1930s and the 1980s, in various institutions such as 'Poor Houses' and special hospitals. In the eighteenth century, signing was initially promoted amongst deaf children and adults but, because of the tre-mendous influence of Darwin who viewed all disabled children as 'defectives', attempts were soon made to ban signing and to stop deaf people from marrying for fear more and more deaf children would be produced. In Ancient Greece, those children born obviously disabled were killed at birth because they were seen as 'a form of retribution from the gods' (Harrison, 1995: 10).

Jenks (1996) refers to these two competing discourses of evil vs purity and innocence as the Dionysian and Apollonian conceptions of childhood, and Stainton Rogers (2001) illuminates how discourses of control and welfare linked to these conceptions may come into conflict. So the Children Act (1989) embraces an Apollonian concep-tion, placing child welfare and protection at centre stage. Conversely, the 1991 Criminal Justice Act adopts a Dionysian stance, positioning parents as responsible for restraining *their* children's base criminal instincts. It is, furthermore, acceptable for parents to administer 'loving smacks' to their children in the UK, an anomalous mixed metaphor which suggests violence can be protective and loving, but in any other context, including animal welfare, such behaviour would constitute an assault, a criminal act. Research also evidences that parents administer corporal punishment not for the good of the child but because they perceive it as their right when they want to reassert lost control, punish the child or are angry (Hazel et al., 2003; Brownlie and Anderson, 2006). Sweden's different responses to the rare occasions when children kill other children can also be explained by the Scandinavian countries' much more liberal and 'progressive' rights-centred responses to children (Moss and Petrie, 2002). These include Sweden outlawing corporal punishment in 1979, low child poverty and many other child-centred initiatives such as child-only play spaces.

The history of UK childcare policy also swings between different 'ideal type' typologies of children. These range from children being the property of parents with state intervention a last resort – *laissez faire patriarchy* – to a paternalist, protectionist state role, or to a children's rights and liberation viewpoint, which sees children as an oppressed minority group who should be granted a more adult and autonomous status (Fox Harding, 2001). There has been increasing attention paid to the rights of children and their participation in important decisions about their lives in recent legislation but this is often highly tokenistic (L. Green, 2006). Goldson (2001) also argues children are being increasingly demonized in criminal justice policy and, although the Jamie Bulger case was exceptional, it was used to justify hardening attitudes towards children who were seen as out of control, reckless and threatening. Asylum seeker children are also treated less favourably than other children because the Children Act legislation conflicts with other immigration legislation such as the 2004 Asylum and Immigration Act (S. Cunningham and Tomlinson, 2005). The decline in child mortality and fertility in the last century is also related to our contemporary investment in children both as a 'precious' emotional artefact for adults (Zelizer, 1985; Warner, 1994), and as future productive workers (Lister, 2003; Green, 2006), although these attitudes neglect children's own views or current welfare and happiness.

This section has illustrated how changing opinions about children's temperaments have had a cumulative and confusing impact on how we now view children. We tend to see the child as somehow outside of rather than of society and as either innately innocent or evil, or contradictorily both. Sometimes the two discourses conflict, although we rarely consciously recognize this. Evans (1994) outlines how the socially constructed and familial and institutionally policed boundary between childhood and sexuality leads to two versions of the 'protection from sexual harm' argument: 'One of [protecting] sexual beings from harm because of their immaturity and ignorance and the other of [protecting] the non-sexual from the perversity of sexual indoctrination' (Evans, 1994: 9). The next section will draw strongly on social constructionism to elevate the image of the child as competent, one that has been largely absent within traditional social science and public perspectives.

The Competent Child

Generational power and inequalities

The power adults have over children, economically, physically, emotionally and socially, is a key aspect of the new sociology. Childhood is a minority category where paternalistic adult decisions are made on behalf of children and their 'best interests' (Qvortrup, 2002). Jenks (1996) uses the term *gerontocentrism* as a parallel for *ethnocentrism* (judging other cultures unfavourably by using your own cultural standards as a moral yardstick), to illustrate how children's competences have been undermined by adults. *Adultcentricism* also describes the way in which society is organized for, and seen through, the eyes of adults. 'Old sociology' saw the child as an adjunct or possession of the parent or adult. Hence, not only did adults tend to speak for children in terms of research, but researchers unilaterally set the research agenda. They often interpreted children's actions without investigating children's understandings or even observing their behaviour, for example by asking parents questions about their children. In statistical representations children were traditionally grouped homogenously together as dependants under categories such as family income, father's occupation and parents' education (Qvortrup, 1997), although family income alone gives little indication about how and on whom that income is spent, men often controlling the flow of money and benefitting more from it (Pahl, 1989). In these statistical studies, children emerged as 'items' parents spend their time caring for or their money on, leaving us with minimal understanding of how children spend their time outside structured settings and what useful things they may do or say.

The new sociologists therefore turned their attention to generational and other inequalities and exposed childhood as a subordinated social status (Mayall, 2002; S. Jackson and Scott, 2000). In one study, children explained that, although negotiations and bargaining were common, they would be more likely to do what their parents asked but not what their siblings wanted. This was not only because they felt parents as adults held legitimate power but, more importantly, because they were aware of their dependency and parental ability to curtail their activities and deprive them of resources (Punch, 2005). Sociologists have also advocated new methods of researching with children which often involve prolonged interaction with them, for example ethnographic research, interviews, diaries and drawing. The emphasis is on engaging with children on their own terms, eliciting what children really think, feel and do rather than what children think adults do or do not want to know, which is in itself an effect of power inequalities. The ways in which children both possess power and agency and are simultaneously denied them by adults have been illuminated. For example, an analysis of corporeal power shows adults arbitrarily subject small children to unreciprocated hugs and pats and the horrors of kissing undesirable relatives as well as punitive corporal punishments (Hood-Williams, 1990).

Rewriting perceptions of children

The 'new sociology' depicts the child as an active, competent, reflective human entity who has ideas, skills, abilities and power. Initially seen as a participatory *social actor*, one who acts in and on their worlds, recent work progresses a child to a *social agent*, someone who has an effect or impact (Mayall, 2002), a much stronger term (James and James, 2004). By historically, politically and culturally contextualizing children and illuminating the many ways children have lived and been represented, sociology also negates the image of the universal, homogenous child, thus overturning earlier psychological and sociological views of children as biologically programmed robots, inert experimental objects of psychological laboratories or over-socialized cultural dopes (Wrong, 1961).

Corsaro (1997) advocates substituting the old term 'socialization' with *interpretive reproduction*, elucidating the creative, innovative aspects of children's cultures and their contributions to society whilst still acknowledging the constraints imposed upon them. Thorne (1993) shows that children do not directly reproduce adult conceptions of gender but play with them, sometimes conforming to stereotypes, at other times resisting, changing or parodying them. Christensen (1993) illustrates how younger children's fascination with, and desire to show and talk about, their newly encountered minor bruises and scratches is misinterpreted and negated by adults, thinking they are complaining about nothing and not being aware these are actually new experiences for these children. An early ethnographic study of a cancer ward showed how the majority of the children were aware of their terminal diagnoses because they had inventively listened outside doors, accurately interpreting adult conversations, but they protected their parents and other adults from this knowledge and discussed the issues with other children (Bluebond-Langner, 1978).

The Opies' research (1959, 1969) illuminated the importance of peer cultures, children's language, games, folklore and story telling, much being passed down historically, as well as showing how adults' and children's cultures have become sharply differentiated. Children's favourite games then were daring or subversive, those least favoured by adults or which adults demonstrated minimal proficiency in, such as skipping. Their most desirable sweets were those with garish colours and inedible names like traffic light lollipops and gob-stoppers. However, there is now concern that children's restricted freedom outside the home, as discussed later in the chapter (H. Cunningham, 2006), and the power of highly structured activities and new technological entertainment may threaten these cultures, stunt-ing creativity and imagination.

The traditional assumptions that 'adults know best' and what the most important issues are for children are not reinforced by recent research. In one Australian school study of 9- to 12-year-olds, peer bullying was high on the children's agenda in relation to distressing issues but did not even feature on the teachers' parallel list (Howard and Johnson, 2000). In another study one sexually abused teenager expressed great anger that her mother had not intervened, report-ing her mother was consistently saying she would know if anyone was hurting her children and would protect them. In this particular study, all the teenagers were scathing about adults 'protecting' them from sexual knowledge as younger children, because they felt that, if they had had an age-appropriate awareness of what sexual abuse was, they would at least have had a chance of understanding what was happening and telling someone (Green, 2001).

'Imprisoned for their own good?'

Risk management and trying to eliminate risk have additionally had a profound influence on children's freedom. Rosier, an American soci-ologist, recounts how, when her father was 7 in the 1940s, every week he was offered the choice of going with his parents to a cinema about 5 miles away or playing outside with his friends in the neighbour-hood until their return. Rosier recollects a childhood a generation later where, although at night she had to endure babysitters until the age of about 10, she was relatively free to explore her natural environment for hours in the afternoons and early evenings (Rosier and Kinney, 2005). Rosier then goes on to show how in the USA (and the UK is similar) children's freedom to explore the neighbourhood environs alone has become increasingly restricted because of adult paranoia about stranger abuse and accidents. This impacts upon children's perceptions and elevated fears too (Wells, 2005), and leads to children being perceived as more dependent, vulnerable and less competent than before. A recent UK survey revealed only 49 per cent of parents would ever allow their children aged 5–10 to play unsupervised outside their front door in contrast to the over 65s, nearly half of whom played outside every day, with their now grown-up children enjoying similar freedom when children (Living Streets, 2009). Disabled children, for example deaf children, are also likely to be subject to an even more restrictive environment, justified under the guise of parental protectiveness (Young et al., 2008).

There has been a noticeable decrease in the number of children killed in traffic accidents, falling from 7.5 per 1,000 children in 1970 to 4.5 at the end of the twentieth century (H. Cunningham, 2006), but, given that 'the home habitat' of a typical 8-year-old has shrunk by a factor of nine in a generation, then it may warrant consideration whether this mortality decline has been worth the price children have paid for it. The image of a middle-class child, cosseted yet imprisoned behind the windows of a parental car whilst being shuttled to different venues in an endless roundabout of adult-directed, structured activities, such as after-school homework and sports clubs, is evocative (Lee, 2001). Working-class children and youths, in contrast, tend to have greater freedom and mobility and in urban areas are more likely to 'hang around' the streets, but are conversely type-cast as dangerous vandals and hoodlums and perceived of as an unruly threat to society.

If we travel back to the eighteenth and nineteenth centuries, children from the age of a few years old would be expected to work, and although we would not want young children to sell wares on the street, operate dangerous equipment or clean chimneys now, children *could* do these things (H. Cunningham, 2006). They were also accustomed to confronting distressing events like serious illness and death (see chapter 8 for elaboration). Many children still work in low economic resource countries like India, and child labour is often unequivocally denounced as morally wrong by Western countries, sometimes without an acknowledgement that it may give children greater independence, skills and autonomy, or be vital for their or the whole family's survival. In the UK childhood has been increasingly prolonged, from 1972 when the school leaving age rose from 14 to 16 to now when most children are in training or education until 18, many into their early or mid twenties. These extended childhoods can be linked to political and socio-economic factors, such as economic recessions and the demise in youth employment opportunities and unskilled labour from the 1980s onwards (see chapters 4 and 5 for further discussion on this). However, it is rarely acknowledged we still have a covert child labour force, because children who work, care or

kill challenge childhood as an idealized time of carefree play, innocence and little responsibility. Our largely invisible child labour force
includes children who are the main carers for ill or disabled relatives,
children working in the family business or those who have considerable domestic or childcare responsibility because parents work long
paid hours. Other children work in shops, garages, gardens, markets,
or on building sites and in hotels, work which can be dangerous, is
very poorly paid and often contravenes child law and employment
legislation. This work tends to be performed by poor or working-class
children, often impacting on their educational performance (Stack
and McKechnie, 2002; Lavalette, 2005)

New Technology

Children have become savvy about the use of new technology, but at
the same time, through chat rooms and social networking, they are
at risk of being duped by abusive adult strangers posing as other children, who build up trust with the child before they attempt to abuse
them, although the risk is low. However, with over one-third of 7-year-
olds using the internet and 90 per cent of 13-year-olds interacting with
networking websites, it is not surprising some commentators are concerned about the potential which exists, particularly for those already
disadvantaged and possessing low self-esteem, to be further targeted
and bullied by their peers (James, 2009). In 1983 Postman argued that
new media such as television – and now the internet – have destroyed
childhood by giving children access to the same information as adults
rather than allowing adults to introduce them slowly to taboo and
difficult subjects such as sex, violence and death. However, these difficult issues are part of life and recurrent themes in many children's
traditional fairytales such as the Grimm brothers' stories. After all,
what could be more frightening than two children who are aban-
doned by their parents and then by chance find another apparently
benign parental figure who actually wants to kill and eat them – the
main plotline in *Hansel and Gretel*? This, however, is a different issue
from those of potential peer bullying and adult net abuse mentioned
above, and suggests that new technology brings with it both benefits
and risks, both of which require far greater research and analysis.

There is concern that the violent and formulaic nature of many
popular computer or console games gives out unrealistic and individualist messages about how problems are best resolved. They also work
on the lowest common denominator, emotional gratification basis
and are calculatingly compelling and compulsive (and predictable)
in a way real-life, negotiated and collaborative games and the real
world rarely are (Warner, 1994). But new technology is often given a

bad press, and when radio and television were first introduced they were denounced by some commentators as being a corrupting influence (Buckingham, 2001). It is also highly unlikely that participating in violent games or watching videos will in themselves lead a child to become violent, and most research shows that children's behaviour is influenced by a multiplicity of different factors. There are ongoing debates, however, about how much electronic media and technology controls children and to what extent they can subvert their intended influences. Research on sex in the media appears to negate media panic that children are 'growing up too fast', and children appear aware of what they should understand and they present themselves very much as knowing the boundaries and self-censoring when they reach them (Buckingham and Bragg, 2005). Claims that many of the games played on media consoles lead to, or in themselves constitute, antisocial and individualistic behaviour have been countered by the argument children often talk about and collaborate on these games and are discerning consumers. Conversely, Kline (2005) sees the relationship between children and the media as heavily unequal and mediatized companies as amoral, their only concern being maximization of profit. The way supermarkets shamelessly used to strategically place confectionery within toddlers' grasps at the end of checkouts is an earlier example. Similarly, designer goods are currently marketed as status elevators successfully to the children (and parents) who can least afford them – for example, the saleability of new designer trainers being piloted in the poorest black ghettos in the USA (N. Klein, 2000). Companies marketing their products to children also spend phenomenal amounts of time and money 'knowing' children and researching their likes, dislikes, interpretations, thoughts, hopes and even dreams (Schor, 2004).

This section has shown children are active and competent in many areas, but adults often undermine competence and restrict their autonomy because of adult fears, not allowing children to take any real risks or build up knowledgeable repertories to deal with unsure or potentially risky situations. This situation was exemplified recently when a postgraduate social work student in her mid-twenties, who still lived with her parents, on placement in a not particularly dangerous area, asked her astonished supervisor if she would accompany her to the bus stop at 7 p.m. because she felt unsafe walking around alone in the evening.

Social Divisions and Inequalities in Children's Lives

Children's lives are highly diverse, affected not only by culture and dominant temporal notions of childhood but also by the impact of gender, race, social class, disability and sexuality and associated oppression and discrimination. Although Thorne's (1993) study showed much subversion and resistance, other studies have revealed the regularizing power of gender with children. Small children often exclude gender-atypical peers from their activities, using the term 'pouf' as an insult, comprehending its negativity but not its meaning. As children grow older, gender regulation strategies become more sophisticated, but boys still focus mainly on their male peers and draw on insults referring to women and male homosexuality such as 'gay boy', 'faggot' or ' you're a right girl' to police gender atypical and non-heterosexual behaviour, inaccurately conflating sexuality and gender. Their targets tend to be gentle, emotionally vulnerable boys, who resist macho competitive behaviour, rough and tumble play fighting or haranguing girls (Mac an Ghaill, 1994 L. Green, 1998). In one ethnographic study, primary school boys were observed pulling the bra straps of embarrassed early developing girls, and calling them names such as 'big tits', 'period bag' and 'slag' (Renold, 2002). Toys and clothes are still highly genderized and hierarchicalized according to gender. In one US study, boys refused to watch commercials featuring girls, although girls watched those with either sex in (Seiner, 2005). In countries such as India, Bangladesh and China, being female engenders even more serious consequences. Even though illegal, sex-selective abortion, female infanticide and also generalized abuse and neglect of girls are common, due to ingrained social and religious norms which valorize male children and devalue female children and women (L. Green and Taylor, 2010).

In relation to social class, although there have been ongoing debates about definition and measurement, poverty and social exclusion are key constituents. Poverty can be *absolute*, relating to one's basic needs for food, water and shelter, or *comparative/relative* in relation to norms and standards in the population studied. Gordon et al. (2000), using a definition of poverty as an income 50 per cent below the average household income, estimated 4.4 million out of a total of 11.3 million children living in the UK were then subject to relative poverty. One in five children currently live in poverty, despite Britain being one of the most affluent countries in the world. This number increases for lone-parent children, around 50 per cent being poor, with rates of poverty for black African, Pakistani and Bangladeshi children being more than double those for white children, with Bangladeshi children being the most disadvantaged (L. Platt, 2007).

Gordon et al. (2000) conducted a survey of UK parents but ironically did not elicit children's views, reinforcing criticisms made earlier regarding parents speaking on behalf of children. They found 92 per cent of parents thought being unable to afford to celebrate a special occasion was an indicator of poverty, although only 53 per cent thought not being able to invite a child's friend for a meal once a fortnight constituted poverty. Various studies directly eliciting children's viewpoints, however, show children are acutely aware of poverty. Many talked evocatively about 'relative deprivation' and not being able to afford to attend a school trip, go to the cinema with friends, invite them round or purchase designer labels. Other children described 'absolute deprivation/poverty' such as being cold and not having much food in the house. Some children reported that both forms of deprivation/poverty made them feel miserable and different from their peers (Montgomery and Burr, 2003), although other children still identified poverty as absolute and distant, associating it with images of tramps and starving, third-world children and not associating poverty with their less affluent peers. Children born to poor families are more likely to be of a low birth weight and to live in crowded or damp conditions. They are also at higher risk of suffering domestic accidents such as house fires, and having health problems, in addition to doing less well at school. This legacy extends into adulthood, impacting on their educational, occupational and health life chances (Child Poverty Action Group (CPAG), 2001).

In 2008/9 New Labour's pledge of halving child poverty by 2010 looked unlikely to be fulfilled and New Labour had not even met its target of reducing child poverty by a quarter by 2005 in 2008 (Elliot, 2008; Gentleman, 2009). Inequality in Britain is higher than in many other European countries such as the Scandinavian nations who have more progressive, redistributive tax schemes, and the gap between rich and poor in the UK continues to widen. Yet as we live in a neo-liberal capitalist democracy, freedom, liberty and the profit motive are defended to protect the rights of the rich whilst subjugating and depriving others (Novak, 2002; Lavalette, 2005). New Labour has heralded 'work' as a way out of poverty yet recent statistics show the majority of children in poverty have at least one parent working (Gentleman, 2009). A 2007 United Nations Children's Fund (UNICEF) Report, drawing on forty different indicators, also lists the welfare of children in the UK bottom in a comparison of twenty-one affluent countries (*Child Poverty in Perspective*, 2007). Children in the UK were amongst the poorest and most neglected. Additionally, they ranked low in other key areas such as relationships and happiness, but, unsurprisingly, given our children's increasingly restricted freedom to roam alone, Britain scored better on health and safety. Research conducted for the CPAG ranked the UK twenty-fourth out of twenty-nine European countries for child wellbeing, with only Romania,

Bulgaria, Latvia, Lithuania and Malta faring worse (*The Guardian*, 2009).

As regards disabled children, until the 2001 Special Educational Needs and Disability Act, many received segregated education in special schools, where little was expected from them and they received inferior schooling, impacting on future life chances. Since then, many more children have been integrated into mainstream education, although problems still exist. These include some children missing play periods because of sessions being scheduled at the same time with, for example, speech and language therapists or physiotherapists, or because the disabled children were too embarrassed to request additional help in front of other children. Despite this, Wolley's research (2005) found many positives since integration, including decreases in negative stereotypes among other children, some of whom saw the disabled children simply as their friends and did not invoke common public perceptions that disability is a personal, individualized tragedy and that disabled children should be pitied. Although much literature is dominated by the view that having a disabled child is difficult, lonely and isolating, as Harrison's research into mothers in Belfast (1995) found, in other studies the professionals were judged by parents as being profoundly negative while the parents themselves were very positive about their disabled children and the joy they brought (Kearney and Griffin, 2001).

Conclusion

This chapter has critiqued how child development is conceptualized within traditional psychology, highlighting problematic issues such as its biological determinism and its culturally specific, linear, universalistic approach to children as well as its positivistic tendency to parade itself as a disinterested neutral seeker of knowledge. Its peripheralization of the social was also deemed problematic. If you look back to chapter 2 after reading this chapter, it will become more apparent how polarized sociology and psychology are. Traditional socialization theories emanating from sociology were also criticized because, like psychology, they homogenize the child and see development as a one-way process. The child, according to socialization, is society's sponge as opposed to in psychology which asserts children are a genetically programmed and naturally developing 'human becoming'. An alternative viewpoint was then advanced from the 'new sociology of childhood' theorists who focus on inequalities relating not only to generational power imbalances but also to other social divisions, such as social class and gender. They also concentrate on the child in the present and their actions, agency and peer cultures, rather than setting the child in default mode as an adult in waiting and as automatically deficient. Much of children's 'deficiency' can be attributed to adults' treatment of them, and attitudes and conceptions of children were shown to be strongly related to the historical and social context, childhood being a highly unstable category. The new sociology illuminates children's competencies but also reveals the effects adults' paternalist attitudes and fears have on children's lives.

When examining both developmental psychology and the new sociology, although they appear to be diametrically opposed, both help us to understand children and childhood and both have strengths and weaknesses. Many contemporary psychologists are much more socially aware and politicized than previously. The new critical developmental psychology also helps to contextualize psychology's political positioning and origins. Some of the new critical psychologists and the new sociologists are radical constructionists and completely repudiate any notions of development as biological (Stainton Rogers and Stainton Rogers, 1992; Morss, 1996). Others see psychology as an important discipline and fear, contra Morss, that to repudiate developmental psychology completely is to 'throw out the baby with the bathwater' (Lee, 2001: 54; Walkerdine, 2004). Lee, a sociologist, who, tellingly, also has a Ph.D. in psychology asks 'how does the "being" child change if that change is not thought of as the supplementation of a natural lack?' (2001: 54) and draws on sociologists as well as psychologists to try to understand the separability of children and adults (Lee, 2005). Like the recent productive collaboration of sociologists with other disciplines, collaboration with developmental psychology seems desperately overdue, although many might dissent, asserting the two disciplines are too dissonant ever to work together. The chapter will conclude here with the optimistic words of Valerie Walkerdine, a well-known critical psychologist, who argues persuasively that we need to move beyond the dualism of psychology and sociology:

> It is not helpful simply to replace interiority with exteriority, individual with social . . ., because all that achieves is to leave the dualism which created the problem in the first place intact. If it is clear there is no essential state of childhood or adulthood, what we need to understand is how people of particular ages become subjects . . . (and) how those classic aspects of psychology, learning, reasoning and emotions and so forth are produced as part of social practices . . . Could it be that children as subjects are created as both beings and becoming . . . yet also in a way in which they are constantly apprenticed into new practices? (Walkerdine, 2004: 102–7)

Reflection and discussion questions

Evaluate the key criticisms of traditional child psychology made by critical psychologists and the new sociologists of childhood.

Are cultural, social and historical constructions of childhood important? Why?

Compare and contrast sociological and psychological understandings of children and childhood.

Recommended reading

Jenks' (1996) short key text on childhood or James et al.'s (1998) edited book on constructions of childhood are excellent places to start reading about the sociology of childhood, although they are now slightly dated. More recent books include those written by Wyness (2006) and Mayall (2000). Burman's critical analysis of traditional developmental psychology (1994, updated 2007), written by a psychologist, is also well worth reading. The journals *Childhood* and *Children and Society*, although to some extent multi-disciplinary journals, contain many critical and analytical articles on children and childhood.

Adolescence and Youth

This chapter analyses psychological notions of adolescence and sociological notions of youth, taking into account historical and cross-comparative perspectives and changes in welfare policy. Adolescence and youth are recent terms describing a transitional, semi-dependent state between childhood and adulthood. The term 'childhood' extends further, encompassing early and middle childhood and adolescence up until 18 years of age, but there are many inconsistencies relating to when certain forms of autonomy, rights and responsibilities are granted, although many occur during adolescence/youth. In England the age of criminal responsibility is 10, sexual consent 16, and the right to purchase cigarettes, vote or consume alcohol in a public house 18. One can marry at 18, or 16 with parental consent, yet one can enlist in the army without parental consent at 16 and, ironically, full welfare benefits or adult wages are not granted until the early to mid twenties (Mizen, 2004).

Initially within this chapter, early psychological claims of adolescence as a 'naturally' traumatic developmental stage are evaluated, followed by an analysis of physical, cognitive and psychosocial changes. In the latter sociological part of the chapter, psychology's view of adolescence as troubled is shown to have reinforced and sustained enduring representations of young people as both dangerous and vulnerable. Youth transitions and historical changes in relation to employment and higher education are then analysed, followed by an examination of young people's lifestyles and beliefs.

Adolescence and psychology

Adolescence is generally accepted as a bio-psychological concept and often associated uncritically with white Western psychological understandings. G. Stanley Hall (1904), who was concerned mainly with misbehaving boys, initially conceptualized it as a biologically influenced 'natural' time of 'Sturm and Drang' or 'storm and stress'. This belief that adolescence 'exists' as a universal, 'naturally' turbulent developmental stage has strongly influenced sociological, psychological, media and policy understandings ever since: 'there is concern for any adolescent who does not progress through this time without showing some sort of disruption and turmoil' (Fitzgerald, 2005: 795).

Influenced by early philosophers such as Rousseau (1712–78), Hall wrote of a metamorphosis between childhood and adulthood, puberty signifying a new birth, paralleling the evolutionary development of the human race from savagery to perceived civilization. This genetically encoded experiential history was recapitulated into individuals' physiological and psychological development, adolescence occurring when hormonal changes lead to physical changes and psychological trauma before the onset of 'mature' adulthood. Later psychologists challenged Hall, claiming adolescence for most was a relatively stable and untroubled period (Coleman and Hendry, 1999; Arnett, 1999; Herbert, 2008). Psychological problems in children and teenagers have, however, increased steadily since the early 1980s (Collishaw et al., 2004), but it cannot be assumed these are problems *of* adolescence, and they may be a cohort or social generation phenomenon. One major problem with this traditional psychological conception of adolescence is therefore not the belief that certain biological changes potentially associated with cognitive development, physical development and puberty generally take place during this period (although significant timing variations exist historically and cross-culturally), but the conclusion that they inevitably adversely impact upon young people's social and psychological functioning.

In the nineteenth century, 'adolescence' did not exist, with the vast majority of working-class children in the UK being in full-time employment by the age of 12 (Coward, 1999). Globally there are also still cultures where girls can be married and boys enlisted as soldiers at 12 (C. Beckett, 2002), or where preordained rites of passage involve girls transitioning to women or boys to men through a short process of ceremonial initiation rather than the prolonged intermediate period we know as adolescence. Much debate still exists within the anthropological literature about whether adolescence is a cross-cultural phenomenon for both sexes, applies only to boys universally or only occurs in complex societies where it takes a significant time to learn adult skills. In many cultures the notion of adolescence as a troubled time is also absent (Montgomery, 2009).

Difficulties ascertaining when adolescence commences and ends render it problematic as a developmental stage. If puberty is the start, some girls start to menstruate at 9 years old, others at 14 or 15, but surely 9-year-olds cannot be regarded as adolescents? And what physical markers should define the beginning of puberty for boys? Does adolescence then finish with the termination of puberty, and what physiological markers indicate this? Even more confusingly, what psychologists regard as having an unpredictable physiological beginning, they see as having an unclear social end: 'It is generally agreed that adolescence begins in biology (the variable time of puberty) and ends in culture (the even more variable point at which young people are deemed "responsible" and "independent" by society)' (Herbert, 2008: 368).

The impact society has on adolescents' behaviour regarding physical changes is also a moot point, even amongst traditional developmental psychologists. Thornton (2008: 491–4) argues that the media have wrongly interpreted the rapid proliferation of new neural connections in the adolescent brain as preceding and causing stereotypically assumed adolescent behaviour such as impulsivity and risk taking. Rigorous neurological reviews show hormones may only affect the brain indirectly (Sisk and Zehr, 2005). The delayed cognitive development of the 'wild children' also evidences that genetic potential must be coordinated with favourable environmental influences to be fulfilled. Thornton (2008) asserts that at adolescence a learning process, moving from novice to potential expert, takes place, in relation to slowly acquiring new skills and making increasingly accurate decisions, which affects brain structures, indicating a two-way reciprocal process between brain and behaviour, with the social also a profound influence on both.

K. Berger (2005), conversely (although acknowledging their complex relationship), claims that increasing hormone levels both precede and cause rapid shifts in emotional extremes from elation to despair, additionally precipitating sexual thoughts in boys (but not girls) and 'producing' negative mood changes related to the menstrual cycle in girls. Berger initially states that hormone levels only contribute minimally to adolescents' moods and sexual behaviour but then contradictorily asserts 'hormones *directly* cause moods and emotions to change more quickly in adolescence than in childhood and adulthood [and] *directly* make adolescents seek sexual activity, which makes them emotional, aroused and frustrated' (2005: 343 – my emphasis). This recourse to the biological for an explanation of adolescent behaviour is, however, not limited to textbooks, but can be found, unevidenced, even in academic peer-reviewed articles, Moffit stating 'the coincidence of puberty with the rise in the prevalence of delinquent behaviour compels me to look for clues in adolescent development' (1993: 686).

What is absent in most psychological accounts is the potentially profound influence of social factors, although these are considered peripherally. Might the fact that boys seem more overtly interested in sex than girls, as Berger claims, be far less likely to be associated with hormone levels and more likely to be affected by gendered and inequitable social influences which celebrate heterosexual adolescent male sexual activity and negate female activity, boys being 'represented as desiring agents and girls simply as the victims of male desire' (Hockey and James, 2003: 144)? Could the negative menstrual cycle emotions girls experience also be more associated with cultural notions of menstruation as 'a curse', unclean and polluting (Prendergast, 1995), compounded by early developing girls being sexually harassed by male peers (Renold, 2002), rather than a simple product of hormonal levels? Berger mentions US studies showing that early maturing pubertal girls tend to suffer lower self-esteem, more depression and a poorer body image than other girls (Siegel et al., 1999) and may be teased by boys. She then ironically excuses the boys' behaviour, uncritically attributing it to them 'being awed by the sexual [female] creature in their midst' (K. Berger, 2005: 346).

Conversely, in other societies, menarche, the first onset of menstruation, is a joyful event ritually and communally celebrated. For example, a Kung girl from Africa's Kalahari Desert experiencing her first period must sit down and silently wait. When the women realize she is missing, they find her and lift her up, as her feet are not allowed to touch the ground, returning her to the village. She is then placed in a small grass seclusion hut and the women perform an uninhibited celebration of womanhood around her during which they sing, dance and clap and disrobe apart from a small pubic covering (Konner, 1991). In this context, would early maturing girls be affected by the same negative emotions during their menstrual cycle as their Western counterparts?

The examples above suggest adolescence is not only a cultural artefact but a problematic concept even within its own discipline, psychology. Psychology now generally acknowledges definitional difficulties but refuses to discard adolescence as a specific developmental stage, stressing adolescence's variability in beginning and ending, and mentioning cross-cultural differences. However, many non-Western cultures possess no conception of adolescence, suggesting their cultural practices are being straitjacketed into Western understandings. Embracing a wide definition of adolescence, commencing with biology and ending with culture, a girl could become adolescent when she first menstruated at 9 and adult at 12 in some cultures if she marries and assumes adult responsibilities then. Conversely she could remain an adolescent until the mid twenties in a Western culture if she enters higher education but remains greatly dependent on her family. However, given these rather intractable problems, might psychology still help us to comprehend young people's development during this nebulous and contested period? The next four subsections will concentrate on physical, cognitive, moral and psychosocial development during adolescence, focusing on an evaluation of key theorists such as Piaget, Kohlberg and Erikson.

Physical Development and Adolescence

In all cultures, between about 9 and 15 years, most children enter puberty, a transitional stage between biological physical immaturity and full physical and sexually reproductive maturity. Puberty starts with a physical signal from the hypothalamus in the brain to increase the production of growth hormones which stimulate the growth of all body tissue including primary and secondary sex organs. Both oestrogen and testosterone are present in both sexes before, during and after puberty. Additional testosterone production in boys leads to full development of testicles and sperm production, followed by their first, often nocturnal, ejaculation. These changes occur alongside the testes enlarging, the penis lengthening, the thickening and reddening of the scrotum and the appearance of pubic, facial and other bodily hair, as well as the deepening of the voice. Surprisingly, 65 per cent of boys also experience some short-lived breast development.

Increased oestrogen and progesterone in girls leads to mature eggs being released and the capacity for reproduction, often signalled by the first period. The first sign of sexual development is a small rise around the nipples, a breast bud, although full breast development tends not to occur until the end of puberty. Breast buds are followed by the growth of pubic hair and the further growth of the uterus and ovaries, alongside a thickening of the vaginal lining. However, the pelvic inlet, the opening of the birth canal, develops slower, only reaching full maturity when girls are around 18, suggesting giving birth could pose greater risks for younger adolescents (Bogin, 1999).

Both sexes experience an overall 'growth spurt' lasting two to three years, alongside these sexual developmental changes, where they grow faster than since they were babies, girls tending to experience this earlier than boys. Most reach 98 per cent of their adult height by the end of this period (Sinclair and Dangerfield, 1998). However, not all parts or functions of the body develop in synchronicity. The gangly, awkward and uncoordinated appearance and excessive fatigue of some adolescents therefore can have a physiological basis (Cole et al., 2005). Growth during this period extends from the extremities to the core (opposite to neonatal and infant development) with the fingers and toes growing faster than the hands and the feet, and the torso developing last (K. Berger, 2005). Changes in body fat and overall body shape also occur with boys losing fat during adolescence and acquiring a more muscled, angular appearance in contrast to girls, who retain a higher fat-to-muscle ratio, endowing them with a more rounded form. Relatively minor changes can also occur which may cause anguish, such as the development of acne caused by changes in the oil and sweat glands of the skin.

Prior to puberty there is little difference between the sexes in terms of strength but it has been argued that not only are boys taller than girls after puberty by an average of 5 inches but also, even when the sexes are the same size and weight, boys are stronger in terms of being able to engage in sport for longer periods than girls and in force exerted per ounce of muscle (Cole et al., 2005). However, sociological research shows that boys are more encouraged in, and engage more with, sport and physical activities than girls (see Green and Taylor, 2010). This difference, in conjunction with the cultural models and policing girls receive in terms of maintaining a very slender body shape and low weight (Cartner-Morley, 2007), may have a significant effect on how girls' bodies develop during adolescence and their strength and height after puberty. Examples of this pressure include the emergence of pro-anorexia networking websites and the recent much-discussed comment made by the model Kate Moss – 'nothing tastes better than skinny feels' (*Independent*, 20.11.2009). Therefore, how the social and cultural context in itself shapes biology must be considered alongside 'normal' biological maturation and their mutual interaction. Young people are biologically at their healthiest during this period and are much less likely to be affected by any degenerative or age-related conditions than adults. Psychology does concede that cultural factors might impact on ill health, leading to illnesses such as anorexia and bulimia nervosa which disproportionately affect women, but the extent to which social factors, including gender and power, may impact on health is understated.

Adolescence and cognitive development

Piaget posited that a new logical structure develops in the brains of adolescents from 12 onwards – *formal operations*. This involves a shift away from concrete thinking to more flexible, hypothetico-deductive and abstract modes of thought, but some adolescents and adults never progress beyond *concrete operations*. Formal operations involve higher-order or logical thinking – the ability to evaluate a range of possibilities, be critical of received wisdom, reason analogously and reflect on abstract notions rooted in philosophy, politics or religion. Although Piaget is a constructivist in the sense that he saw cognition as developing simultaneously both from genetic bases and from experiential knowledge, there have been many criticisms of his theory of cognitive development, even at the formal operations stage.

One key criticism was that children could think logically at a much earlier stage than Piaget claimed if the tasks set made cultural sense and they were motivated to engage (see Donaldson, 1978). Piaget's defenders, however, argued that children were not being set alternative tasks of the same complexity as by Piaget, and additionally these new tasks could be solved in ways not requiring logical thought. This debate raged for approximately a decade without a consensus about what might be a 'pure', accurate test for children's logical competence (Thornton, 2008). Researchers eventually agreed that what was important was not children's success or failure at a particular test but the processes they went through, which needed further study, as you can succeed or fail in tasks in many different ways, success not necessarily indicating logical competence. Adolescents also have as much difficulty in applying logical reasoning as younger children and even if they can apply it in some situations, they do not necessarily do so in others, even highly literate and intelligent adolescents (Thornton, 2008). In contemporary, rural, premodern societies with minimal formal education, abstract and logical reasoning often appears absent in adolescence and adult thought. Even in Western cultures, in one study, only teenagers who had been directly educated about how to reason, through using abstract principles of algebra, were able to understand logical necessity (Morris and Sloutsky, 1998). Modern psychologists therefore generally concur that logical reasoning is not a natural, developmental, cross-cultural adolescent or even adult stage, but a taught cultural artefact (Thornton, 2002, 2008; Kuhn, 2006). Mental models reflecting how we comprehend the world and factual information we possess may be more important than logical reasoning, in how we reach our inferences and decisions. If this is the case, then 'the mystery may be less of a question of why human beings are so bad at understanding logical principles, and more a matter of how so many of us manage to grasp them at all' (Thornton, 2002: 101).

Although consensus exists that adolescents rarely fully develop Piaget's abstract reasoning, they do make more effective decisions than younger children, but it is not clear why and how they are made. Changes in brain structure herald significant production of neural connections, reductions in little-used neural pathways and greater myelination of nerves (myelin is a white substance which forms a protective sheath around nerve fibres). These allow more effective neural message conduction, but this cannot be explicitly linked to specific behaviour or cognition. Adolescents also make more use of *availability*, *intuitive* or *representative heuristics* than younger children.

Heuristics relate to quick, intuitive decisions being made on the basis of feelings and from assumptions derived from our past knowledge and generalizations. Their conclusions therefore seem instinctively right but are wrong far more often than conclusions derived from careful analytic thought (Moshman, 2000). When conclusions derived from logical analytical thought contradict adolescents' beliefs, they are also less likely to accept them and more likely to find unnecessary fault with them. Adolescents are, despite this, surprisingly less likely to draw on heuristics than adults, suggesting adults may in some areas be more biased and less logical than adolescents (Klaczynski, 2000). Hypothetico-deductive (analytical) reasoning, although logically flawless and more time-consuming, can also lead to wrong decisions.

Some psychologists argue reasoning and knowledge are domain-specific, so one may excel in logical reasoning in an area one is very knowledgeable about but not in others. If this hypothesis is accepted, Piaget's stage theory is more likely to be an uneven patchy affair, focusing on topics, rather than a clear-cut transition from one stage to another, with domain-specific knowledge rendering children superior to adults on some tasks. Reviewing the information provided above also does not really help us to understand why adolescents make more effective decisions than younger children, although it could be a combination of more logical thinking, more effective heuristic decisions due to accumulated experience, and more domain-specific expertise.

Moral Development

Piaget and Kohlberg, both cognitive developmentalists, are considered the most significant contributors to the field of moral development. Freud also argued that the development of one's super ego or conscience becomes more sophisticated during adolescence. Piaget's early cognitive work (1932/1965) asserted that children's moral reasoning shifted from morality dictated by higher authorities, such as parents and teachers, and judged on an action's consequences, to a position where underlying intentions and a more flexible socially interactive approach were more important. Therefore, younger children see someone who breaks fifteen cups accidentally as naughtier than someone who breaks one cup deliberately. They generally refrain from actions such as stealing because they think they will be reprimanded, not because they reason stealing is wrong. This first stage of Piagetian morality, *the morality of constraint*, applies to children up to 7–8 years. From then up until about 10 years, the *transitional period* occurs, where children develop more reciprocal and peer- or group-orientated rules. By 11–12, the stage of *autonomous* or *relative morality* emerges, in which children reject authoritarianism and see rules as the product of group consent and potentially changeable, and view fairness and intent as paramount. Research in different countries has overall substantiated this, but the quality of peer/group interaction, not its mere existence, is important. Other studies have shown intentionality, counter Piaget, can sometimes be taken into account by younger children.

Kohlberg (1976) later developed a more sophisticated, Piaget-influenced, three-level, six-stage, chronological, age-related model of moral reasoning. The most famous vignette he used was of Heinz. Heinz's wife was presented in this hypothetical scenario as dying of cancer although one new expensive drug might save her, but the pharmacist who discovered it was charging ten times the price it cost to produce. With everything he could borrow and save Heinz could only accumulate half the price. Heinz tried unsuccessfully to negotiate with the pharmacist about paying less or the rest in instalments. Children were given this information and then asked whether Heinz should steal the drug and why.

During Kohlberg's first *pre-conventional level* (operational up to middle childhood), stage 1 is egocentric and focuses on imposed rules, whereas stage 2 is more about exchange (for example, 'if you give me some sweets I'll share my can of lemonade'), self-interest, avoiding punishment and attaining rewards. Children at stage 1 tend to say Heinz should not steal the drug because he will get sent to prison, or he should steal it because he might get into trouble if his wife dies. At stage 2, children give a response such as that Heinz should steal the drug because his wife would do the same for him or because he loves her and wants her to live.

At level 2, *conventional morality* (occurring at 13–16), stage 3 initially involves meeting others' expectations and gaining approval, whilst the fourth stage is more focused on the social system and upholding agreements/laws. Children at stage 3 are concerned either that, if Heinz steals the drug, he will be seen as a criminal, or that, if not, he will be seen as an uncaring, negligent husband. At stage 4, children concentrate on social institutions like marriage and the law and connected obligations. They stress either that a husband has responsibility for his wife, therefore stealing the drug is justified, or conversely that he should not steal it because, if everyone stole what they needed but could not afford, society would stop functioning effectively.

The third level, *post conventional morality*, commences with stage 5 involving adhering to a social contract and ensuring that individual rights such as life and liberty are upheld, alongside a utilitarianist commitment to sacrificing some principles if the majority benefits.

Stage 6 involves a greater commitment to breaking laws to uphold universal self-chosen ethical principles. In Western countries, level 2 stage 4 reasoning emerges at adolescence, although stage 3 is still more dominant (Colby et al., 1983), with level 3 stage 5 only emerging in very few people by young adulthood and many never reaching it. There is little evidence for stage 6, although it may occur in extraordinary circumstances such as during World War II when European gentiles rescued Jews destined for extermination. They therefore transcended individual societal rules, living by their own morals (Olliner and Olliner, 1988). At the post conventional morality stage more abstract reasoning takes place and children responded with answers to the Heinz dilemma showing commitment to broad principles. They therefore gave responses such as 'a life is worth more than profit', or that one should not steal because there might be equally deserving people who need that drug, positing the way forward being to campaign for the drug to be available to everyone who needs it.

Most research evidences that children broadly progress through the stages in the order predicted by Kohlberg, although the transition is not discontinuous to the point that, when once a stage is reached, individuals rarely reason at a lower stage. Adolescents reason at lower than expected stages sometimes, or utilize different stages simultaneously when it is concordant with their goals (Rest, 1979). Other criticisms of Kohlberg centre on the fact that his understanding of morality emanated from a Western liberal democratic perspective. Research utilizing Kohlberg's methods shows, in some small rural societies with little formal education, neither children nor adults reach stage 4 and the post conventional level. Stages 1 and 2 and occasionally 3 are often the highest reached with leaders occasionally reaching the fourth stage (Snarey, 1995). This may be because the harmonious functioning of the group, often achieved by adhering to preordained rules, may be regarded as more important than individual liberties or civil rights. This could lead to non-Western societies being judged as possessing less advanced moral reasoning than Western societies, without an understanding of their cultures.

Other approaches have conversely found that most cultures could, according to different methods and criteria from those utilized by Kohlberg, be judged as attaining post conventional morality by adulthood (Gielen and Markoulis, 1994). The DTI test, rather than asking children and adults to reason why they give particular answers, gives them an easier task – a fixed list of answers to draw from (Rest et al., 1999). This test shows individuals simultaneously drawing on arguments from both stage 1 and stage 3, but also suggests smaller cultural differences than previously assumed. An examination of very different religions, despite ongoing debates around whether any moral absolutes exist (Blackburn, 2001), seems to show similar ethical principles (Armstrong, 1999). There also seems to be a difference in how people reason morally when social conventions are accorded a moral dimension as opposed to when issues involving broader, more abstract instances of social justice are separated from convention or cultural beliefs, in that cultural beliefs impede logical moral reasoning.

Gilligan (1977) argues that, because girls are more likely to favour an interpersonal ethic or *morality of care* than boys, their reasoning is more likely to be judged as less developed. However, research has not demonstrated differential, gendered stage achievement, although it has been conceded Kohlberg neglected this area of morality (Thornton, 2008). Although a relationship between moral reasoning and moral action exists, they often fail to coincide. In one study, 3- to 11-year-olds were told about children cheating on a task involving moving ping-pong balls from a bucket to a jar without using their hands, and then asked to complete the same task. After this, only 40 per cent of the younger and 25 per cent of the older children were prepared to cheat (Subbotsky, 1993). However, when they were actually party to observing another child cheat and lie successfully, 80 per cent of younger children cheated although 50 per cent of older children were still honest. Such behaviour seems to reinforce Kohlberg's and Piaget's claims older children are more likely to consider the social context and abstract issues of fairness and thus have attained a higher level of moral reasoning, although the relationship between moral reasoning and moral action is still tenous.

Psychosocial Development and Adolescent Identity

According to Erikson's psychosocial model, the final childhood developmental task is to overcome the dilemma of 'identity versus role confusion', ideally forming a coherent and mature sense of identity before adulthood. Marcia (1966) tested out two dimensions of Erikson's theory – (i) crisis/exploration, and (ii) commitment in relation to occupation and political and religious beliefs, identifying four patterns. *Identity achievement* occurs with the adolescent thinking through various options and deciding on one of these, for example choosing a particular university because it is highly rated for a particular subject or becoming a Quaker because it is an egalitarian, pacifist religion. *Identity foreclosure* occurs with commitments adopted uncritically on the basis of tradition or others' expectations. So an adolescent may vote for a political party their parents belong to or follow their father into a trade as a plasterer. Adolescents adopting both these patterns seem secure although Erikson posited foreclosure as a negative process. Questioning one's identity may, however, be a privilege only accorded to the affluent in Western liberal democracies as opposed to the Western poor and those inhabiting more rural, less complex societies.

Identity moratorium occurs when adolescents are in a state of flux or crisis and are experimenting with different identities and asking themselves reflective questions. These may be sexual (Am I heterosexual, gay, bisexual, not sure, or would I prefer not to be labelled at all?), or vocational/academic (Should I study Music at university, which I enjoy but it would be hard to earn a moderate living, or shall I study Computing which pays well but which I don't enjoy?), or social (Shall I become a bohemian Maverick, a conformist morally vacuous citizen or an anarchic Punk rocker?). Here they have not yet reached a committed identity position but Erikson positions this stage as the potential precursor to achievement. The fourth position Marcia identified was *identity diffusion*, characterized by adolescent apathy and little enthusiasm for succeeding in any area. Erikson also mentions *negative identity*, where an oppositional identity has been forged in rebellion against parental or societal values, but not been rationally thought through. This may not be a problem if you become an avant-garde artist in opposition to your family's conformity and respectable professional careers, but if you become a drug dealer when your father is a high court judge or drop out of college if your mother is an academic, it may be problematic (Thornton, 2008). Erikson thinks this stage represents attention-seeking behaviour and occurs predominantly due to unsupportive parental behaviour.

US research mostly substantiates Erikson's theory, one study showing identity confusion drops from 46 per cent in early adolescence to 13 per cent after college, and identity achievement increases from 5 to 40 per cent (Waterman, 1985), although full identity achievement is more likely to occur in late adolescence and early adulthood than before. Erikson's theory is also corroborated by research on autobiographical memory (Conway and Holmes, 2004). Criticisms and modifications of Erikson's theory and Marcia's development of it relate to identity development being more relevant to post-industrial Western societies than other less technological societies (Sneed, Schwartz and Cross, 2006). In the latter, adulthood tends to be attained much earlier and occupational and social roles are often ascribed and non-negotiable, divergence attracting disapproval, punishment or even exclusion. Identity achievement may also occur in some areas at adolescence but not in others (Grotevant, 1998). How one experiences or gains identity will also depend not only upon societal values but also upon parenting styles and peer relationships, and both strictly disciplinarian parenting and negligible rules and boundaries have negative consequences (Maccoby, 2000).

Racial Identity

Identity is seen as a lifelong quest by Erikson, although it assumes particular prominence in adolescence. Since Erikson, both psychologists and sociologists have interrogated, researched and developed different concepts of identity, although sociology generally views identity as more fluid, heterogeneous and multifaceted than does psychology. Furthermore, two forms of identity are seen as especially important during adolescence and young adulthood, racial identity and gender identity, although racial identity will be explored here. Racial, ethnic and cultural identities are often seen as synonymous, but they are overlapping rather than the same. Racial identity refers to identity via now much discredited biological 'racial' features such as skin colour. Cultural and ethnic identity may involve 'racial' aspects, but refers more specifically to particular cultural practices and beliefs. One of the most well-known and earliest conceptualizations of racial identity is Cross' (1971) psychological *nigrescence* model which posits that black individuals experience a resocialization experience. During this they are deemed to progress from an unawareness of race to a profound awareness of different races, racisms and discrimination. This results initially in an exclusive commitment to their black community and finally in mixing with many cultures, alongside an awareness of how some cultures may be discriminated against.

One criticism of Cross' model is its assumption individuals are unaware of their and others' races before they attain identity. To concentrate only on one aspect of identity also denies identity's complexity and flux (Green, 2004) and that it may be comprised of or influenced by many facets such as gender, social class, sexual orientation, parental and community influence and one's interests and commitments, not just race. Also, among mixed-heritage individuals – 400,000 of whom were under 19 in the 2001 census (Owen, 2007) – some had a protean and flexible identity, identifying as black, white or mixed race at different times or in different situations (Alibhai Brown, 2001; Brunsma and Rockquemore, 2002). Children's schools' racial mixes (Tizard and Phoenix, 1993) and social class (Katz, 1996) also affect racial identity. In some studies middle-class children saw themselves as free to choose their identity and were more likely to identify as mixed race rather than black than were working-class children (perhaps being buffered to some extent from racism by their privileged class position). Some mixed heritage adolescents also reject any kind of racial identification, preferring to identify as 'human race' (Christian, 2000; Brunsma and Rockquemore, 2002).

Bronfenbrenner's Ecological Theory

Although no comprehensive theories of child or adolescent normative development have superseded Freud, Piaget or Erikson, despite claims of their declining influence (Steinberg and Morris, 2001), in 1979 Bronfenbrenner conceptualized and drew up a developmental ecological systems theory. This profoundly influenced child and particularly adolescent psychological research from the late 1980s onwards, also emerging within vocational disciplines such as social work and teaching. Bronfenbrenner's model (1979) positions the child's world as being organized within a set of nested structures, much like a set of Russian dolls, and encourages developmental psychologists to examine the interaction between the individual and various contexts. The *microsystem* is the direct environment the child interacts with, the *mesosystem* represents the relationships between microsystems, the *exosystem* encompasses settings the child is not a part of but that nevertheless impact upon him/her and the *macrosystem* represents the wider cultural context within which all the other systems are located.

Subsequently, a number of psychological studies emerged which considered interpersonal and wider contexts. They showed, for example, contra Hall that parental alienation and extreme delinquency are the exception, not the norm, although minor disagreements and bickering were found to be normal – particularly in early adolescence – and are impacted upon by ethnicity and social class. Ecologically influenced research also revealed that adolescents often become closer to peers than to parents and preferentially confide in them. Despite this, other research also seems to show that parental control and monitoring predict better adolescent development than their absence, as do better sibling relationships, despite conflict occurring more with siblings than parents. Adolescents have also been found to select friends highly similar in social class and background, personality and interests. Adolescent bullying is, furthermore, influenced by gender in that males are more likely to perpetrate direct bullying via verbal or physical attacks whereas girls' bullying is more covert and relational. Adolescents' romantic attachments are also influenced by early attachment experiences but peer relationships can mediate previous negative influences and can intervene both positively and negatively in relation to activities, interests, friendships and romances. Adolescents involved in voluntary, civic and political work have also been found to emanate from more middle-class families, to have more altruistic personalities and more often to be female (see reviews by Steinberg and Morris, 2001, and Smetana et al., 2006, for further references in relation to these ecologically influenced studies).

What is interesting, however, is that, although social work academics sometimes interpret the ecological model in terms of studying political influences and inequalities (e.g. Jack, 2000), this is rarely the case with developmental psychological researchers who tend to shy away from these areas. This evasion is evidenced by the research above which mainly deals with the mesosystem and suggested by the following citation: 'While it is true that a disproportionate share of many social problems touch the lives of poor and non white youth, the majority of these adolescents develop in psychologically healthy ways and it makes little sense to focus the study of these youth on adolescent malady' (Steinberg and Morris, 2001: 96).

The authors of this particular review on adolescence, who are influential US psychologists, continue further to lament the perceived loss of the study of the individual adolescent 'amidst all this focus on context, diversity and biology' (2001: 101), demonstrating their disinterest in and unease with not only the political and structural context but the ecological theory as a whole and too much attention being paid to difference or context at any level.

To conclude this section on adolescent psychology, the relationship between biology and behaviour has been examined and found not to have a causal link, although significant physical, cognitive, moral and psychosocial changes take place during adolescence. A paradox, however, exists, for although many psychologists repudiate early psychological claims that biology causes hormonal/neurological changes linked to adolescent distress, Erikson's notion of an adolescent identity crisis seems to represent Hall's storm and stress thesis, albeit in a less biologically determinist form. The discontinuous stage-like characteristics of developmental psychology are also unconfirmed by more recent research, using different methodology, which reveals development to be highly complex. Later researchers have shown that inferences or interpretations drawn from laboratory experiments are often wrong and rarely externally valid in terms of real world application. Sensitivity to intent, the social context, structural factors and inequalities, and individuals' understanding of the research may also enable some younger individuals to think or morally reason in much more sophisticated and analytical ways than the early studies suggested. The fact that individuals may draw on a variety of different stage or level discourses concurrently, or use one level to solve one problem and another level to solve another, or may have achieved identity in one area but not in others, furthermore suggests major problems with discontinuous stage theories.

That adolescents who are able to reason at higher cognitive and moral levels often do not choose to do so, or deliberately negate logical thinking when it goes against their preconceived notions, also suggests the situation is much more involved than previously assumed. It is, furthermore, an irony that psychology's prime commitment to biology and genetics renders it unable to accept the structural and cultural context as paramount, even when recent research stresses this. Although studies influenced by the ecological model are increasing, the individual adolescent is still centre stage and structural influences often neglected or played down. However, despite these shortcomings, traditional developmental psychology does offer us some useful ways of trying to understand biological, psychosocial and cognitive processes in adolescents.

Youth and sociology

France (2007) locates 'the discovery of adolescence' in the age of reason and early Victorian modernity, when the new social science disciplines were accruing professional and scientific status. Hall's theoretical underpinnings of adolescence worryingly fused middle-class patriarchal values, Christian theology and Darwinian evolutionary theory to explain the problems of 'youth', but his theory was generally accepted as scientific 'truth', profoundly influencing the professions and policy from then on. The attraction lay in demystifying young people's problems by positing them as homogeneous and 'natural' but still indicative of lower thought processes and therefore potentially requiring control. The sociological study of youth therefore cannot be contextualized without understanding how Hall's exposition of adolescence, although now mostly discredited, preceded it. Sociology, however, mostly avoids the term 'adolescence' because of its bio-psychological connotations, utilizing the term 'youth' in preference.

The concept of youth is amorphous in sociology, although it seems to encompass a potentially longer time span than adolescence, extending from around the early teens until potentially the mid twenties. Sociology's youth is a transitional period but, unlike psychology's discontinuous, defined developmental stages, sociology inclines more to flexible, ragged and unclear transitions, acknowledged as Western but with 'neither a clear nor a chronological beginning or end' (Coles, 1995: 7). Rather than developing 'objective' universal theories of youth, sociologists analyse the influence of social structures on how youth is constituted, whether they be functionalist sociologists who see society as benevolent, meritocratic and governed by consensus, or critical sociologists, seeing structural inequalities relating to gender, ethnicity or social class as paramount. Sociology therefore differs from psychology, not just in its retreat from biology and individual psychology and psychopathology, but because it locates 'youth' differently, dependent upon such contextual factors as historical time period, cultural and spatial location, political and media representations and social discourses. Parsons, an early functionalist sociologist, positioned youth as a distinct generational cohort subject to socialization processes (1942), with Eisenstadt (1956) stressing young people's peer cultures as important for easing them into adult roles. 'Youth generation', further expounded upon by Wyn and Woodman (2007), views young people simultaneously creating historical constellations and being constituted by them, each generation having a particular generational consciousness mediated by structural inequalities. The post 1970s youth generation are therefore characterized more by consumption than were previous generations, but those without disposable income to exhibit 'conspicuous consumption' and buy the latest 'hip' clothes and music are often seen as 'style failures', subject to social exclusion and status loss (Croghan et al., 2006).

Dangerous Youth

Responses to young people are still dominated by hegemonic (powerful and ideologically influenced) and inherited notions of individualistic risk and danger. These are classed, racialized and gendered but rarely acknowledged as such. Young people are therefore seen either as posing a risk to others, for example through youth crime, antisocial behaviour or school exclusion (Stephen and Squires, 2004), or as vulnerable and at risk of harm from others, indicating the enduring influence of Hall's conception of a 'troubled' adolescence and Jenks' Apollonian and Dionysian notions of childhood. In a recent Australian study examining how young people were depicted in national and electronic print media, key discourses identified were young people (i) as needing help (54 per cent), (ii) as victims (14 per cent), (iii) as problematic without ameliorating factors (20 per cent), and (iv) as successful (10 per cent) (Bolzan, 2005). 88 per cent of all media items therefore saw young people as problematic and, as Rose (1991) has argued, there has been a tendency to group all young people who receive such labels together as potentially dangerous. However, girls are seen as more at risk, particularly sexually, than boys, and ethnic minority and working-class boys depicted as more threatening than middle-class boys (Griffin, 2001).

Contemporary moral panics about youth centre around young people's sexual behaviour, 'binge drinking' and drug consumption, young people being represented as irresponsible, disrespectful to adults, easily addicted and involved in increasing street violence and unsafe sex whilst intoxicated. Evidence does suggest rising alcohol consumption influenced by successful marketing of alcopops and cheap shots of cocktails or spirits (Measham, 2007), alongside increasing sporadic and regular 'normalized' drug use. However, measurement is difficult, with one Home Office study defining 'binge drinking' perhaps rather unrealistically as getting drunk once a month (Richardson and Budd, 2003). Many young people's drug and alcohol use is argued to be far less problematic than depicted (France, 2007; Furlong and Cartmel, 2007), although class and gender dimensions are important. Middle-class youngsters tend to consume 'soft' drugs but drug use is influenced by locality, culture, income and supply, with poor, unemployed youth more at risk of dependence on 'hard' drugs such as heroin (Leitner et al., 1993). Girls' increasing alcohol consumption, furthermore, may relate to their increasing freedom and perceived sexual equality. With previous generations, heavy drinking was predominantly a macho pastime, girls' movements and drinking constrained because of fears of sexual promiscuity or exploitation and their lower disposable income, although young women's autonomy has always been demonized historically (Jackson and Tinkler, 2007).

A welfarist, rehabilitative strand has mostly disappeared in youth justice policy. Since 1997 more authoritarian legislation has led to increasingly punitive measures such as custodial sentences and imprisoning parents of truanting children (Muncie, 2007). These ignore children's welfare and rights, placing responsibility on mostly disadvantaged young people and their parents, who already suffer considerable victimization. Young people, particularly marginalized groups, are therefore increasingly likely to be subject to adult mistrust, institutionalized surveillance and regulation (Kelly, 2003). France (2008) correspondingly shows how current public policy is shaped by an underdeveloped and methodologically problematic 'science of prevention'. This identifies relationships between numerous risk factors and future problems (although the causal mechanisms are complex and individual prediction difficult), which then 'justify' intervention into the lives of children who have not committed crimes on the ephemeral suggestion they may do so later.

How our society treats our young people is, however, rarely commented on by the media, and young people's problems are individualized and pathologized in much policy. Although government guidelines recommend only children under 14 who are persistent offenders or have committed a very heinous crime should be locked up, a recent Barnardo's study found less than one-third of 12- to 14-year-olds in prison whom they surveyed met these criteria.

In addition, more than half of the children in custody were known to have been abused, with more than a third living with known offenders and a third having witnessed adult domestic violence (Dickson, 2009). Furthermore, in comparative terms, a 2007 UNICEF survey ranked Britain's treatment of young people lowest out of twenty-one developed countries, and a recent United Nations Committee Report on the Rights of the Child berated Britain for demonizing young people, many of whom were marginalized, impoverished and criminalized (Bosely, 2007a). Many young people therefore continue to be mistreated not only in a micro sense through familial abuse and neglect, but institutionally in state care, custody and education, as well as through wider societal structures allowing young people to remain in poverty (Corby, 2004). Although we live in an age of risk reflexivity and uncertainty (Beck, 1992, 2000; Giddens, 1991), in which young people appear to navigate uncertain pathways to adulthood confronting 'illusory' endless options – known as the 'epistemological fallacy' (Furlong and Cartmel, 2007) – alongside risks and uncertainties, marginalized youth accumulate significantly greater risks than they realistically represent to others.

Youth Transitions and Historical Changes

Changes in youth employment and unemployment

Coles (1995) identifies three important social transitions characterizing youth's experiences to adulthood, from full-time education to full-time work, from family of origin to family of destination, and from residing in the family home to independent living. These factors differ according to historical, structural, geographical and global factors. In the 1970s the UK was an industrialized, labour-intensive society with full employment. Working-class male youths left school at 16 and easily found secure employment in factories, on building sites or as apprentices, although opportunities differed by gender and race/ethnicity (Cohen, 1997). Even now a huge gender pay gap exists, with girls pushed more into trades like hairdressing and boys into more technological apprenticeships, resulting in a 26 per cent pay gap, with the average female apprentice in 2007 earning £113 per week compared to a male average of £153 (F. Abrams, 2007). Since the 1970s, increasing labour-saving technological innovations and global capitalism's transfer of industrial work to cheaper developing countries, alongside recurrent national and international economic crises, heralded by the 1973 OPEC oil crisis and symbolized by the current global recession, have also led to a profound restructuring of employment. This has resulted in declines in the quantity and quality

of youth jobs available, particularly affecting those with few qualifications (K. Roberts, 1997; France, 2007; Furlong and Cartmel, 2007). The
UK is now post-industrial, producing few goods, and mining or refin-
ing few natural resources. Most jobs are in the financial and service
industries, with many, such as call centre posts, being casualized
with poor conditions and pay. Recent official figures for NEETs – those
not in education, work or training – aged 19–24 rose from 629,000 in
2000 to 651,000 in 2008, with females outstripping males by 139,000
(Lipsett, 2009a). These are significant factors separating the post 1970s
and Baby Boomer (post World War II) youth generations.

The expansion of higher education

In the UK and Europe, higher education (HE) has expanded phenomenally but is now levelling off. In 1974 there were 650,000 students,
but in 2009 there were 2.7 million (A. Beckett, 2009). However, government pledges of 50 per cent of young people being in HE by 2010
seem overly optimistic. In 2007, 39.8 per cent of 18- to 30-year-olds
were in HE, up by only 0.6 per cent from 39.2 per cent in 1999, despite
attempts at widening participation (Lipsett, 2008). We are, however,
now seen as a learning society, with both opportunities and pressures related to entering HE or undertaking vocational qualifications
increasing. In the 1980s, alongside increases in youth unemployment,
obligatory youth training schemes emerged. These were criticized by
some as concealment and surveillance technologies, merely watching
young people and keeping them off unemployment registers, rather
than equipping them for gainful employment, which for the most
part did not exist. These were superseded by many vocational qualifications and pre-university equivalents to 'A' levels. Both 'A' level
pass rates and the grades attained have incrementally increased year
on year since the early 1980s. They reached a 97 per cent pass rate in
2007, with nearly one in ten 'A'-level students achieving three grade
A passes, helped somewhat by students being allowed to re-sit exams
and coursework. GCSEs and 'A' levels have therefore been subject to
contested accusations of academic 'dumbing down' (McVeigh, 2007).
More A grades were also awarded to girls, pupils attending private
schools and those living in the South (Shepherd, 2009d) compared to
pupils from low-income families, with only 0.5 per cent (176 out of
300,000 pupils) of those eligible for free school meals attaining three
A grade 'A' levels in 2007 (Curtis, 2008).

Structural inequalities therefore also manifest themselves in education. Girls' slightly better GCSE and 'A' level results have provoked
simplistic moral panics about contemporary education favouring girls
and disadvantaging boys (Epstein, 1998; Griffin, 2001). These obscure
the fact that only some disadvantaged white working-class and ethnic

minority boys are underperforming. Tripartite education (superseded by comprehensivization in the late 1970s), which streamed 11-year-olds into grammar schools for academic pupils, secondary moderns for the less able, and technical, vocational schools, also practised gendered discrimination by selecting equal numbers of boys and girls for grammar schools, although girls statistically performed better in the 11+ exams. Willis (1977) identified an anti-education masculinist culture amongst working-class boys which still exists, arguably contributing to their continuing poor educational success, a fact rarely addressed. The difference then was that the boys knew that they could without difficulty walk into a job without qualifications.

Today, with the increasing expansion of higher education and contracting youth employment, more working-class pupils attend university, but this does not necessarily enhance their employment opportunities in comparison to the 1970s. It merely renders competition for jobs intense, leaving disadvantaged working-class youth who are without qualifications, such as homeless youth and care leavers, more vulnerable. Half of all first-time job market entrants have a degree. Although few are negative about university education, those graduating in 1999 were on average earning 10 per cent less than those who had graduated only four years before, with female graduates earning 9 per cent less than males. Many graduates now occupy positions not previously occupied by graduates and they often do not establish a clear career trajectory until ten years after graduation (D. Williams, 2005). The term 'slackers' or 'Generation X' also currently describes groups of young people extensively overqualified for the jobs they can procure, subsequently retreating into an aimless lifestyle of successive McJobs and engaging with 'trash media' (Osgerby, 2004).

Higher education, like primary and secondary education, still mirrors previous social class patterns with the dimmer middle-class students now benefiting more from higher education than the industrious, intelligent working class. Children from the richest 2 per cent of households are more than four and a half times as likely to study at high-status universities than children from average households. Children from the most affluent 25 per cent of families – judged by having two cars and 4+-bedroomed houses – occupy 55 per cent of places at high-ranking universities, compared with students from the poorest 25 per cent of households, typically living in flats or terraced houses, who make up 6.3 per cent (Shepherd, 2009a). Similar results are found when postcode analyses of poor and affluent areas are conducted (Shepherd, 2009b). Many working-class students are concentrated in the post-1992 universities, previously polytechnics, which have lower academic credibility than the elite research-oriented universities (Forsyth and Furlong, 2000), although working-class youth are still more likely to leave education at the minimum age than middle- and upper-class students. Poorer students are also disadvantaged by the withdrawal of maintenance grants and the institution of fees in the 1990s. This has led to many doing extensive paid work to fund their degree, which not only impacts on attrition (students dropping out or failing) and final degree grade but leads to a greater likelihood of attending a university near home. Middle- and upper-class students, in contrast, are more likely to have parents who help to fund their education and their move away from home to a more academically recognized university. Their parents also mobilize strategies and resources, such as private schools, private tutoring and social networking, to ensure educational advantage for their children (Ball, 2003).

For the top graduate jobs, not only was the 'hard currency' of qualifications required – elite universities being seen as providing the best graduates – but 'softer currency', such as leadership, interpersonal skills, appearance and even accent, were essential factors, yet again favouring middle-class graduates (Brown and Hesketh with Williams, 2004). Recent research on social mobility also found most of those entering the top professions, such as medicine and law, were from the most affluent families: 75 per cent of judges, 70 per cent of top finance directors and over 50 per cent of all the top jobs went to those privately educated, who constitute only 7 per cent of all school children the same age (Millburn, 2009), suggesting elitist control and privilege and a 'closed shop' mentality.

The profound changes in youth employment and higher education have inevitably extended the transition from full-time education to work for today's post-1970s generation, delaying independent living and family formation. Living with parents has become more flexible and less linear, with some young people working away from home for a few years then returning home to do a degree or save for a house. Others stay in education, not leaving the family home until their education is finished, which could be in their mid twenties. When young people settle down consequently occurs later, although working-class and disadvantaged youth are more likely to become single parents at much younger ages, with homeless youth and those from state-care backgrounds living independently much earlier, regardless of parenthood. Willis (1977) regarded one marker of the transition to adulthood as 'the pay-packet' but, with high youth unemployment and increasing participation in higher education, this is no longer relevant. Similarly, can a young person in their mid twenties be regarded as an adult if they have never been financially or emotionally independent?

Hilpern (2008a) argues university is not the rite of passage (to adult-hood) it once was, because some parents are effectively managing all their children's affairs for many years after they are legally adults, a phenomenon colloquially termed 'helicopter parenting'. Hilpern (2008a) cites parents launching appeals against university grades, negotiating their children's work salaries and conditions, and even managing their bank account. The term 'black hawk parents', a vari-ation on helicopter parenting, describes parents who are prepared to resort to dishonest or illegal activities to ensure educational and occupational advantage for their children (Macleod, 2008), including writing or purchasing essays for their offspring.

Youth transitions and social capital

Young people's transitions, as well as their leisure pursuits and con-sumption patterns, seem to be structured by their socio-economic position. *Social capital* has also been a useful way of showing the rela-tionship between process and outcome. Bourdieu (1984) identifies how various forms of capital – i.e. the resources one has economically, educationally, culturally and politically, or can mobilize – lead to advantage and disadvantage, to different aspirations and 'tastes', and fundamentally different ways of thinking and being for socially dif-ferent classes. These are unconsciously embodied in the way we talk and think, and in our corporeal presentation – our 'habitus'. Later work by Putnam (2000) differentiates further between *bonding capital* (inward-looking resources and support) which lead working-class and disadvantaged young people to remain in their own locality and draw support and trust from within it, and *bridging capital*. Bridging capital refers to more dependence on outward-looking resources and drawing on heterogeneous and geographically differentiated resources to 'get ahead' rather than 'get by', which is more middle-class.

Recent Economic and Social Research (ESCR) neighbourhood studies found that working-class young people depended more on bonding capital and friends and family, which disadvantaged them in terms of careers and jobs (Holland et al., 2007). One young working-class black youth, offered an elite university sports scholarship instead attended his local college because he feared leaving his familiar, pre-dominantly black neighbourhood. Another intellectually promising white working-class young woman was studying nursing at her local college because of single parenthood and because that was the upper limit of her and her mother's expectations of her, career-wise. Bould (2003) researched different neighbourhoods and the social capital they imbue in the USA, finding in affluent neighbourhoods everyone would look out for risky teenage behaviour, dealing with it collec-tively 'in house'. In more disadvantaged areas, support was rarely forthcoming from neighbours or police and there was a fear of involving the authorities because of potential repercussions. This shows how even bonding capital may be weak in the more deprived areas.

Youth, Identity, Politics and Values

Identity is more social, dynamic and multifaceted in sociology than in psychology (Jenkins, 1996). Erikson, for example, sees identity as something to be 'achieved' as opposed to the sociological view of fluidity and multiplicity. This sees identity shifting and possessing multiple facets, both ascribed through structures of power and achieved through our own agency, subjectivity and understanding of our narratives and family history. Our identity is as much about positioning ourselves through our identification with and attachment to those we see as similar, through kinship, class, race, gender, sexuality, or musical or sports alliances, as it is about *dis-identification* – distancing ourselves from what we are not (Lawler, 2008). Some people also have the power to ascribe both positive identifies to themselves and negative or non-identities to others. Young working-class people deemed by the media as dangerous and undeserving, or young gay people depicted by politicians, religious leaders and peers as unnatural and deviant, have to either accept such negative identities or work hard to disavow them or resignify them, two examples being the partial positive reclamation of the word 'nigger' by black rappers and 'queer' by gay youth.

Although class identity was important in the 1960s and 1970s, the fragmentation of class alongside the rise of the individualist consumer society has led to young people often identifying themselves through consumption (Miles, 2000). They see their identity as their 'own' achievement – a reflexive individual and lifelong project of body and self to be worked on (Giddens, 1991). This obscures the hidden advantages being middle class or white or male may bring. The following section will deal with youth subcultures and lifestyles, the power consumerism has and how the countervailing political and social climate has had an influence on the values of the post-1970s youth generation. In the 1960s and 1970s, alongside the 'hippy' counterculture and emerging social movements such as gay, black, women's, disability rights and anti war movements, many young people identified with collectivist values such as justice and equality. Contemporary youth in the UK and across Europe seem since then to have acquired more inward-looking, less collectivist values.

In a study of 12- to 25-year-olds of different social classes, genders, sexual orientations and ethnicities in Slovakia and the UK, Stainton Rogers et al. (2004) found, mirroring many other recent studies, that most young people valued their friends and family first, placed importance on health, 'happiness' and hedonism, were cynical about organized party politics and were very individualist. However, debates ensue about whether weakened participation in traditional politics suggests political apathy or a different approach. Although young people today may have little understanding of or affinity with structural issues such as sex, class and race discrimination, they are often engaged with single-issue politics such as the anti-vivisection movement and involved in one-off demonstrations, petitions or boycotts (Furlong and Cartmel, 2007). In a European study, 70 per cent of young people said they would pay higher taxes to prevent environmental damage (Haerpfer et al., 2002).

From Youth Subcultures to Youth Lifestyles

In the 1960s and 1970s, a group of mainly male middle-class, Marxist sociologists conducted ethnographic studies on easily accessible disadvantaged working-class male youths and their 'deviant' and criminal subcultures, often presenting their behaviour as constituting intentional resistance against ruling-class oppression (Griffin, 2001). Other researchers concentrated on white working-class subcultural groups, such as the Teddy boys, Skinheads, Mods and Rockers, and Punks, and their specific music and dress codes. They theorized how these groups were subject to moral panics and the amplification of any deviant acts they committed on the inaccurate pretext they were a risk to the status quo (Cohen, 1997). This research was important for showing how the media manipulated certain groups, and challenged the psychological storm and stress thesis. However, the researchers were rightly criticized for often imbuing working-class youth with a class consciousness they did not possess (Osgerby, 2004), and for ignoring young white women and ethnic minority youths (Griffin, 2001).

Research in the 1970s and 1980s revealed the more bedroom-based culture of girls, which involved listening to pop music, applying make-up, practising dancing, chatting and comparing sexual notes (McRobbie, 1978). In the 1980s, girls' autonomy was constrained by societal and parental sexual double standards (Halson, 1991; Lees, 1993). In the 1990s, girls' more public lives involved pop fandom and identifying with and potentially adopting more subversive and active forms of femininity such as those modelled by Riot Girl and Madonna. McRobbie (1994) later analysed the changing face of girls' magazines. These commenced with the compliant femininity, and 'trust and obey your man' romantic messages promulgated by *Jackie* in the 1970s. These discourses were often intercepted by the readership critically and ambivalently (suggesting such messages were not always fully believed or followed). Far more candidly (hetero)sexual and sassy magazines, containing glossy articles on fashion, music and beauty, then emerged in the 1980s and 1990s.

Other researchers in the 1980s and 1990s exposed the surveillance, marginalization and multiple oppression of minority youth across racial, sexual, class, gender and disability dimensions (Mac an Ghaill, 1994; Griffin, 2001). Gilroy (2002) exposed pervasive racism in the lives of black youths and, in July 2001, youth race riots occurred in deprived Northern towns such as Oldham, Burnley and Bradford. Although, initially, racism and social deprivations were taken into account, the blame was quickly placed on the individuals and insufficient racial integration. Moral panic then ensued about rap music and threatening black youth. However, many young Pakistani people in Britain were born there, identifying strongly as British citizens in terms of rights and belonging, very clearly expressed in their enthusiasm for British football but also seeing Islam as important to their identities (Hussain and Bagguley, 2005). Unlike their first-generation parents, they are very vocal against racism and about their rights as British citizens. Many Somali young adults, although also born here, often have their claims to being British denied because of their skin colour and have to contend with and negotiate being seen as British in Somalia and as Somali in the UK. They therefore often invest in and prioritize their Muslim identity over and above racial, gendered or ethno-national elements of self (Valentine and Sporton, 2009).

Many black (and increasingly white) youngsters, furthermore, fuse cultural influences and invoke *bricolage* (the forging together of a number of disparate elements to create something new) and hybridity in their tastes and in relation to music, television viewing habits and mixed dress styles. Some Asian teenage girls may, for example, wear traditional cultural dress with Western-style high-heeled shoes and make-up, and embrace both Western and Bollywood films. They may match the way they behave and act with the setting they are in – for example, behaving and dressing at home in a fairly traditional manner, and in a more Western way when out with their work colleagues or non-Asian friends. Some other studies have shown black and white youth mixing amicably with each other and some white youth even emulating black dress, hair and music styles. In Back's (1996) study of an urban mixed-ethnic community, although many of the white and Afro-caribbean youths mixed amicably together, there was much exclusion and racist harassment of Vietnamese young people by both groups.

There has also been a shift from seeing certain groups of young people, who identify with each other and share material circumstances, clothes styles and musical and leisure tastes, as indicating specific subcultural groupings to more postmodernist views. Advocates of the latter viewpoint claim the term 'youth lifestyles' is more relevant to contemporary society, where consumption is the main mediator of identity (e.g. Miles, 2000). Groups such as those involved in the 1980s dance scene are presented as individualistic neo-tribes (A. Bennett, 1999; Maffesoli, 1996), loose groupings unconnected with class, gender or ethnicity that conglomerate for specific activities such as raves but have very little else in common. However, Shildrick and MacDonald (2006) and Blackman (2005) argue that youth cultural and group identities are still hugely influenced by class, gender and racial formations and subculture. They lambast some of the post-subcultural researchers for concentrating on interesting, highly stylized middle-class groupings rather than the more ordinary and less flamboyant subcultures of poorer and excluded youth (Shildrick, 2003). Bose (2003), for example, showed how young black and Asian youths were frequently excluded, or self excluded because of fear of discrimination, from popular cultural venues in Manchester.

The term 'chav' has also acquired derogatory overtones and is associated with vulgar, unintelligent, potentially violent young working-class people with showy jewellery and clothes. Although chavs have been satirized in comedy shows, exemplified by Vicky Pollard from *Little Britain* and Lauren from *The Catherine Tate Show*, a real debate exists as to whether chavs are a disadvantaged subcultural group separated from the 'Chav Nots' by social deprivation and anti-educational attitudes (Nayak, 2006; Kneen, 2007). Other research with disadvantaged youth in the North found they mainly remained with their geographical peer group, their leisure centred around 'hanging out' on street corners, their consumption clearly linked to and shaped by geographical and material constraints (Shildrick and MacDonald, 2006).

Consumption documented in the 1920s associated with dancehalls, the cinema and magazines, exploded during the 'youthquake' of the 1950s and 1960s due to significant increases in disposable income (Miles, 2000) and teenagers were targeted as a specific marketing group (M. Abrams, 1959). Youth was depicted as a vibrant 'fun' time, young people acting as the trail blazers for style, images fundamentally diverging from previous negative conceptions. Today's youth still have disposable income and are avid consumers but the big difference, other than the advent of branding, consumerist society, is the impact of the new technology. The young tend to be depicted as media saturated and savvy, a new 'net' generation. Many extensively use mobile phones and the internet for communication, entertainment and information, communicating via email and participating in virtual reality online gaming, internet chat rooms and social network-ing sites such as Facebook or Bebo. The mobile phone has also been used as both a communication and bargaining tool between parents and children, parents seeing it as extending control, and children and young people as a way of negotiating curfews (S. Williams and Williams, 2005).

There are also gendered and ethnic differences in how mobiles are used and, although they have generally been found to be used for contact between friends and family, coordinating activities, forging and sustaining intimate relationships and digital gift giving, one study of British Pakistani Muslims aged 14–25 found they additionally used mobiles for texting to Pakistan because it was cheap. These par-ticular young males said they could not be parted from their phones and would rather go out and forget their key than their mobile, although a few participants were fed up of being expected to be con-tinually available and deliberately left phones at home or pretended the battery had run down (Green and Singleton, 2007). The young males viewed the female-to-female longer conversations as inferior 'gossip' but their male conversations as instrumental. They also liked being able to text feelings and emotions to girls and flirt with them without the possibility of instant, visible rejection. The young people also used mixed languages in both text and talk, and Punjabi was used when they did not want non-Muslim others within earshot to understand what they were saying. The phones were also status symbols, and slim, sleek and silver was the 'in look'. Their wallpapers, phone covers, screensavers and ringtones also revealed gendered and ethnic choices and identities.

Some young people, however, still remain on the other side of the digital divide and have limited access to new technology. Although 75 per cent of 9- to 19-year-olds have home internet access (Livingstone et al., 2005), this still leaves 25 per cent who don't. Similarly, although 80 per cent of young people own mobile phones, using them regu-larly, again 20 per cent are excluded (Mintel, 2003). These tend to be from poorer families and blame themselves for being unable to keep up with new technology (Holloway and Valentine, 2003). The new technology also offers young people new ways of communicating, evaluating more unstructured, differently presented information and increasing expertise in Information and Comunication Technology (ICT), which those without access may be disadvantaged by, particu-larly in relation to future employability.

There are also concerns that excessive use of the internet or games consoles can either incite violence in young people or render them vacuous couch potatoes. However, as with the research on younger children, there is no clear-cut evidence of a causal relationship with violence or other fears being realized (Buckingham, 2002). One concern exists that, since market branding in the 1980s, young people feel they can only acquire status from buying brands. Views diverge here, with some theorists seeing young people as sufficiently cynical and discerning to know what they want to buy and view. Fiske (1989), for example, cited young urban Aborigines subverting the original colonial meanings explicit in the Old Western films, and cheering and applauding when the Indians killed or captured white men or carried 'their' women off. Other commentators stress caution, acknowledging choices exist but only within the constraints of the economic interests of the dominant groups within society, emphasizing that disadvantaged groups are more vulnerable to manipulation through brand advertising (N. Klein, 2000). Therefore, although extensive marketing for a particular product may flop, global capitalism and consumerism only continue to exist by eternally manufacturing new desires which can never be sated.

Conclusion

This chapter has briefly reviewed key theories and research on the psychology of adolescence and the sociology of youth, although adolescence covers a narrower chronological period between the early and late teen period, whereas youth can extend to the mid twenties. Adolescent psychology places considerable emphasis on physical changes and their relationship with cognitive, moral and psychosocial developments, although many psychologists now concede adolescence's socially constructed nature, questioning claims that there is a causal effect between hormonal and physical changes and social behaviour, notably around distressed or antisocial behaviour. Psychological perspectives are, however, useful as they document the physical changes that occur, and show how children's cognitive abilities, including their moral reasoning, change during adolescence and how their behaviour may be related to experimenting with their potential future identities and life plans. The sociology of youth explores how changing social structure and the socio-economic and political climate impact significantly upon young people's experiences and identities over time. Areas focused on included the perceptions of youth as a dangerous and irresponsible group, youth employment and the expansion of higher education, social capital and youth, identity and values and the power of consumerism and new technology. Gender, race and social class were also shown to impact profoundly upon young people's identities and experiences.

Reflection and discussion questions

Why might psychology's understanding and theorization of adolescence be seen as problematic and deficient?

Why are adolescents and young people frequently represented as troubled, 'in trouble' or troublesome?

Document and analyse recent changes in youth unemployment and higher education.

Recommended reading

Coleman and Hendry's UK psychological text on adolescence (1999) is an accessible, socially aware and well-written text, but now a little dated. Journal articles by Steinberg and Morris (2001) and Smetana et al. (2006) are comprehensive but fairly traditional reviews of the psychological literature on adolescence, but draw predominantly from US research. UK books by Mizen (2004), Roche et al. (2004), France (2007) and Furlong and Cartmel (2007) on the sociology of youth are highly sensitive to social change and social inequalities. *Adolescence* is a useful journal to consult for recent psychological research on adolescence, whilst the *Journal of Youth Studies* is excellent for sociological and social policy orientated research and theorizing.

Young Adulthood

CHAPTER

05

Young adulthood normally ranges from 18 to 40 within psychology, whereas sociologists rarely group their research with adults according to age categories, rendering direct comparison between psychology and sociology difficult. Adolescent psychology being so linked to physiology and puberty, thus covering a narrower period than youth in sociology (which extends until the mid twenties), further compounds this difficulty. The psychological section of this chapter will therefore analyse physical development, cognitive development and psychosocial changes from 18 onwards. Claims for a new developmental period, 'emergent adulthood', will also be examined. Following on, the changing nature of young adulthood will be analysed from a sociological vantage point with specific reference to transitions into and markers of adulthood and the importance and role of work, leisure, friends and family. Following this, similarities and differences in the ways the two disciplines understand and interpret young adulthood will then be examined.

Psychology and young adulthood

Physical Changes and Development

Girls generally reach maximum height by 16 and boys by 18, but other growth processes, including muscle and fat augmentation, continue until the mid twenties, although because of greater body muscle mass in males they tend to be stronger (Berger, 2005). For both sexes strength and speed increase throughout the twenties, peaking around 30, young adults excelling at most sports and physical activities. All one's body systems, including circulatory, respiratory, digestive and sexual reproductive, are most efficient in one's twenties, with young adults less affected by naturally occurring diseases and disability than older age groups.

When young people require health treatment, causes are often environmental or cultural, and strongly influenced by gender. These include car accidents, alcohol or drug misuse, eating disorders and self-inflicted and other-directed violence (Green and Taylor, 2010), young men being the most likely agitators and recipients of violence. However, subtle slow signs of senescence, when overall growth finishes and a gradual age-related decline begins, commence in the twenties but are rarely apparent until the thirties or later. Collagen – connective bodily tissue – decreases about 1 per cent per year from the age of 20, eventually resulting in thinning, less elastic and more wrinkled skin. In the twenties lung capacity starts to diminish, with slow declines from about 30 in kidney function, sight and hearing, and the beginning of greying hair. Psychologists do, however, concede many factors could impact upon both achievements and these declines, such as general health, ethnicity/race, social class and genetic predispositions. Men's socialization into being competitive, expressing strength and concealing vulnerability may lead to them not only placing themselves in risk situations but also to males seeing preventative or 'curative' health care as unmasculine (Berger, 2005).

Cognitive Changes

The pattern for cognitive development mirrors that of physical development. Young adults peak in most areas such as intelligence and general cognition, although psychiatric illnesses such as schizophrenia (which often emerges in late adolescence or early adulthood) may significantly impair cognition. Younger adults perform better than older age groups on measures of both short-term and long-term memory. However, one recent study questioned whether or not older adults' declining ability to attend to auditory stimuli when background noise was present was due to age-related cognitive declines, because, when individual differences in age-related hearing loss were adjusted for, there were no differences in cognitive ability to process and attend to auditory stimuli (Murphy et al., 2002). Young adults are generally more proficient at fluid intelligence, which depends less on experience and education and more on how fast you respond and abstract reasoning, although Schaie's US longitudinal study (1989) showed no decline in crystallized or fluid intelligence before middle or late adulthood in some individuals. In other studies middle and late-age adults have shown gains on crystallized but rarely on fluid intelligence. According to Schaie's longitudinal and cross-sectional research, global or overall IQ scores rise in early adulthood, remaining fairly constant until about 60 (Schaie, 1983b).

In relation to post-Piagetian approaches, some theorists assert that the stage of *formal operations* is not the final one and that *post-formal operations* can be detected in some young adults. Since not all problems can realistically be approached with time-consuming, abstract, hypothetical evaluations which lead to clear unequivocal solutions, it has been argued that, consequently, a more pragmatic flexible approach takes over (Labouvie-Vief, 1980). This involves combining objective analytical thought with subjective thought, derived from these young adults' viewpoints and experiences (Sinnott, 1998) as they realize many answers may be provisional. They therefore generate more possible solutions to hypothetical problems than adolescents (Blanchard Fields, 1999), combining logic and emotion whereas adolescents often think in polarized ways, believing a problem has one right solution. Arlin (1984) argues post-formal thinking is characterized by problem finding as well as problem solving, and is most advanced when incorporating dialectical thinking which involves synthesizing opposing ideas. There is little consensus over whether such thinking represents a loss or a progression from Piaget's stages but it is generally seen as a reasonable adult adaptation in the face of complex, multifaceted and unclear cognitive tasks. Cultural backgrounds also impact, with those of Chinese or Asian heritage thinking more holistically and contextually and being more compromise orientated whereas Americans manifest more polarized and less contextual thinking (Peng and Nisbett, 1999; Nisbett et al., 2001). In young and middle adulthood when we are confronted with many difficult ethical dilemmas and mix with people who have different philosophical outlooks, again a more flexible approach takes precedence regarding moral reasoning for some young adults.

Psychosocial Changes

Erikson's sixth and seventh stages are both relevant to young adulthood. 'Intimacy vs isolation' relates to fusing your identity with someone else's without fearing abandonment or losing yourself, thus attaining a secure intimate partnership. 'Generativity vs stagnation' is about motivation to achieve and the feeling of cumulatively accomplishing something, whether that is bringing up children well, being promoted in your career, exercising creativity or developing certain skills. Although Erikson was writing in the mid twentieth century, contemporary life span psychologists also view the central tasks in young adulthood as successful intimate partnerships and friendships, and generativity in relation to work and parenthood (Bee, 1994; Berger, 2005). This suggests the key psychosocial issues have changed little in the last fifty years, although contemporary psychologists now discuss areas seldom mentioned fifty years ago, such as lesbian and gay relationships, childless couples, divorce, surrogate parents and domestic violence.

Levinson (1978, 1986), based on detailed interviews with forty 35- to 40-year-old American men from different but not comprehensive occupational categories, also developed an influential account of phases in adult life. Levinson subdivides early young adulthood into two sub-stages. At 17–22 men become more autonomous, envisioning a 'Dream' of certain life goals they would like to attain, such as financial wealth, occupational achievement or becoming an elite sportsman. At 22–28, they enter the adult world more fully, forging a special intimate partner relationship and progressing in work. The age 30 transition stage (28–33) involves re-evaluation and possible repositioning of one's goals before the 'settling down' phase in one's late thirties when career and family trajectory are more formally established. An important feature of early adulthood is also having a mentor offering guidance and support.

Levinson and Erikson have subsequently been criticized for basing most of their theories on men but a review of four unpublished studies showed some of Levinson's phases were also relevant for women although there were differences (Roberts and Newton, 1987). These included women's 'Dreams' envisioning occupation as less central than marriage and family, often subordinating their needs and dreams to support their husbands' aspirations. Even professional career women rarely had mentors or had experienced profound difficulty finding one. The age 30 transition was interesting because women who had submerged all into family life became more individualistic, whereas more career orientated females tended to become more family focused. The thirties were less clearly defined than for men as a settling period, possibly because the combination of work and family obligations meant women were not secure in a career path and were still largely responsible for childcare and housework. If one person's 'Dream' is subverted or quashed by the other partner, the relationship can be in serious jeopardy. Durkin (1995) cites the example of John McEnroe, the tennis player, telling his wife, Tatum O'Neal, the actress, he would not allow her to make films while leaving their children with a stranger, which led to her filing for divorce.

Psychologists think young adults need to achieve some emotional separation from their parents, and studies have shown close friends provide more pleasure and support and induce more self-awareness than family relationships (Bukowski et al., 1996; Pahl and Spencer, 1996), probably because of the choice element and less self-censoring occurring in friendships. In one study what induced the move from acquaintance to friend surprisingly included perceived physical attractiveness, even amongst same-sex, platonic friendships, as well as more obvious factors such as openness to doing activities together, frequent acquaintance and the absence of 'unacceptable' character-istics. Such exclusionary characteristics could range from different religious or political beliefs to acting on prejudicial stereotypes such as racism and homophobia (Fehr, 1996). Clear gender differences have, however, been found in same-sex friendships. Women are gen-erally more prepared to disclose vulnerability and be intimate and supportive with their close friends whereas men's friendships at this age are mostly based on joint activities and sharing common inter-ests, although both sexes seem equally satisfied with their same-sex friendships. Sibling relationships are also important because they tend to be the most enduring life relationship, siblings sharing both childhood experiences and genetic material (Durkin, 1995).

Sternberg (1986) asserts 'falling in love' must be followed by inti-macy and commitment for a relationship to endure. The Western romantic ideal of all three occurring together is difficult to achieve because passion is often heightened by unfamiliarity and dimmed by routine and commitment, and because modern Western marriage is represented as an exclusive relationship which fulfils all emotional and sexual needs (Reibstein and Richards, 1992). The more similar partners are in terms of background, interests, personality and goals, the more the relationship is likely to be successful, known as the homogamy or homophily principle (D. Cramer, 1998).

Successful close friendships or long-term relationships are often profoundly influenced by earlier attachment experiences and sub-sequent internal working models, although some people are able to analyse pathological childhood attachments and forge a new, healthier working model. People with different working models also describe themselves and partner expectations differently. Those with insecure working models are more likely to be lonely (Hazan and Shaver, 1987) with avoidant subjects reporting less intensive love experiences, and insecure and avoidant participants having more, but fewer enduring love affairs than secure subjects (Feeney and Noller, 1992; Feeny et al., 1993). Warm and sensitive family attachment style at adolescence also positively influenced future attachments, including romantic relationships. Young adults from violent paren-tal backgrounds in a simulated marital conflict experiment were more likely to attribute blame and predict negative outcomes and to report aggressive conflict in their own relationships than those from non-violent backgrounds (Duggan et al., 2001).

Early attachment styles, furthermore, significantly impact on coping styles, distress experienced and support sought (Mikulincer et al., 1993) and later attachments with children (Rossi and Rossi, 1990).

However, regardless of attachment style, responses to distress seem more intense in younger than older adulthood. In one study, where apparently disparaging remarks were made about the participants, greater anger, inquisitiveness and negativity were expressed by the younger adults although both younger and older adults expressed equivalent sadness (Charles and Carstensen, 2008). This suggests that, as one ages, volatile and confrontational behaviours reduce, and the ability to use more passive emotional regulation strategies increases, regardless of background (Blanchard Fields and Coats, 2008). Defence mechanisms (discussed in the chapters on childhood) have also been found to be more maladaptive, involving acting out and passive aggression, with younger as opposed to older adults (Segal et al., 2007).

Young people are also more likely to suppress negative emotions than older adults, which is less healthy than reappraising the situation to minimize negative or increase positive emotions. Young men have been found to suppress negative emotion more than young women (John and Gross, 2004), and lifelong gender socialization practices which constrain men from showing vulnerability but encourage women to do so may be relevant. Although regret is experienced throughout the life course (Landman, 1987) and can impact on overall wellbeing, all age groups tend to use downward social comparisons to improve threatened self-esteem (Zeelenberg and Peters, 2007). Younger people have more time to rectify adverse situations and therefore resort to downward social comparisons less frequently than older adults (Bauer et al., 2008).

In relationships women are more likely to fulfil the role of kin keeper for both partners and be the emotional linchpin between friends and family, smoothing out arguments, for example, and maintaining contact via Xmas cards and phone calls (Durkin, 1995). In relation to notions of generativity, work and parenthood, partnership satisfaction plummets after the birth of a first child. Parental work hours (paid and unpaid) also increase and leisure time decreases (Kluwer et al., 2002) with a role overload occurring when both parents work, women often undertaking a double or triple shift whereby, alongside paid employment, they assume most domestic and childcare responsibility. Durkin (1995) extensively investigates the social psychological literature on gender, finding it central to young adulthood, particularly in relation to domestic divisions of labour. Although men are becoming more involved in childcare and housework and the couple's gender role ideologies impact upon this, Durkin (1995), drawing from numerous studies conducted in the 1980s and 1990s, finds the man's contribution is only estimated to be 20–30 per cent of total housework, although men perceive their contributions as higher. In Sweden men were far more involved in housework than men in the USA, suggesting long-term social policy change, such as the Swedish government's pursuit of gender equality, possibly may have had some effect (Wright et al., 1992).When young adults do not have their own biological or non-biological children, they may attain generativity by involving themselves greatly with relatives' or friends' children or through entering a profession such as teaching or social work which involves close contact with children (Durkin, 1995).

Levinson sees young adulthood as continuing life cycle progress. Although acknowledging some men may not work, find work oppressive or fail to be promoted, his model nevertheless seems to be a patriarchal white middle-class American model that does not adequately consider working-class or ethnic minority men or women, although some of his research participants were blue-collar workers. Women, whom Levinson ignored until much later (1996), are increasingly participating in the workforce in the Western world and enter higher education in the UK in higher numbers than men (45 per cent of women compared to 35 per cent of men in the 18–30 age bracket, according to 2006–7 figures: Lipsett, 2009b). Despite this, many women work part time compared to men and their occupational attainment is markedly lower. Early psychological theories argued women had been socialized into fear of success. In the 1960s, when male and female students were given a story to complete about a medical student at the top of their class, if the hypothetical student was male, both sexes were positive. If female, the description was generally unfavourable, describing her as physically unattractive, unfriendly and with psychological problems (Horner, 1972). Research since then, however, does not appear to corroborate the notion that fear of success is gendered. Other studies evaluating whether women's work was rated lower or higher than men's have reported mixed results. However, research does tend to corroborate that women have lower expectations and confidence regarding work than men.

A study of Scottish final-year university students (although both men and women espoused egalitarian gender-neutral notions about work and men's and women's competence) showed, when children were brought into the equation, both sexes felt women were more 'biologically' suited to looking after children and/or it was their duty. These students therefore contradictorily revealed an ideology of 'unequal egalitarianism', anticipating inequality outside university life (Wetherall et al., 1987). Subsequent sociological and psychological research shows the accuracy of such anticipation and the frequent reversion to stereotypical gender roles after a child is born (Durkin, 1995).

Emergent Adulthood

In 2000, Arnett proposed a new developmental period between the late teens and mid twenties, which he named *emergent adulthood*. Arnett claimed this involved greater identity experimentation and delays in ideological and relationship commitment and in developing an occupational trajectory in comparison to previous generations, alongside a sense of instability. Arnett's work is rarely discussed in traditional psychology or adolescence textbooks (Côté and Bynner, 2008), although much debate and contestation have ensued. Arnett's notion of identity exploration until the mid twenties would also seem to challenge both Erikson's and Levinson's classical descriptions of the phases of early adulthood and therefore is important to analyse.

Côté and Bynner (2008), sociologists, argue that, although 'emergent adulthood' may be a useful euphemism for describing the current prolonged transitioning into adulthood, there is little evidence it represents a new developmental period, because those not experiencing it must lose out or be deficient in some way (2008: 253), which they assert there is no evidence for. They criticize Arnett for insufficient attention to the part disadvantage, for example, lower social class, may play and question whether identity is always clearly formed even by the mid twenties. They do, however, place emphasis on 'floundering', during which one job after another may be tried in an uncertain employment market where even prospects for many graduates are poor. They concur with Arnett that individuals conceptualize themselves as adults not through the old markers of marriage, employment and financial and emotional independence but through their psychological actions, such as taking responsibility for their behaviour, but they perceive Arnett as overstating the choices all young people are able to make.

Konstam (2008), adopting an implicitly clinical developmental perspective, also examines young adulthood, through interviews with sixty-four 25- to 35-year-old Americans and their parents and employers. She, however, avoids engaging with the question of whether emergent and young adulthood are differentiated, possibly because she finds so much blurring between them (J. L. Tanner, 2008). Konstam highlights the challenges young people face because of their rapidly changing and complex everyday worlds and, because her work deals with later young adulthood, she also depicts the losses involved with transitions to adulthood as well as the gains. One example given is of a 32-year-old married man awaiting the birth of his first child. He dislikes his responsible, well-paid job but, because of family responsibilities, can make fewer choices than his less committed peers. A converse example is a young woman who elects to do low-paid work with little responsibility because it gives her the opportunity to leave work at short notice and travel abroad.

Although Konstam commendably refuses to pathologize this young adult cohort, her research shows some young people experience negative psychological symptoms related to this unclear transition to adulthood. Applying Schwartz's *tyranny of choice* (2004b) she suggests what differentiates this current generation from others is their perception of having significant opportunities and almost limitless choices. Konstam sees this as a difficult challenge, rather than being inevitably beneficial, involving a meandering path to adulthood. Many respondents felt they had gained little personally or occupationally from higher education, using it to fill time and explore themselves. They felt unprepared for work, requesting extensive guidance and mentorship from adults, but parents and employers were unsure how to respond because of their very different life trajectories. Employers found the young people challenging to manage. They viewed them as technologically proficient but simultaneously over-dependent on technology, and good at work/home life balance but often to the detriment of a strong commitment to work, although they requested much support there from their line managers. Research in the UK closely mirrors Konstam's findings. Many young people have observed their parents work consistently long hours, showing unquestioning commitment to employers, and then subsequently watching their pension schemes decrease in value, sometimes being defrauded by the very employer they showed such loyalty to – one alleged example being previous employees of Murdoch and the *Daily Mirror*. Many young adults are consequently rebelling against the traditional work ethic, resigning from inflexible, unfulfilling jobs with poor conditions and limited promotional opportunities and confidently challenging authority. However, this generation have never (until now, 2008–10 and ongoing) experienced a significant economic recession and, given increasing youth unemployment and the influx of work-hungry graduates from other countries, young people may have to rethink (Asthana, 2008; Hilpern, 2008b).

Arnett's model is a useful counterpoint to earlier stage models limited by the time they were written in, such as Levinson's and Erikson's. Konstam's work is a useful empirical exploration of young adulthood from the perspectives of the young adults themselves, their parents and employers. Konstam empathizes with these young people, showing how their perceptions of choice initially bedazzle them but ultimately disappoint, when they are burdened with family and financial responsibilities. They appear overly dependent at work but simultaneously relatively uncommitted to it, confounding employers who expect these often educated individuals to show loyalty, autonomy and initiative. Perhaps one marker for contemporary adulthood should not just be taking responsibility for one's actions but an awareness that following a meandering path to adulthood may have losses as well as gains. Konstam's sample is also fairly unrepresentative as 100 per cent had a college education and 40 per cent were graduates, and perhaps if she had included more ethnic minorities and socially and economically deprived young adults, her findings would have been different.

Arnett's model mirrors the same disadvantages that psychological stage models carry with them, in that they are insufficiently able to take into account social change and structural constraints on choice. Konstam is more flexible but largely ignores structural inequalities and how they impact upon 'real' choices. Both authors, do, nevertheless, demonstrate how different young people's lives are today from those of previous generations and how adulthood may now have to be measured differently.

Sociology and young adulthood

Some difficulty exists within sociology in clearly differentiating between mid to late youth and the early part of young adulthood as the two clearly converge in many aspects. Issues in the previous chapter additionally relevant to early, young adulthood include media depictions of young people as dangerous, the transition from an industrialized to a consumerist society, and changes in youth employment. The chapter also began to examine the contemporary relevance of traditional markers of adulthood, such as waged work, independence and long-term relationships. Changes in higher education were furthermore evaluated, and youth identities, political beliefs, subcultures and lifestyles were examined in the context of structured inequalities. This section builds on these themes, in addition to examining the experience of the latter period of young adulthood and placing greater emphasis on friendships, relationships and parenthood. Initially there will be an analysis of transitions into adulthood. Changes in family and intimate relationships will then be evaluated as will employment changes, and the importance and effects of new technology, sport and leisure.

Transitions into and Markers of Contemporary Adulthood

Strong claims have been made that life courses are now de-institutionalized or de-standardized (Heelas et al., 1996; Lash and Urry, 1987) and that key markers of 'previous' life courses, often historically related to chronological age, are irrelevant in individualized societies (Beck, 1992). Therefore, young people are now often represented as confronting choice biographies (Du Bois-Reymond, 1998) and fragmented adulthoods (Côté, 2000). These claims are difficult to evaluate because what constitutes adulthood today is contested and unclear. Qualitative and quantitative studies often have divergent findings, depending on sample size and constituencies, what questions have been asked and interpretation of findings/results. Significant differences exist between the experiences of young adulthood in the post-industrial and developing nations and between different groups within one nation. Some commentators also judge adulthood on historical markers, suggesting today's young adults are immature and irresponsible, whilst others argue that, because society is so different today, new criteria for judging adulthood are needed.

One study of 4,666 Belgians aged 18–36 found little evidence individualization had replaced the traditional standardized life course, in both idealized views of the right time for key events such as marriage, childbearing or starting work *and* when this actually occurred, although prolonged education and cohabitation occasionally led to work, parenthood and marriage occurring a couple of years later than in previous generations (Elchardus and Smits, 2006). The Comparative Families and Transitions in Europe project (Biggart et al., 2003) also showed respondents' future expectations were traditional and linear. Elchardus and Smits suggest this proclaimed 'yo-yoization of the life cycle' and reversal of normative sequences is rare due to age-related institutional processes such as compulsory schooling, access to pensions, and biological age restrictions such as capacity for reproduction. However, they acknowledge tradition has been replaced by personal choice in many young people's accounts.

Research, principally on Norway and Britain, found engaging with adulthood was highly influenced by structural inequalities, but most participants' accounts centred on autonomy and choice, alongside deafening silences about inequality, again suggesting the prominence but not necessarily the accuracy of the individualized choice and agency thesis. Brannen and Nilsen (2005) identified four groups: (i) deferred adults, those characterized by living with parents and long-term financial dependence; (ii) those living semi-independently; (iii) those who experienced precarious early unsupported entry into adulthood, but were 'getting by' and were often themselves parents or cohabiting already; and (iv) those whose living situations varied but who had clear future plans. Some deferrers were in vocational training or were university students but had no clear future goals, which the authors suggest implies a denial of ageing and rejection of full adulthood. Others in the clearly planned-out futures group, such as English Asian men studying law and Norwegian shipyard workers following their fathers' occupational route, saw the future as unproblematic. However, those with the fewest financial, economic and cultural resources often fell prey to their beliefs in autonomy and choice: 'Individualisation as ideology can . . . [disadvantage] those whose lives are more at the mercy of structural constraints . . . in relation to market liberalism . . . Individual rights to freedom of choice are defined in terms of consumption . . . emphasised at the expense of political rights and citizenship' (Brannen and Nilsen, 2005: 424).

A qualitative interview study with fifty-eight young people and their parents in the United Kingdom, Norway and Spain (Holdsworth and Morgan, 2005), showed leaving home is no longer related to other significant events such as going to university, getting a job or getting married, which the authors interpret as a move towards a more individualized biography. In the UK and Norway, leaving home generally occurred in the late teens and early twenties, but in Spain many lived with parents until their thirties. The young people associated adulthood with markers such as financial independence, psychological initiative, agency and autonomy. Those in the UK and Norway saw independence as freedom from parental constraint, with Spanish respondents somewhat understandably disagreeing. This was, however, a small unrepresentative qualitative study. The Office for National Statistics reported in *Social Trends* that 18 per cent of young women and 29 per cent of young men aged 20–34 now live at home with their parents, compared with 15 per cent of women and 27 per cent of men in 2000, positing economic reasons for the increase, such as the quadrupling of numbers entering higher education in the last four decades and rising house prices, the average first-time buyer now being 29 years old (Collinson, 2009). A 2007 Eurobarometer survey of 15- to 30-year-olds found 44 per cent lived with parents because of lack of affordable housing, 38 per cent cited economic pressures, and 12 per cent wanted 'the comforts of home' but not the responsibilities (Carvel, 2009a).

Thomson et al.'s (2004) longitudinal biographical study of 100 UK young people, aged 15 to 24 years, from contrasting social backgrounds, explored their evolving and sometimes paradoxical views of adulthood. Mirroring other UK research, transitions to adulthood were structured by social class with accelerated transitions occurring for those with few economic and family resources, such as those from care backgrounds and socially deprived neighbourhoods (Webster et al., 2004) and extended transitions more the norm for the middle classes (Bynner, 2002). Thomson's research suggests significant debate about what constitutes adulthood, whether it is legal rights and responsibilities, chronological age, competence, completing education or entering full-time work. In the first interviews conducted, the young adults stressed responsibilities, legal markers, the quality of their relationships, taking care of others, and competence. There was a division between a relational understanding of adulthood involving consideration for and care of others (for example within parenthood), and an individualized view involving self, increasing independence, autonomy and choice. The young people moved between these different positions at different times. Both education and work were seen as sources of adult competence and recognition, as were an involvement in criminality for some, parenthood, voluntary work or adult leisure activities such as clubbing. However, these activities were clearly structured by both class and gender, young parenthood being disproportionately shouldered by working-class girls.

Blatterer's (2007) research with Australian young men (aged 25–35) rejects the 'delayed adulthood' hypothesis based on later family formation or delayed labour market entry. Blatterer proposes a new form of adulthood, contesting claims that young adults' leisure practices such as playing computer games or reading *Harry Potter*, evidence hedonistic consumerism, infantilization or the eschewing of adulthood (Furedi, 2003), depicted in the media by terms such as 'twixters', 'kidults', 'adulescents' and 'KIPPERS' ('kids in parents' pockets eroding retirement savings'). The standardized adulthood young people tend to be judged against existed in a short period between the Second World War and the 1973 OPEC oil crisis, during which labour market stability enabled gendered heterosexual nuclear family formation and employment entry to be relatively fixed in time. Because of current unstable labour markets and the claimed transformation of intimacy to a more reciprocal rather than a traditional duty-bound arrangement (Giddens, 1992), Blatterer argues that clear markers and transitions are rarely possible or desirable. Blatterer's respondents recognized significant differences between the generations, normalizing change and uncertainty in their young adult lives, particularly regarding employment. They were more individualistic and fatalistic than the preceding generation, but Blatterer rejects claims today's young adults are selfish and self-obsessed, asserting that their living-for-the-present paradigms and constant self-reflexivity (Beck, 1992) are logical responses to systemic uncertainty (Bauman, 2001).

One US interview study with law and business university students found many underestimated work and economic insecurity and were over-confident about their potential to earn consistently high incomes, do interesting jobs and have successful families. As in Wetherall et al.'s study, the men tokenistically supported gender equality and valued educated females but envisaged their partner would be responsible for childcare. Their female peers wanted partnership equality but were not hopeful about attaining it (Orrange, 2007).

Gender and young adulthood

Views and experiences of adulthood appear from many studies, as suggested above, to be profoundly affected by gender. One US interview study of forty-two, largely white, middle-class women in their early twenties, found most semi-consciously incorporated aspects of 'living feminism' into their viewpoints (Aronson, 2008), perceiving adulthood as characterized by independence/self-reliance, self-development and uncertainty. Secure intimate relationships were seen as optional, for those with and without children, and not as a marker of adulthood, although the mostly heterosexual women aspired to egalitarian relationships. The importance of self and of identity development was expressed disproportionately by middle-class college women who viewed university attendance as certain, although many experienced graduation and starting, or looking for, work as stressful. The working-class women saw work as more important than self-development, but work uncertainty was undifferentiated by class. One respondent was more certain about her tattoos than her career trajectory and most respondents thought they had a lot of choices, but contradictorily struggled for good opportunities. Aronson suggests career uncertainty may be gendered and some respondents were highly competent but viewed success as luck, paralleling other studies where men tend to attribute success to competence and failure to bad luck, whereas women attribute success to luck and failure to incompetence.

Davis (2007) in another US study of how gender ideology and egalitarianism impacted upon a representative sample of 14- to 17- and 22- to 25-year-olds found initially adolescents' gender ideologies were highly influenced by their families of origin, including whether their mothers were college graduates. Over time, egalitarian social background characteristics lost their protective impact and individuals' own experiences became more important. Those married by 21 and those with children in their mid twenties were less egalitarian than those not married at that age, and less egalitarian than their former selves before they had children. A study utilizing the British Household Panel Survey (BHPS) examined young women's work/family trajectories and, when focusing on a specific period of the life course using simple analytical strategies, found their life courses to be heterogeneous and complex (Aassve et al., 2007). Although Hakim (2003) argued women hold three enduring life choice preferences – (i) mostly work (20 per cent), whereby women remain childless or have children later, (ii) mostly family (20 per cent), where women exit the workplace if work threatens family, or (iii) a combination of the two (60 per cent) – the data from this study show greater complexity. There was no evidence any young women were exclusively family focused, though some were more family than work orientated. Most combined work and family, although in very diverse ways, following oblique and circuitous pathways, and a continuous attachment to work was evident.

Work

With the move to a post-industrial society, much employment has shifted to the service and financial sectors, and casualized labour and part-time and short-term contract jobs have expanded, although sociology rarely differentiates between young and middle adulthood when examining work patterns. Many younger adults who have not yet established an occupational trajectory are likely to be those in the poorest, most insecure jobs. Call-centre work has increased exponentially and often involves young adults, poor conditions, low pay, little autonomy and close surveillance, call centres recently being compared to the nineteenth-century 'satanic' textile mills (by the Trades Union Congress, which is Britain's largest civil service union: Edemariam, 2010). A deepening economic recession predicted to be long-term, including increasing national debt, unemployment and deflation, has been documented in the last two years (2008–10). Most affected will be 18- to 34-year-olds as half have debts of up to £10,000, with a fifth owing more, a third have no savings, and many worryingly reported insufficient understanding of financial products (Osborne, 2008). The gulf between those who attended prestigious universities, the new universities and those without higher education credentials is also likely to widen, with those entering the job market earlier even more prone to unemployment than before (Hinscliff, 2008). Between October and December 2008, 38,000 young people aged 18–24 were made redundant, about 25 per cent of the overall total in that age group, and a Children's Society Report surveyed 17- to 19-year-olds and found 22 per cent could not find jobs (Carvel, 2009b).

Emotional labour, gender and work stress

Much employment today also involves emotional labour (Hochschild, 1983), expressing or suppressing specific emotions so members of the public feel empathized with or even intimidated – for example, by debt collectors. Emotional labour is frequently feminized, involving aesthetic and sexual work, whereby employees are expected to look and sound a certain way, for example female flight attendants or waitresses. This can negatively affect employees' emotional lives when they routinely express unfelt emotions and recite heavily scripted responses. Professional women involved in emotional labour within nursing, teaching and social work were also, according to analysis of the 1999 BHPS, more likely than male peers in the same professions to be stressed and fatigued (Barron and West, 2007). Jobs with a high caring component were initially associated with women, 'natural vocationality' and the private sphere (the family, domesticity and childcare within the home) and still accrue lower pay and status. Men often experience these jobs differently and, unlike women in traditionally male jobs, such as accountancy, benefit from easier promotion, associated with gendered preferential hiring. In one study, male residential workers were often channelled into male specialities and encouraged to perform tasks associated with stereotypical masculinity, such as those involving finance and management, which are highly valued and rewarded (Green et al., 2001) and arguably less stressful than the work of direct caring within these jobs.

Rose, using BHPS data found pay, employment security, influence over hours worked and promotion opportunities were more important than the intrinsic nature of work itself, although those in specific professions, such as medicine, often express a vocational orientation in which job satisfaction is central. Work-related stress additionally impacts greatly upon job satisfaction. Interestingly, in one job satisfaction league table, those rating job satisfaction the highest, and within the top ten of over eighty different occupations were miscellaneous childcare workers, hairdressers, farm workers, educational assistants and gardeners. These jobs tend not to be well paid or to involve great responsibility, but they do involve variety and autonomy. Conversely laboratory technicians, assembly line workers and primary school teachers were in the bottom ten jobs, where employees often have minimal control over their work or its environment (M. Rose, 2003).

The growth of part-time work increased from 4 per cent of workers in 1951 to 21 per cent in 2004, 81 per cent of whom were women (*Social Trends*, 2005). Women's paid work has also increased, from 43 per cent of 15- to 59-year-olds economically active in 1951 to 73 per cent in 2005, whereas men who were economically active aged 15–64 declined from 96 per cent to 83 per cent in the same period (*Social Trends*, 2006). Women are more economically active now for many reasons, including the demise of the full-time housewife, increasing elective singledom, the declining birth rate, the mechanization of housework, higher divorce levels and rising debt in a consumer society (Fulcher and Scott, 2007), although they have more fragmented careers than men (Fenton and Dermott, 2006). Britain also has a punitive overwork culture, British employees working the longest hours of all Europeans with considerably fewer holidays (Bunting, 2004a).

U. Beck (2000) argues our paid working lives are increasingly insecure and fragmented, 'new capitalism' leading to individuals becoming distrustful, detached and lacking work roots. As firms become increasingly flexible – for example, 24-hour supermarkets and telephone answering lines – employees work longer and more unstructured hours. Long working hours in one area of the economy impact on others, so as mothers increasingly enter the workforce and work long hours, so too must they ensure childcare provision. Reay (2005) agues middle-class women are only able to devote so much time to their children's education because working-class women undertake their household domestic tasks. Increases in the number of working women, encouraged by New Labour's 'welfare to work' programmes, which target, amongst other groups, single, mostly female parents, is also causing a care deficit as those who previously cared for elderly relatives, neighbours and children are now often doing paid work. Nearly a third of all working mothers also rely on informal childcare provision from grandparents (Carvel, 2009a). A 2004 Eurobarometer survey found 66 per cent of female and 42 per cent of male workers were combining paid work with household chores and childcare for at least twelve extra hours a week. There were, however, significant national differences, with liberal, market-oriented countries like the UK having far less state regulation of working-time options than Sweden and the Netherlands. In this survey the UK was also singled out by a large predominance of poor-quality part-time work, long working hours, and little employment protection for women after maternity leave.

Although women are attaining higher qualifications, having greater access to higher-level occupations and the pay gap and occupational segregation between full-time male and female workers have narrowed, this has not occurred with part-time work. So, although a minority of women have high-status, well-paid work, 'the traditional "female" pattern of women in low level low paid jobs who disengage for some time after childbirth persists' (Bottero, 2000). Joshi et al.'s (2007) statistical analysis also argues that, for full-time work, although raw data appear to show some convergence in the gender pay gap, when the data are controlled for work experience and women's increasing qualifications, if the typical full-time working woman had been paid at men's rates, she would have received higher pay than the typical man. Women's disadvantages in high-status occupations persist, with ongoing increases in the gender pay gap for women in senior posts. An extensive Institute of Directors study found women earned 26 per cent less than their male equivalents (Ward, 2007) and male university professors in Britain were paid an average of 13.9 per cent more than female professors in 2007–8, compared with 13.7 per cent more the previous year, women only constituting 18.7 per cent of university professors (Shepherd, 2009c). The best systems for ensuring women's participation and equality are those in which, proportionally, a similar number of women and men are in full-time positions; few jobs require more than forty-five hours per week; the state regulates work conditions rather than them being subject to collective bargaining (Plantenega, 2003); and employers recognize family obligations, and alternative childcare is accessible and affordable – in all of which the UK falls down badly (Gornick and Meyers, 2003).

The reality of 'the new man' who contributes significantly more to childcare and domestic tasks than in previous generations is also being challenged. Although men witnessing their children's births has increased from 8.5 per cent of fathers in the 1950s (Lewis-Stempel, 2001) to over 90 per cent of married or cohabiting fathers now (Kiernan, 2003), men still see the 'breadwinning' role as their most important contribution to family life (Hatten et al., 2002). Despite this, the number of stay-at-home fathers has almost doubled to 200,000 since 1993, but this number is very small compared to that of stay-at-home mothers, who totalled 2.1 million in 2007 (Morrison, 2007). La Valle et al. (2002) found 30 per cent of fathers working full-time doing more than forty-eight hours per week, with another study revealing that, while a third of fathers worked more than fifty hours, less than a quarter of non-fathers worked these hours (Mattheson and Summerfield, 2001). A Canadian study in which fathers were the principal child caregivers showed, though they initially felt very uncomfortable, particularly in female dominated environments such as playgroups, they often acclimatized, built trust with others and became skilled at relationships and care work. However, interestingly, they continued to identify themselves in ways indicating prestigious masculinity, such as through their risk taking and sports expertise (Doucet, 2006).

Disability and employment

Disabled young adults are likely to have lower qualifications than their non-disabled peers and to be unemployed or underemployed, often depending on benefits. When hidden unemployment is considered, the unemployment rate was 18.3 per cent for disabled people, and 6.4 per cent for the non-disabled (Labour Force Survey, Spring, 2003) and the former are six times more likely to be refused an interview than non-disabled applicants, even when they have requisite skills and qualifications (Hyde, 2006). Employers are often unhappy about providing specialist support despite the 'reasonable adjustments' stipulations for employers set out in the Disability Discrimination Act. They are also influenced by mass media depictions of disabled people as dependent and pitiful, stereotypes ironically exacerbated by disability charities who use such images emotionally as a way of attracting maximum donations. Alternatively, disabled people, particularly those with mental heath problems, often scare people and are seen as dangerous because of high-profile media coverage of rare examples of mentally ill people being violent, when they are far more likely to be introverted and confused. The traditional medical model of disability saw disabled people as unfortunate victims who could not gain satisfactory employment because their disabilities prevented it. The social model conversely argues persuasively that it is society that disables individuals through discrimination and insufficient social provision, not their disability. Young men and women with learning disabilities are also at significant risk of sexual exploitation, as well as routine verbal harassment and theft in public arenas (Cooke and Ellis, 2004), which may inhibit them from searching for work or may make family members over-protective.

Race, ethnicity and employment

The situation with race and ethnicity – both contested concepts – and employment is complex. Inequalities revealed by earnings, however, reveal a more pessimistic picture than comparison by social class. In 2000, white men earned an average of £300 per week, black Caribbean men £250, Pakistani men £230 and Bangladeshi men under £150 (*Social Trends*, 2002). The inequalities could have been caused by individual, cultural or institutional racism, cultural differences, class inequalities, differential skills and qualifications or a combination of these. Mason (2006) finds Chinese and Indian men are concentrated either at the bottom or the top of the labour market, which makes statistical analyses difficult to make sense of. Many ethnic minorities are also spatially concentrated in specific regions such as London, the West Midlands and many Northern cities, which may also affect their earnings. Although they are consistently at higher risk of unemployment than white people, this is exacerbated by rising unemployment and economic recessions. Whilst male unemployment for British and Irish men was 5 per cent, and only 7 per cent for Indians, it increased to 20 per cent for Bangladeshi males and 24 per cent for Bangladeshi women versus 4 per cent for white women. Although the under-25s suffered the most, only 12 per cent of young white males were unemployed compared to over 40 per cent of their Bangladeshi male peers (Mason, 2006). A *Guardian* newspaper article drawing on research from The Institute for Public Policy showed the situation has worsened recently and reported 48 per cent of black youths aged 16–24 were currently unemployed, compared with 31 per cent of their Asian and 20 per cent of their white peers (Ramesh, 2010).

Leisure and Sport

Although aspects of paid or unpaid work may be pleasurable, people engage in leisure for enjoyment outside work. Many tastes and habits have flourished in recent years such as the popularity of television, the internet and foreign holidays. However, leisure activities take place in different spheres, such as inside and outside the home. They may be passive and privatized as in watching DVDs alone, or active such as running, or both active and collaborative such as playing football. These divisions blur with the rise of synchronous conversation on the internet and digital game playing with people on distant continents. The privatization of leisure is a long-term trend in the UK (Roberts, 1996), strengthened by the popularity of TV, the internet and online shopping and gaming, as well as gardening, decorating and the rise of the 'DIY Warrior'. Leisure is also dictated by social class – even what type of newspaper you read, what kind of alcoholic and non-alcoholic drinks you partake of, and what art or music you appreciate (Bourdieu, 1984). Ironically, as the middle class accrue more spending power to afford consumer goods, they now have less time to enjoy them (Roberts, 1996).

Young adults, particularly those without offspring are more likely to engage in leisure outside the home – such as clubbing, football matches and visits to public houses and cinemas – than middle-aged or older adults because of disposable income, lack of dependants and the importance of the peer group. The notion of leisure as play is often ignored for adults because of its association with children, fantasy and development. However, many activities that both young and middle-aged adults engage in, such as collecting objects, hang-gliding, mountaineering and international backpacking, can be seen as specialized play. Kjolsrod (2003) draws not only from Freudian perspectives which see such play as an escape from reality, but also from sociological perspectives which see such actions as proving autonomy and contributing to ontological security (a stable and secure mental state where we view our life as having positive meaning). Gaming, as in betting and competitive sports, brings excitement, relieves boredom and is related to general risk experiences. Specialized play may also balance one aspect of identity (secure repetitive occupational stability) with, for example, the fear, visceral discomfort and unpredictability of engaging with dangerous sports.

Leisure is gendered, with both 'the modern girl' of the 1920s and the 'ladette' of the 1990s being constructed negatively as folk devils by the media – sexually precocious, coarse, selfish and aping the worst excesses of men's drinking and aggressive behaviour – but ironically also being seen to infiltrate typical male provinces such as the public house illegitimately and to risk their health through 'dangerous' sexual practices and alcohol consumption (C. Jackson and Tinkler, 2007).

Using the British Cohort Study, studying those born in 1970 to adult life and beyond, social class differences were discerned between those participating in organized leisure, such as the Scouts and church clubs, and those attending youth clubs. Those involved in organized leisure were more educationally successful and came from more affluent families, whereas those attending youth clubs emanated from poor socio-economic backgrounds, had low birth weights, little confidence and often engaged in antisocial behaviours. They were also more likely to be 'socially excluded' by age 30 than adolescents using any other leisure facilities, even those using community centres and sports centres, which recruit and attract young people independent of background (Feinstein et al. 2006). Another study utilizing the same data source, but looking at the 1958 and 1970 cohorts, followed to age 33 and 30 respectively, found a clear relationship between physical leisure activity and psychological wellbeing fifteen years later for both cohorts, but no evidence that physical activity ameliorated or affected inequalities in health (Sacker and Cable, 2005). In a review of qualitative studies, Allender et al. (2006) found young and middle-aged adults do sport and exercise for a multiplicity of reasons, including self-development; honing their skills; as an escape from routine; for competitive reasons; to keep fit and healthy; and because they enjoyed the social networks and camaraderie.

New Technology

New technology is also likely to be a major part of many young adults' leisure and work activities. Although midlife adults are likely to be comfortable and familiar with technology such as the telephone, television and radio, most have had to learn to use computers, mobile phones and the internet as adults, and as a result are less familiar with them than young adults who have grown up with these technologies. Mobile phone texting is commonplace with young adults, as is use of the internet. Hardey (2002) argues the internet is ideal for studying Giddens' notion of the more contingent and mutual pure relationship which only survives if both parties open up to each other and are satisfied. In Hardey's research into internet dating, his respondents felt the reciprocal yet disembodied email communication they engaged in gave them control. Turn-taking enabled them to reveal intimate details about themselves and receive similar information from others that neither would have been likely to reveal on an initial face-to-face encounter. They also discussed both the advantages and disadvantages of knowing what someone looked like before you met them, although some respondents stated emphatically that, regardless of how well they got on over the internet, if they were not attracted to the other person physically when they met, the relationship would go no further.

Zhao (2006) also asserts the internet has fundamentally changed how we interact. Although previously we would telephone someone familiar on the other side the world, such as a partner, close friend or family member, networking sites such as *Facebook* and *Bebo* allow us to meet electronically and 'make friends' with complete strangers, although surveillance, for example by insurance companies, digital bullying and harassment, as well as identity theft, are also increasing on these sites. Electronic text chat occurs frequently on the internet, in situations such as digital gaming, and on hobby, interest and discussion sites. Chat rooms allow 'the permanence of writing and the synchronicity of speaking . . . an entirely new (disembodied) mode of contact' (Zhao 2006: 462). Asynchronous messaging such as email allows the reader to decide when, how and whether they will respond. Some are sceptical of these disembodied communications, seeing them as antisocial and inferior to face-to-face relationships (Kraut et al., 1998; Nie et al., 2002) while others see these as equally valid, but different types of relationships (Thompson, 1995). Support groups for people such as adults abused as children or transsexual teenagers have also, in some cases, led to their members claiming that these 'anonymous' disembodied relationships have substantially changed their lives for the better (Chayko, 2002; Groskop, 2009).

Furthermore, human beings have been found not only to interact socially with pets and deities in ways they would with humans but also to interact with new technology similarly. It is not that people believe these entities are actually human, as the ability to differentiate human and non-human develops in infancy, but they still manage to engage us emotionally and communicatively. Drawing from various studies, Cerulo (2009) gives the example of people being polite to robots, computers and avatars (residents of online worlds such as Second Life), responding to praise from them, regarding them as team members, 'liking' those whose personalities and characteristics resembled their own, and rating those sounding masculine as outgoing and intelligent and those sounding feminine as knowledgeable about emotions. Technosynchricity also enables us to experience artificially simulated environments temporarily as real, as with new architectural technology enabling us to walk into and interact with a virtual environment, such as a building, which currently has no material existence.

Relationships, Friends and Acquaintances in Young Adulthood

Changing family structures and practices

Early sociological work focused on traditional nuclear family structures (heterosexual mother, father and children) and their alleged universality and importance for socializing children and stabilizing adult personalities, positively stressing highly gendered marital roles (Parsons and Bales, 1951). Others saw the nuclear family as an emotionally overloaded electrical circuit, where isolated individuals scapegoated and traumatized each other (Laing and Esterson, 1964; Leach, 1967). Feminists saw, and still view, the family as an unequal, patriarchal institution where well-documented domestic violence and child abuse regularly occur and women disproportionately undertake the lion's share of domestic and childcare tasks. In one large Canadian study, for example, men's housework contribution not only was much lower than that of their female partners but declined further after each child was born (Baxter et al., 2008). Marxists viewed the family as benefiting capitalism as wives serviced their husbands for work and cared for children unpaid but were also a reserve army of labour when capitalism needed them. Later work argues that family practices in terms of support, activities done together, communication, care and intimacy are far more important than structure (Morgan, 1996). Family structure is, however, also becoming highly complex and heterogeneous.

With new reproductive technology, a couple's child may not be biologically related to either of them even if the mother has given birth, if both sperm and egg donors were used. Children may be officially or informally adopted or fostered with no biological relationship to those parenting them. Young adults may regard friends as family, or family as friends, or blur the two. Gay couples might enter into negotiated relationships with other gay or heterosexual people to produce children, and complex parenting and family relationships may be agreed. With rising divorce rates, children may live with half- and stepsiblings across a number of reconstituted families, with solo living, cohabitation, non-residential relationships, decreasing fertility and children born outside marriage becoming increasingly common (Ware et al., 2007).

Although divorce and remarriage are often commonly regarded as detrimental to children, careful analysis of longitudinal research has shown that, although many children will suffer short-term upset when parents separate, the vast majority are resilient and able to cope and may even benefit. If children suffer long-term from divorce, it is how the parents conduct their relationship with each other and in respect of their children before, during and after the divorce that is the crucial factor, not the divorce itself (Hetherington, 2003). Pets are, furthermore, frequently regarded as family. Dogs, cats, horse, fish and even parrots have been mentioned as family, without any prompts, in terms of attachment, company, support and interaction (Charles and Davies, 2008), with US studies revealing 85 per cent of dog owners and 78 per cent of cat owners regard their animals as full family members in terms of interaction, some travelling regularly with them and reporting feeling closer to their pets than their mothers (see Cerulo, 2009).

Demographic changes

If demographic statistics are examined, the mean age for marriage rose from 22 in the 1960s to 28.9 years by 2004 (ONS, 2006), cohabiting before marriage rose from 4 per cent of couples residing in the same property in 1966 to 68 per cent in 1993 (Pullinger and Summerfield, 1993), and in the 1990s 70 per cent of new relationships were cohabiting ones (Buck and Scott, 1994). From the 1960s to the 1990s the number of childless couples doubled to 20 per cent, fertility dropping from 2.93 children to 1.8, although fertility is now increasing again. In 1980 only 12 per cent of births occurred outside marriage but by 2004 this was 42 per cent (ONS, 2006). Although some of these changes are relevant to all adults, first marriage and childbearing are mostly likely to occur in young adulthood, although there are a small but significant number of women bearing children during and after their forties, and some men produce children much older. Despite these changes, using longitudinal census data from the ONS between 1981 and 2001, Ware et al. (2007) still found a third of residencies in England and Wales contained couples with at least one dependent child, showing the continuing importance of this family formation. This has occurred, ironically, at the same time as lone person and lone parent households are increasing, 29 per cent of households comprising single people in 2005 (*Social Trends*, 2006). However, transitions into and out of nuclear families are very different from in earlier eras, with much cohabitation, divorce and remarriage, and reconstituted families and stepchildren making up many contemporary nuclear families.

Ethnic family formations and practices are often invisibilized in general statistical representations and percentage averages. There are indications of higher rates of divorce, separation and single parenthood amongst South Asian Hindus and Sikhs, despite their religions seeing marriage as sacrosanct, than for South Asian Muslims – although still much lower than the general population (Babb et al., 2006). Associations made between family dishonour and divorce and the likelihood of mothers and daughters being stigmatized or expelled by their community inhibit Muslim South Asian women from initiating divorces, although anecdotal evidence suggests divorce is on the increase (Rani, 2007; Guru, 2009). Black families are conversely more likely to be female-headed lone-parent families than white or South Asian families, recent figures estimating 60 per cent (Owen, 2006). This living arrangement has been fairly stable over the last thirty years, mirroring family structures of lower working-class families in the Caribbean region (Goulbourne, 2001).

Changing attitudes to divorce, cohabitation, illegitimate children and gay partnerships

The rising divorce rate can be partially explained by increasing social acceptability accompanied by legal changes making divorces 'no fault', potentially easier, quicker and cheaper. Cohabitees are generally no longer viewed negatively, as 'living in sin' or as uncommitted (Park et al., 2001). A Scottish study of 20- to 29-year-old cohabiting couples found they expressed great commitment to their relationship, many anticipating marrying or staying together long-term (Jamieson et al., 2002). To have a child 'outside wedlock' fifty years ago was shameful, and derogatory terms such as 'illegitimate child' and 'bastard', then commonplace, are rarely heard these days. The greater number of childless couples could be attributed to much greater control over reproduction and voluntary infertility, as well as work becoming increasingly important for women.

As regards gay relationships, because of stigma and the previous criminalization and psychiatrization of homosexuality until the 1970s, many gay people hid their sexual orientation, often living an exclusively heterosexual, or double, life. Gay men even had their own invented language, *Polari*, and bodily codes for recognizing each other. Recent legislation has allowed gay couples to foster, adopt and enter into a civil partnership, which, although largely legally equivalent to marriage, is embraced by some couples whilst others see it as an inferior, second-class alternative, or unnecessary (Barr and McCann, 2005). Some gay couples are still very reticent about their sexuality, and discrimination continues and is embedded in everyday language and in political and religious rhetoric. Young gay adolescents and adults consequently often suffer mental health problems disproportionately, homophobic bullying being well documented but often unacknowledged and unchallenged in schools, higher education, workplaces and within sport (e.g. Trotter, 2009).

Celibacy, singledom and non-residential relationships

Celibacy may be a positive short- or long-term choice for some young or even middle-aged adults, or chosen for professional reasons such as becoming a priest, or it may be involuntary for a variety of reasons. Involuntary female celibates in one British study were often introverted, highly educated and ambitious, but the men conversely were more likely to be lower-class and unemployed (Kiernan, 1988). In another study, the participants (n = 82), modal age 25–34, had diverse backgrounds and sexualities and included virgins, those previously in sexual relationships and those currently in sexless partnerships (Donnelly et al., 2001). This study found many participants were painfully shy, some revealed body image problems and most expressed unhappiness about celibacy and felt 'off time' in their sexual relationships.

Other small-scale qualitative studies examine rising trends such as singledom and non residential relationships. In 1979, 19 per cent of people did not live with a partner, but by 2004 it was 29 per cent (Roseneil, 2006). People in long-term committed relationships living apart are sometimes known as LATS (living alone togethers) or distance relaters, or these relationships are conceptualized as commuter marriages. Of these, 80 per cent are aged under 40 (Haskey, 2005), most being middle-class. Many LATS had significant caring responsibilities for children or dependent relatives, important careers in different locations or did not want to disrupt previously planned life trajectories (Roseneil, 2006; Holmes, 2006). Many had married or cohabited before, and in Roseneil's study they could be divided into: (i) those who did not want to live together, often because of past relationship distress or because they valued time alone and their independence; (ii) those who did want to cohabit but were unable to; and (iii) those who were currently unsure. Demonstrating emotional caring for each other over a distance, keeping in regular contact and communicating even very mundane everyday matters were important sustaining factors.

Lewis' (2001) young single women felt proud of being independent and living alone but Macvarish's (2006) slightly older women aged 34 to 50, thus bridging young and middle adulthood, saw singledom more ambivalently, fearing being ill and alone when old or being pitied by others. Reynold's (2006) discursive analysis of the reflections of thirty single women (aged 30–60) on previous intimate relationships with men found many self-blamed for unequal sharing of housework, or their ex-partner's dishonesty or domestic violence. They also saw relationships as time-limited and ending when they needed to, again showing some affinity with Giddens' notions of the pure relationship, terminated when it no longer gives satisfaction to one or both partners.

Intergenerational family transmissions

US research shows much intergenerational support is from parent to young, then adult child, identifying three main categories: (i) advice and support from parents, (ii) donation of material items such as money; and (iii) provision of services such as household chores. UK research shows different patterns impacted upon by declining fertility, women working, gender, cultural, geographical and historical factors and social class (Myles, 2002; Brannen, 2006). For example, in Britain many of the current grandparent generation have experienced full university grants, increased savings, subsidized owner occupation and better-paid jobs and pensions than preceding or following generations. They are therefore more able to help their children financially than earlier or later generations, although class divisions still impact significantly. In some of the working-class families there was a tradition of – often gendered – reciprocity. So, grandmothers might care for children whilst daughters worked but would in turn be cared for themselves by daughters when elderly, with sons and fathers tending to give more moral or material support. In other families, particularly middle-class ones, far less reciprocity was noted, particularly towards the older generation. Some individuals stressed self-reliance but remained conspiciously silent about how they had been helped by their families, and others transposed all responsibility for their and others' care onto the welfare state (Brannen, 2003).

Middle-class families may be more geographically/occupationally mobile, which could partially explain lower intergenerational transmission, although 4 out of 10 people remain in the same local authority throughout their lives and only 1 in 100 households move significant distances away. Of people who have a living parent, 50 per cent also see them and any eldest children at least once a week, and half of these have only half an hour's travel to do so (Pooley et al., 2005). The little research conducted also often ignores how intergenerational support and transmission may also extend from children to adults, as in the case of young carers – children or teenagers who are the main carer for a chronically ill or disabled parent or relative. Also, because of a generational digital divide, middle-aged and older adults are more likely to ask their children and grandchildren for help with new technology such as the internet and email. Below is a rather delightful quote taken from a recent Swedish study:

> Grandpa: Can you teach me how it works then? (To Anton, 10 years old)
> Grandma: Yes teach Grandpa how it works.
> Anton : Yeah.
>
> (Aarsand, 2007)

Friends and family

The term 'families of choice' originated from studies in which gay people saw their friends more as family than their biological family (e.g. Weeks et al., 2001) but could be increasingly applicable to het-erosexuals with declining fertility and rising divorce rates (O'Connor, 1999) and perhaps to university students living away from home. However, a recent longitudinal study shows that, although bounda-ries have blurred, the suggestion families of choice are replacing 'given' family in terms of expectations, commitment and interactions is overstated (Pahl and Spencer, 2004).

Although there is increasing interest in friendships and new electronic forms of making new friends or being reacquainted with old ones emerging (e.g. the Facebook, Bebo and Friends Reunited networking websites), few studies consider how friendships change across the life course according to cohort, generation or experiences of ageing, although there is some evidence social class is important. One longitudinal study of people aged from 16 to 76+ found for the younger age groups, particularly those aged 16–25, partners replaced non-kin friends as their nominated closest friend (Pahl and Spencer, 2004; Pahl and Pevalin, 2005). Friendship is also seen as less dyadic than within psychology. Friendships may be initiated and sustained not only according to the *homophily* (similarity) principle but because of situational circumstances, and serve different needs – you may befriend someone you like and see frequently at work but it may not survive you moving jobs or areas. You make friends with the mother of your child's best friend because of their shared activities, or you slowly become acquainted with your neighbour who feeds your cats when you are away and realize you have much in common. One relationship could be strongly linked with the joint friendships two couples have, yet another may help to maintain one person's individuality and separate interests (Eve, 2002). Furthermore, people regard 'true' friends as those who support them in difficult times such as divorce or serious illness. Friendship groups also seem to be made at different times, coming in clusters, so friends from school or university days may be very different from those made much later via a hobby or at work.

Conclusion

This chapter has examined young adulthood from sociological and psychological perspectives. Psychology identifies physical and psychological changes in young adulthood, revealing this as a time where adults peak intellectually and physically and continue to differentiate themselves from their family and forge adult status and separate identities, relationships, families and careers. Despite this they are still learning how to adapt to uncertain, unfamiliar and complex circumstances which may explain why 'post-formal' operations emerge. Furthermore, they are also still relatively underdeveloped in dealing with emotional issues as their responses are less psychologically healthy, and more aggressive and defensive, than those of older adults. Social developmental psychology is also more sensitive than traditional developmental psychology to the environment and structural inequalities such as gender, and some of the methodology employed by social psychologists, such as Wetherall, and the questions they ask and their conclusions are similar to those in some sociological studies. However, psychology is still constrained by its emphasis on discontinuous stages and its relative inability to accommodate to changing circumstances. Although Arnett's and Konstam's work is able to consider how young adults' lives are changing in contemporary society, neither seem particularly aware of structural inequalities such as social class and race/ethnicity.

Sociology, in comparison, is sensitive to structural inequalities and their impact as well as how changing social, technological, economic and historical constellations have fundamentally changed the experience of young adulthood. Although much debate exists around markers of young adulthood or whether de-standardization of the life course has really occurred, sociology is aware of young adults' heterogeneous lives. It draws attention to the double-bind situations some young adults encounter, in which their lives are increasingly constrained by disadvantage, discrimination and poor educational and occupational opportunities whilst they are simultaneously presented with a myriad of limitless choices and opportunities they will never be able to access. Sociology also realizes the living situations of young adults today are very different from those of preceding generations and tries to understand these new situations, such as the rise of non-residential relationships and gay relationships, as well as the increasingly complex relationships between children and adults from reconstituted families, or where new reproductive technology has been used.

Reflection and discussion questions

How does developmental psychology understand and theorize young adulthood?

What is 'emergent adulthood' and is it a useful or relevant concept?

What impact might social divisions and inequalities have on transitions into and experiences of young adulthood?

Recommended reading

Most life span psychology texts have useful sections on young/early adulthood covering biosocial, cognitive and psychosocial development but the majority are American, so are only partially applicable to the UK. Sociology does not deal with young adulthood as an age span per se, but articles on how transitions into and markers of young adulthood are changing, such as those by Thomson et al. (2004) and Blatterer (2007), on changing family structures and practices (e.g. Ware et al., 2007) and on leisure experiences and new technology (e.g. Zhao, 2006; Cerulo, 2009) are useful sources.

CHAPTER 06

Middle Adulthood

Introduction

This chapter examines middle adulthood (otherwise known as midlife or middle age), from psychological and sociological perspectives, despite its historical and contemporary neglect. Brim (1992: 171) referred to midlife as 'the last uncharted territory in human development' and, although there has been progress since then, it still remains the least researched age span (Lachman, 2004). Many studies examine specific issues in an age undifferentiated manner or bridge young and middle adulthood or middle adulthood and old age, ignoring potential age differences. What constitutes middle age is also movable chronologically and in terms of other benchmarks. Midlife currently encapsulates the period between 40 and 60 but if located chronologically via average life expectancy, then the late thirties up until the early forties realistically constitute middle age, but this could change if life expectancy increased. Compulsory retirement in Western countries has also often closely coincided with old age, but, with new anti-age-discrimination legislation in England and rising European statutory retirement ages, could middle age be further extended? Furthermore, if we accept Laslett's notion of the third age in young old age as an extended middle age for those still healthy and affluent, then some 70-year-olds could fit within the middle-age category whilst some unhealthy, socio-economically deprived 40- to 60-year-olds might be excluded.

Although certain factors seem to typify middle adulthood, others, previously seen as midlife markers, are increasingly being revealed as historically specific cohort effects. For example, although most women give birth in their twenties and thirties, some procreate as teenagers, others increasingly in their forties and, with the aid of reproductive technology, a few have even given birth, albeit with donor eggs, in their fifties and sixties. Women today enter full-time education and the labour market in higher numbers than before, and many adult children still live at home. Therefore, even families who conceived children young may still be supporting them as adults, caring for older relatives and potentially managing dual careers. The psychological concept of the 'empty nest', applied to the 1950s traditional full-time housewife whose life was consumed by children and domesticity, and who was depicted as bereft and role-less when her children left home, therefore seems increasingly redundant – if indeed it ever existed, which some studies cited in this chapter question. Lay persons' accounts normally associate middle age with more stable and sedentary living and some inevitable physical decline, as well as paradoxically some trauma, hence the infamous notion of a midlife crisis.

This chapter analyses psychological concepts and studies pertinent to the midlife. It initially examines physical and cognitive changes, then evaluates psychosocial factors, assessing how relevant traditional stage theories are for contemporary middle age, particularly their claims of a universal midlife crisis. A sociological analysis follows but, because of the limited and uneven research available, it often deals with selective and quite idiosyncratic aspects of midlife, such as women's disrupted sleep patterns and men's penchant for motorbikes and 1970s rock music. Although much sociological research on the family exists, it is often age undifferentiated or tends to invisibilize midlife. For example, Allan and Crow's (2001) edited text initially deals with changing families and, after this, becoming adult, but then marriage, cohabitation and step-families are covered in an age undifferentiated manner before chapter 8 engages with families in later life. There is, however, some literature focused on the generation who now mostly inhabit middle age, more commonly known as Baby Boomers (although this also includes some of the young old), and how certain historical events affect their ideologies, lives and current society.

Psychology and middle adulthood

Physical Changes

During middle adulthood the cumulative effects of primary and secondary ageing become more noticeable, but rarely have significant effects until later adulthood. Primary ageing refers to biologically inevitable, chronological ageing which may vary slightly across and between individuals because of genetic variations. Secondary ageing refers to the ways in which such biological ageing may be exacerbated or hastened due to the effects of negative structural, cultural or environmental factors or processes, such as an enduring poor diet caused by poverty. Both sexes become more susceptible to developing osteoporosis, involving a decrease in calcium density leading to more porous, brittle bones and a greater risk of fractures. Individuals are at very low risk of infections and respiratory problems, although, if they succumb, recovery periods are likely to be longer than in young adults. However, middle adults' risk of disability and chronic illnesses and mortality associated with these (including cancer, heart disease, cardiovascular diseases, high blood pressure and arthritis) rises considerably. In comparison, young adults are rarely substantially affected by or die from these diseases. The risk factors for some cancers and for heart disease are smoking, obesity and minimal exercise, with heredity having a significant impact on predisposition to heart disease but a less clear impact on some cancers, and high blood pressure and cholesterol levels also acting as risk factors for heart disease but not cancer (Bee, 1994). The probability of both disability and chronic disease rises considerably during mid-life but it is still relatively low overall, although social class and status are important factors and behavioural changes can consequently reduce the probability of contracting these diseases or minimize their negative effects.

Appearance gradually changes during middle age. Wrinkles become more apparent, hair greyer and thinner, and greater fat distribution to the stomach occurs in both sexes (sometimes colloquially referred to as 'middle-aged spread'), as well as around the chin and the buttocks (Whitbourne, 2001). Hearing, sight and smell decline. Individuals become more short-sighted and less able to tolerate glare and differentiate between very high and low tones, with men's hearing declining twice as fast as women's (Pearson et al., 1995). These declines seem to be a 'normal' and non-preventable part of ageing although secondary ageing can accelerate the process. For example, working with noisy pneumatic drills or being a heavy metal musician may exacerbate or hasten 'normal' hearing losses. Normal declines often have little effect as glasses generally rectify short-sightedness and, even at age 50, 75 per cent of women and 65 per cent of men can hear a whisper 3 feet away. They therefore could not be considered to have significant hearing difficulties (Pearson et al., 1995).

According to Bee (1994) the most life-changing event in midlife for women is the menopause, officially defined as being reached a year after the last period. Menopause occurs typically in most parts of the world at between 49 and 51 although malnourishment, smoking or a genetic predisposition may lead to earlier menopause, and up to 8 per cent of women experience menopause before age 40 (Weg, 1987). Menopause involves a set of changes over a number of years. The ovaries slowly produce less oestrogen and progesterone, leading to irregular menstruation and eventually to its complete cessation, signalling complete inability to reproduce. However, women's fertility also declines significantly even in the years from 35 to 40 and the risk of spontaneous miscarriage or abnormalities increases. Oestrogen declines also lead to genital tissue loss, to the uterus and vagina shrinking and the vaginal walls becoming thinner, less elastic and producing less lubrication during intercourse. The most noticeable symptom of the menopause is a hot flush, the sensation of heat spreading over you accompanied by a flushed chest and face. It generally only lasts a few minutes, but is often followed by voluble sweating and occurs more nocturnally. After the menopause, bone loss related to lowered oestrogen levels is quite pronounced and women are at much higher risk of osteoporosis then. Regular weight bearing exercise improves bone density for both sexes, although, if the activity ceases, so do the benefits. Some women resort to hormone replacement therapy, but the evidence in relation to its benefits and risk is conflicting and continually changing (Bosely, 2007b).

Both psychological and physical symptoms experienced during menopause seem variable and culturally influenced (Shore, 1999). The menopause in the USA and the UK has traditionally been conceptualized negatively as an illness, with women in countries where it is seen positively reporting fewer physical or mental symptoms. Most life span psychology textbooks, however, pay little attention to the social significance of the menopause or the use of HRT for symptom control and thereby implicitly medicalize it. However, feminist perspectives locate the menopause critically within a biomedical perspective as a 'deficiency disease', an influential and enduring view initially put forward by Robert Wilson in his book *Forever Feminine* (1966). Shore's (1999) qualitative study of ten white middle-class British woman aged 43–60 years revealed that they associated the menopause negatively with the onslaught of old age, but did not mourn no longer being able to have children. Most ignored any information about the menopause unless it came from their perceived 'experts', the medical profession, perceiving it as an unwelcome biomedical phenomenon they must endure.

For men there is no equivalent dramatic decline in hormone levels or reproductive function; nevertheless, there are slow-onset age-related declines in men's reproductive faculties, resulting in less healthy and mobile sperm. Despite no reliable evidence supporting a male menopause, in the 1920s and 1930s thousands of 'menopausal' men in Europe and the Unites States underwent operations in which monkeys' or goats' sex glands were grafted onto their testicles to augment their supposedly ailing supply of sex hormones. Male menopause was, however, totally disproven by the mid 1950s, disappearing from the medical radar, although popular magazines periodically reasserted its existence. In the 1990s the male menopause re-emerged alongside the public's belief that medicine could now cure any condition. Despite disavowal by reputable medics, pharmaceutical companies produced various testosterone replacement therapies to treat the fallacious condition now renamed as *andropause* and men, particularly in the USA, visited doctors there who prescribed these ineffectual 'remedies' (Watkins, 2007).

Cognitive Changes

In the early twentieth century psychologists believed, based on cross-sectional IQ tests, that significant cognitive and intellectual decline occurred from age 20 and was pronounced by midlife. However, with increasing understanding about the limitations of both IQ tests and cross-sectional testing, and the development of new forms of testing, such as longitudinal testing, which showed different results, doubts emerged. Due to the different educational, occupational and life experiences of different cohorts (and perhaps better nutrition and environmental conditions), average IQ increased significantly in developed countries throughout the twentieth century, with each cohort, a phenomenon known as the Flynn effect (Flynn, 1987). Therefore, although cross-sectional tests seemed to compare matched groups at different ages, these groups were in fact very dissimilar. Later longitudinal research, with the same groups retested over time, showed most 36-year-olds were still improving on tests of vocabulary and comprehension (Bayley, 1966). The disadvantage, however, with longitudinal tests is that retesting improves scores, which may show learning not intelligence. Furthermore, many lower scorers drop out, skewing average scores.

Schaie (1983a) therefore developed an improved design called cross-sequential research which involved both longitudinal and cross-sectional testing, so, although he was retesting his original subjects, he was also continually adding in new groups of subjects and comparing the new groups' scores with those who had been retested, thus improving the validity of the results. Both Schaie (1996) and Baltes and Graf (1996) on the basis of research with hundreds of older Germans and Americans, found not until the eighties do significant intellectual declines occur, and middle-agers generally increase or maintain their overall intelligence. Although processing speed and working memory generally show some declines in middle age (Baltes et al., 1999), verbal memory, vocabulary, inductive reasoning and spatial orientation generally improve (Schaie and Willis, 2002), and whatever declines do occur can generally be compensated for by experience and resources (Miller and Lachman, 2000).

Researchers also became wary of talking about one global type of intelligence and started to subdivide intelligence into different spheres, such as numerical, visual, spatial and vocabulary. It also became evident that, although midlifers become less proficient on tests measuring fluid intelligence, which require quick responses and processing and abstract thought, crystallized intelligence and tacit knowledge, which draw on previous skills and accumulated knowledge, do not decline and may increase. Sternberg (2003) formulates three different types of basic intelligence: *analytical intelligence* draws on learning, remembering, strategy, selection and verbal and logical skills, many of the skills required for academic thought; *creative intelligence* demonstrates the ability to be innovative and flexible and think in uncommon or lateral ways; and *practical intelligence* involves adapting one's behaviour to a specific situation and managing diverse situations successfully, but it cannot be measured in any standard IQ test. There is no inevitable decline in middle age in creative intelligence although declines in analytical intelligence have been measured.

Simonton analysed famous contemporary and past scientists, finding most produced their defining work at around age 40. This was, however, not due to optimal brain function but because of greater productivity around that age, and their overall work quality still remained high until their sixties (Horner et al., 1986; Simonton, 1988). With artists and musicians, for whom creativity is important, a peak may be reached later or maintained longer. When expert judges rated the lifetime pieces of 172 composers, later life works, sometimes known as swan songs, were often the most outstanding (Simonton, 1991). In an experimental study of creativity in which groups of 28- to 35-year-olds, 45- to 55-year-olds and 65- to 75-year-olds managed a hypothetical developing country called Shamba, the middle-aged group performed as well as the young group on strategy, planning and managing emergencies. The only difference was that they requested less extra information and made fewer suggestions (Streufert et al., 1990). The older group performed far less efficiently but this could have been because of the unfamiliarity of the tasks and associated declining fluid intelligence, and because types of creativity different from those deployed by artists were required. However, fierce debates about different intelligences and appropriate operationalization and measurement continue, with a new form of intelligence, emotional intelligence (EI), being labelled problematic. EI seems similar to Sternberg's practical intelligence as it involves a sophisticated ability to process emotion-relevant stimuli to successfully guide thought and behaviour. Some researchers view EI as a specific collection of mental abilities, whereas others, conversely, see it as dictated by positive dispositional traits such as optimism and self-esteem, thus causing confusion conceptually and empirically (Mayer et al., 2008). Therefore, although findings about different types of intelligence give us greater understanding of cognitive ability in middle and old age, they must be viewed with caution.

Labouvie-Vief (1982) argued that young adults tend to shift away from operational problem solving to a more pragmatic flexible approach, more noticeable in middle adulthood. Asked to recall in writing a story they had read immediately before, younger adults were more likely to recollect actual events chronologically whereas midlife adults tended to interpret the characters psychologically and précis and decipher the story (Adams, 1991). This suggests at middle age either we are less able to encode very specific detail (a cognitive decline), compensating by summarizing and making sense of a situation, or we may be more likely to think pragmatically, which could represent 'loss in the service of growth' rather than compensation for a decline. Labouvie-Vief proposes the latter, but further research is required.

Psychosocial Changes

The midlife crisis?

The time period between 40 and 65 is seen by Erikson as one in which the challenges of being generative, retaining one's ego identity, and not stagnating or succumbing to despair inevitably affect how we experience old age and death. Jung (1971) claimed the transition to midlife is difficult and new goals need to be set, the main task being *individuation*, which involves trying to equilibrate all aspects of one's psyche and integrating the feminine (*anima*) and masculine (*animus*) aspects of personality. Levinson asserts that ages 40–45 represent the midlife transition, a crisis period when men review their past, present and possible futures, asking searching questions about whether they have or will achieve their 'Dream'. Levinson sees the crisis triggered by retrospection stemming from awareness of the decremental ageing process and watching parents or friends die and children becoming adults, alongside wanting to reconcile aspects of themselves submerged whilst focusing on their careers. During this time, 32 out of 40 of Levinson's subjects reported some instability and turmoil. After 45, the age of the oldest of his subjects, Levinson becomes speculative although he does argue that the transition at age 50 may involve some resolution of the early midlife transition, by possibly changing aspects of one's life. Levinson's later research (1996) with women found 'homemakers' encountered significantly more regret during midlife than career women and desired a life extending out from marriage and family.

Is this conception of a midlife crisis – shared by the lay public, Erikson, Jung and Levinson – mythological, an outdated historical cohort effect, a feature solely of modern Western societies or a universal global phenomenon? The question is difficult to answer, firstly because clear, agreed-upon definitions of what constitutes a midlife crisis rarely accompany discussion. Secondly, what defines middle age chronologically and psychosocially in contemporary Western societies may have no parallels in less developed societies, or may evolve historically. Midlife situations may also vary greatly according to gender, ethnicity and social class, and according to personality, which in itself may be impacted upon by past experiences, rather than constituting inborn inherited characteristics. The studies examined below also show conflicting evidence and viewpoints.

Psychologists in the 1980s who tried to replicate Levinson's findings of a midlife crisis according to different measures and indicators found little substantiating evidence with either sex (Chiriboga, 1989; Hunter and Sundel, 1989). Hendry and Kloep (2002), however, argue that at midlife we are limited by physical changes, such as menopause preventing childbirth, and decreasing strength, alongside constraints on new opportunities, and ongoing responsibilities such as children. They see midlife as a period of stocktaking and deciding whether to settle for what one has – 'happy stagnation' – or engaging with new challenges. They suggest that high control – low demand and low control – low demand situations, for example in work, lead to satisfied stagnation but that high demand – low control situations may overtax individuals' resources, resulting in 'unhappy stagnation'. Some US research shows midlife women often see midlife as a time of confidence derived from successful managing of cumulative life difficulties (Stewart and Ostrove, 1998). Other US studies reveal it to be a time of peak confidence, control and competence but simultaneously as stressful (Lachman et al., 1994). Research also generally confirms that midlifers have more adaptive emotional regulation than younger people (Carstensen et al., 2003 – see also chapter on young adulthood) and peak in their psychosocial competence (Neugarten and Datan, 1974). However, one US study showed that, at the beginning of midlife, 41 per cent of people had both parents alive but, at the end, 77 per cent had no living parents, which may explain some emotional turmoil (Bumpass and Aquilino, 1995).

A study of midlifers' future time perspectives (FTP), examining whether people see their time running out or envisage sufficient time to realize goals, found participants focused on both opportunities and constraints and most were as optimistic as young adults, despite awareness of increasing limitations (Cate and John, 2007). Other research has suggested a dip between young and late midlife with increasing emphasis on loss due to work-related opportunities diminishing and possible health problems emerging later (Staudinger and Bluck, 2001). In a recent large-scale quantitative study of more than 2 million people in over eighty countries, seventy-two developed countries followed a U-shaped life pattern with greater depression in midlife than at any other time, including old age. In the UK, slow-onset depression peaked at age 44 for both sexes, whereas in the USA men peaked at 50 and women at 40 (Oswald and Blanchflower, 2008), with most people recovering by their fifties. The researchers hypothesize recovery involves learning to live with one's strengths and weaknesses whilst quelling previous unattainable aspirations or using social comparison with peers in ways favourable to one's self-concept.

Drawing on case history, psychotherapy and philosophy, Strenger (2009) reaches a similar conclusion, steering a mid point between two cultural myths about midlife – either that one must passively accede to growing limitations, or that, given vision and drive (a view reinforced by our individualist and self-help orientated culture), possibilities are limitless. He therefore argues that an active, aware, self-acceptance at midlife is what diverts crises:

> at midlife . . . our potential has had enough time to express itself and is now embodied in our biography. Misconceptions and illusions we had about ourselves give way to the accumulated evidence of who we are and how we have lived. The freedom of midlife is to fully realise the potential visible in our biography and to focus our energy on making the most of it. Of course, such freedom is not easy to come by (and) self knowledge can be very painful. (Strenger, 2009: 49)

The literature discussed therefore suggests middle age is often experienced as a challenging and ambivalent time, encompassing both negative and positive factors. Nevertheless, marital satisfaction increases then, although it not clear whether this is because more troubled relationships end before midlife, rendering the finding a methodological artefact, or whether it could possibly be cohort-specific. Glenn (1990) found in the USA that, after a 'honeymoon' period, satisfaction dipped for about a decade and then slowly increased throughout middle adulthood. However, increased marital satisfaction may be related more to decreasing relationship problems or possibly lowered expectations than other factors, as in some studies physical affection also decreased simultaneously (Veroff et al., 1981; Swensen et al., 1981). Domestic violence also occurs less with middle-aged couples. Studies have shown that, in middle age, gender convergence occurs in which stereotypically assumed opposite sex traits become more openly adopted, with men expressing vulnerability and sadness and women confidence and assertion (Guttmann,1994; Huyck, 1999). Longitudinal research, however, shows this is less likely to occur with recent cohorts (Moen, 1996), suggesting less rigidity with gender roles today and a cohort or generational effect. In middle adulthood, although one's basic personality changes minimally, a propensity to become slightly more agreeable and conscientious and less neurotic, but simultaneously less open, emerges, in both Western and other nations (Donnellan and Lucas, 2008; McCrae and Allik, 2002), suggesting this is not a constructed but a universal phenomenon and perhaps partially explaining increased marital satisfaction.

Averting midlife crises and constructing life meaning in middle age

What might avert or exacerbate midlife crises depends greatly on the historical and individual situation. Two longitudinal studies of the first generation of US females who had greater career and educational opportunities, found regret and goal planning in early midlife were not necessarily followed by change by age 43. Personality characteristics such as rumination and pessimism, not external barriers, were the major obstacles to change (Stewart and Vandewater, 1999), although it was unclear whether these characteristics were linked to previous life experiences. Cramer (2008), in a longitudinal study from adolescence to late middle age, argues that *identification*, a mature defence mechanism involving changing the self to become more like an admired person or group, increases security. Self-esteem and related 'planful competence' (a psychological term similar to 'agency' in sociology) require successful adult functioning and involve self-confidence, intellectual investment and dependability, but also predict good outcomes in middle adulthood. These are influenced by a combination of the family's socioeconomic status, harmony, consistent boundaries and a stress on achievement in childhood and adolescence (Heyl and Schmitt, 2007). When these were absent, less mature defence mechanisms such as projection and less personality stability emerged. There were, however, exceptions, where previous successful planning and positive identity were challenged in midlife by being unable to advance occupationally or unexpected events such as alcoholism or deaths of loved ones. This led to less mature defence mechanisms being adopted, alongside declining competence and confidence.

Self transcendence, the ability to rise above problems and self-preoccupation, expanding personal boundaries through life experiences such as parenting, acceptance and renewed spirituality also mitigated against depression in midlife (Ellerman and Reed,

2001). Johnston et al. (2004), furthermore, found that, although body dissatisfaction and concern about weight applied to both young and midlife women (exacerbated during midlife by stereotypical images of menopausal women as asexual and ugly), strategies for control – for example, through exercise rather than disordered eating – became healthier in middle age. Factors which could contribute significantly to how one emotionally experiences one's middle age and psychological functioning are also people's accounts of life meaning and personal worth. In one study of college students and middle-aged people, both disproportionately attributed key memories of self-worth to achievement or mastery, and negative self-worth to distressing interpersonal situations (Pillemer et al., 2007). A New Zealand qualitative in-depth study of thirty-eight midlife adults found that, although relationships are of paramount importance to individuals of all ages, midlife was characteristically a time for evaluation, retrospection and introspection and dawning awareness of time left to live rather than time since birth (K. O'Connor and Chamberlain, 1996). This study grouped sources of life meaning into six categories. Relationships with others was key, with 74 per cent of respondents mentioning creativity, 71 per cent personal development, 53 per cent a relationship with nature, 45 per cent religious and spiritual sources and 29 per cent social and political commitments. Nature may, however, have particular relevance in New Zealand where much recreation takes place outdoors and even many city dwellers had rural childhoods.

How one has lived one's life prior to middle age also affects life meaning. One study found creative people, even from age 21, were open, unconventional, autonomous and ambitious, whereas wisdom was predicted by openness and tolerance, often alongside an early commitment to a spiritual or altruistic career (Helson and Srivastava, 2002). Both characteristics were associated with personal growth, creativity giving meaning to life, and wisdom being associated with positive relationships and tolerance, but neither were necessarily associated with one another or simultaneously present. Havighurst (1972) also saw establishing meaningful leisure activities as an important midlife task. These offer escapism, alongside the ability to establish new skills and experiment with roles (e.g. Kleiber, 1999; Freysinger, 1995).

Durkin (1995) argues that, whereas young adults focus on family and educational achievements, middle-aged people tend to focus on their children's lives, and older people on health, retirement and world events, although this does not explain what childless midlife individuals or couples might focus upon. A German study of 392 individuals aged 43–46 years and 61–64 years found older adults' friendships seemed based more on emotional support and congeniality compared with middle-aged friendships that were more associated with openness and mutual interests than agreeableness (Heyl and Schmitt, 2007). This suggests friendships may take on a different character across the life span. Neugarten et al. (1968) also proposed a 'social clock' to explain how social and cultural norms influence adulthood by expecting us to do certain things at certain times/ages whilst discouraging others. They later modified this theory to incorporate changing cultural norms (Neugarten and Neugarten, 1986). Harrup (1989) also differentiates between vertical and horizontal relationships. Most young children's relationships are vertical and asymmetrical in terms of power, dependency and knowledge, but middle adulthood has relationships along both axes, horizontal with peers, siblings and friends but also vertical, with midlifers often exercising considerable power and influence in work and parenting contexts.

Attitudes towards work seem to change in middle age, and status and level of earnings become less important than intrinsic satisfaction. Older workers seem more stable in their jobs and less likely to be absent or job hunting. Average salary and average household income tend to peak. However, during midlife people are more concerned about planning for retirement financially and socially. Due to the collapse of many company pension schemes in England, leading to employees losing all or most of their pension, and increasing unemployment being more likely to affect very young and middle-aged or older workers in the current 'credit crunch', worries about financial security in old age are currently pronounced.

Sociology and middle age

S. Hunt (2005) critiques exaggerated notions of decline and crisis in middle age. He problematizes midlife's increasing medicalization, particularly around the menopause, asserting that as life expectancy increases middle age may now be viewed optimistically and that individuals can construct a positive self-identity, challenging negative social stereotypes around ageing. In Japan, in contrast to the UK, midlife is embraced positively, signalling the commencement of maturity rather than the onset of age-related decline (Lambley, 1995). That said, middle age tends to be neglected within sociology despite a large proportion of the UK population being over 50. Perhaps the very academics who might initiate middle-age research are ensconced in their own midlife crises, although ironically midlifers are invaluable research fodder and consumers for those researching and marketing anti-ageing products. What little sociological literature is accessible is more attuned than psychology to social divisions and to generational and cohort differences, most notably the experience of the Baby Boomers – depending on the commentator, those born either between 1944 and 1965 or between 1946 and 1964, with the latter dates being the most commonly cited – who comprise most mid-lifers today. Sometimes known as the *pivot* or *sandwich generation*, it is assumed their own needs and leisure time are compromised by their paid work, likely to be at its most responsible during midlife, alongside generational pressures in relation to supporting younger and adult children and ageing elderly relatives. This section will analyse ageing, body image and self-perceptions in middle age; leisure and lifestyles; work and time famine; and family and friendship relationships.

Ageing, Self Perception and Body Image during Midlife

Midlife is associated with cognitive and physical decline and often seen as the precursor to old age. These representations are located within an individualistic culture where beauty, particularly female beauty, is seen only in the context of youth and valorized, and where both the body and the self are seen as reflexive projects to be improved upon throughout life. The few studies in this area reinforce this perception but pertain mainly to women, thus overlooking men's experiences. The anti-ageing industry is, furthermore, estimated to be worth over £25 billion pounds. After a BBC TV programme, *Horizon*, in March 2007 concluded that a £17 Boots facial skin product reduced fine lines, product sales increased 2,000 per cent within twenty-four hours, with queues of women clamouring outside the stores for the scientifically proven elixir (D'Souza, 2007). But anti-ageing cream is merely the iceberg tip of an industry which preys on women's insecurity about age. It promises youthful restoration via increasingly expensive and dangerous procedures such as laser treatment, chemical skin peels, facial plastic nip-and-tuck surgery, and fat and collagen injections. A string of reality TV programmes such as *Ten Years Younger* further feed into these insecurities and collude with the anti-ageing industries' solutions.

G. Cooke (2008) argues the infamous Botox does not rejuvenate or cure, but paradoxically paralyses and caricatures, eliminating free expression and concealing the interesting facial character that age and experience endow. Botox also averts further ageing by preventing the facial expressions that produce wrinkles, leaving the face in a state of suspended animation. As a highly toxic poison absorbed by the body, meaning the procedure has to be eternally repeated, Botox is also a perfect example of a *Pharmakon*, the term for a substance that 'cures' *age* socially as it 'poisons' on a physical and human level.

M. Jones (2004) similarly asserts anti-ageing procedures do not recreate youth but diminish and homogenize women's faces, constructing a new life phase – 'stretched middle age':

> nostrils are made smaller during rhinoplasty and ears are pinned back and cut down. Even procedures that seem to make eyes and lips bigger (blepheraplasty, lip enhancement) ... leave them metaphorically closed as they are rendered fixed and less flexible. Removal of 'hooded lids' creates a slightly immobile doll like state . . . No matter what the intentions and desires of its recipients the end effect is they often share a uniform, homogenous look. Furthermore, the 'origins' of beauty have changed . . . people now have cosmetic surgery to look like other(s) who have had cosmetic surgery. (M. Jones, 2004: 96)

Calasanti (2007) argues anti-ageing adverts intersect and reinforce both age and gender discrimination by positing people only have value if they look middle-aged or younger. They represent men and women oppositionally and old age as a loss of gender identity, whilst drawing on white middle-class heterosexual norms of female beauty and male achievement. During midlife, the qualities most culturally valued in women – physical attraction and reproduction potential – decline, whereas those most culturally valued in and by men – competence, power and financial acumen – often increase (Barrett, 2005). In a US study of midlife professional women, who might arguably possess sufficient self-esteem to resist sexist pressure to look youthful, the participants still harboured pervasive but realistic fears of becoming unemployed or underemployed due to discriminatory sexist/ageist ideologies (Trethewey, 2001). Mature men's wrinkles and greying hair are, conversely, often seen as sexy, wise or sophisticated (Fairhurst, 1998). The pressure on men to retain youthfulness is increasing but not to the extent that they are customarily dismissed when reaching a certain age in the same way some publicly visible female employees have been, such as Moira Stuart the newsreader and Arlene Phillips the TV dancing show panellist (Holmwood, 2007), suggesting men are judged primarily on performance and women on appearance.

Trethewey's participants were highly successful in their respective fields but had all either experienced or feared discrimination against them, often colluding with the pressure of conforming to seeming youthfulness, but paradoxically simultaneously resisting too. They all reproduced the master narrative of decline in their accounts of ageing, talking about weight gain, side effects of the menopause and loss of energy, and many feared being seen as asexual. Most also felt isolated at work and saw themselves either as successful tokens in male-dominated fields or as trail blazers, with few female models, mentors or support networks. Some, however, found no longer being seen as sexually desirable at work as liberation and felt they were taken more seriously. Others tried to 'pass' as younger and many were seriously considering cosmetic surgery. Other research suggests many women, but not men, are resorting to cosmetic surgery to avoid occupational age discrimination. The 2005 figures from the British Association of Aesthetic Plastic Surgeons showed significant increases in anti-ageing surgery, it being second only to breast augmentation in popularity. One of the biggest UK plastic surgery organizations also claimed that, while women generally opt for anti-ageing proce-dures, men tend to change a feature they have never been happy with (MacKay, 2006).

The pressure to look or feel young varies cross-culturally. Studies of older and middle-aged individuals comparing the USA to Japan, Finland and Germany (Westerhof et al., 2003) found that reporting feeling younger than one's actual age existed in all countries but was more common in the USA than elsewhere. There, not only is old age more devalued and youth fetishized, but individual responsibility and economic productivity are stressed and there is little social responsi-bility for elderly care. Western women also frequently present with younger self-perceived identities than their chronological male equiv-alents and consistently report feeling younger than they are (Barrett, 2005). However, gender interacts with age, ethnicity and sometimes social class to produce different effects. In one recent study, the white British women were more concerned about the menopause and their ageing facial features than were the predominantly working-class Afro-caribbean, Pakistani and West Indian women. These women were correspondingly more likely to regard the menopause as an indistinct period and to stress general physical symptoms such as tiredness, being far less concerned with their overall appearance and maintaining a youthful façade than their white counterparts (Wray, 2007).

In an earlier UK study of how middle-aged men and women under-stand the implications of ageing, two consistent phrases emerged, 'mutton dressed as lamb' and 'growing old gracefully', both centred on being, acting or looking your age (Fairhurst, 1998). The former was unequivocally negative and applied mostly to women, seen to humiliate themselves by wearing clothes or having hair or make-up deemed too young for their age. Although men rarely applied this phrase to men, and a few men thought women but not men should try to retain a youthful appearance, most thought both sexes 'should make the best of themselves'. This is an ambivalent term which sug-gests decline and compromise. There were some comments from women about being erased as an active human being in midlife, but others viewed it as offering liberation from being a sex object. A few women anticipated old age with dread whereas men did not, but the media continually reinforce such paranoid attitudes, with one female journalist headlining her article on midlife with '. . . I'm an Age-orexic' (D'Souza, 2007), and another newspaper article being subtitled 'There's nothing sadder than a middle-aged woman dressed like a teenager apart from a teenager dressed like a middle-aged woman' (Armstrong, 2007). However, all this female paranoia about ageing is unsurprising given that Western history and art has historically inscribed ageing women's bodies with connotations of ugliness and evil (Friedan, 1993). Witches, for example, in children's fairytale books, are often depicted in this way, but wizards are generally featured as good, if somewhat eccentric, characters whose appearance is not seen as problematic. Due to the focus on youth in the gay male community, gay men are likely to be labelled as middle-aged or older at younger ages than heterosexual men, and their relationships are more predicated on looks and age (Green and Grant, 2008).

Leisure and Sport

Although minimal literature specifically engages with middle age, some limited literature on leisure, sport and working life exists. One study of sport in midlife interviewed twenty-six men and women aged 35–55 who engaged in activities including badminton, long-distance running and attending health clubs. The research revealed a master narrative that 'age is a state of mind', alongside contradictory attempts to deny and resist ageing (Partington et al., 2005). Other narratives depicted midlife as a time of rejuvenation, signalled by a belief that 'life begins at forty', and also its antithesis that one had to gracefully accede to the ageing process. Bodily failure therefore could cause biographical disruption and enforced changes to these sports enthusiasts' predicted life plans, although their discourses were overlapping and ambiguous. One respondent might say, for example, their fitness was still good and they envisaged being active long term, but then a reluctant acceptance of ageing would often intercede and they would ambivalently admit they would only carry on as long as their body allowed. Another participant might explain reluctantly they could no longer compete with younger people but then this would be dismissed by a comment about no longer having time to train or not wanting to be competitive, now thriving more on the camaraderie enjoyed with other athletes.

Tulle (2008) focusing on veteran elite runners aged 48–84, also stresses the disruption to self and identity that an ageing body engenders, invoking Elias' notion of the civilizing process and increasing expected control over one's body, alongside its devaluation in terms of social and sexual capital when ageing and potential or actual bodily failure becomes evident. The 'mask of ageing' phenomenon identified by Featherstone and Wernick (1995), whereby people dis-identify with their aged faces in the mirror, seeing them as a betrayal and their real selves as their younger selves, could also contribute to this disruption and disembodiment of self. The key narrative Tulle's participants revealed was one of tremendous self-discipline in relation to running, it impacting on and often dictating all other areas. However, compromises were inevitable such as giving up par-ticularly demanding endeavours, modifying training to their ageing bodies or competing with others their age, rendering self-esteem and favourable comparison possible.

Kotarba (2005) additionally argues that popular music has been fundamental to growing up and identity since World War II, and is still central to many Baby Boomers' lives. He argues that, as mid-lifers attend concerts much less frequently than young people, the impor-tance of enjoying music in their houses and cars becomes paramount, and adverts for sophisticated music mobile phones and car and home music systems often target boomers. Kotarba, however, is writing about the USA, and in the UK those who spend the most on live music are middle-class 45- to 54-year-olds according to Mintel's research (Johnson, 2007). Many midlifers' histories are also punctuated by romantic memories converging around particular bands or musical tracks. CDs or DVDS are bought as romantic gifts, or anniversaries are celebrated with poignant songs from earlier periods. With many Baby Boomers being grandparents or parents, music also enters into their dialogues with their children and grandchildren. Many reunion and tribute bands have also brought nostalgic middle-agers back to live music scenarios, some attending concerts with their children. Although Kotarba is enthusiastic about midlifers' sustained interest in music, some (presumably younger) music journalists refer nega-tively to the influence the boomers have on popular culture and their 'self indulgent' appreciation of 'colostomy rock' (Harkin, 2006).

Eating habits have also changed for middle-aged people, compared to older people who often retain traditional tastes for British food and conventional preparation techniques. The *Guardian* newspaper last year documented a 36 per cent rise in the sales of Thai, Indian and Chinese meals between 2001 and 2006, and a trebling in the sale of ready meals, as well as showing we eat out more frequently than before (Vidal, 2009). Fixed meals are becoming redundant as we eat faster and at different times. In 1961 people tended to eat at 8 a.m., 1 p.m. and 5.30 p.m. Now Britons breakfast between 7 and 11 a.m., many miss lunch, and evening meals occur between 6 and 10 p.m. Nevertheless, the family meal is still often eaten in a group, and single people often combine eating and socializing. Some groups also prefer fast food, others opt for ethical food such as free-range and organic products and food grown without exploited labour and a third group favour locally grown sustainable food. An academic study using time diaries between 1975 and 2000 corroborated the above claims but additionally found large amounts of time and money were spent on eating out by the more affluent groups, possibly marking social distinction and *conspicuous consumption* – a way of visibly showing others their wealth by how they spend it (Cheng et al., 2007).

Work, Time Famine and Attitudes and Expectations

Work experiences and attitudes differ considerably according to cohort and generation and associated historical and socio-economic experiences. A study of two cohorts of Scottish women born in the 1930s and the 1950s showed, how in very little time, changes in gender relations impacted significantly upon their attitudes, experiences and opportunities. Those living through the austerity of wartime and frequent evacuations, many of whom had lived in houses without inside toilets, regular hot water or a bath or shower, had their children earlier, were more likely to marry and expressed support for more traditional gender roles and attitudes. In comparison those born in the fifties experienced comprehensive welfare state support and increased educational opportunities, the rise of the contraceptive pill and the influence of social movements which included feminism, black power and gay liberation movements, and had much more egalitarian views about gender (K. Hunt, 2002). Middle-aged disabled people today also encounter the dual disadvantage of ageism and disablism with those 45 and above being much less likely to find employment compared to their younger disabled peers. Interestingly, during World War II both young and middle-aged disabled people were actively encouraged to take up employment, doing the jobs that non-disabled conscripts had previously done, but after the war they were integrated into special employment programmes (Hyde, 2006).

An examination of the first wave of Baby Boomers born between 1946 and 1955 reveals they are seen – contradictorily – positively, as bringing new lifestyles and zest as they progress towards retirement, and negatively, as threatening financial disaster because of the projected long-term burdens they may place on health and social care services (Phillipson et al., 2008). Bywater (2006) argues that, in their youth, the boomers were politically and socially innovative, inhabiting 'the glorious window between the Pill and the emergence of AIDS'. Edmunds and Turner (2002), furthermore, suggest boomers were a new generation in aesthetic and sexual terms as well as being the first generation to be fully confronted with a consumer revolution, including rising home ownership, which changed attitudes and life-styles. They are often demonized for this in terms of being blamed for AIDS because of sexually 'permissive' attitudes, and castigated for the supposed breakdown of the family and even environmental problems caused by their apparently excessive consumption, including frequent foreign travel (Phillipson et al., 2008).

Headlines, even in the more 'respectable' newspapers, continually represent the boomers as narcissistic, obsessed with preserving their ageing bodies indefinitely, ludicrous in their consumption of rock music and model train sets and their 'youthful' dress sense and, furthermore, selfish because of excessive consumption and spending their children's inheritances (Frith, 2004; Blacker, 2006; Johnson, 2007). In England midlife men are also berated for their irresponsibility in relation to riding powerful motorbikes and, although between 1996 and 2008 death rates for younger motorcyclists fell by a third, the number of riders aged 40–49 killed or seriously injured doubled (Webster, 2008). Alternatively, the boomers are seen as inspirational figures, fighting social inequalities and war in their youth and now challenging corporate capitalism's neglect of environmental and global ethics (Harkin, 2006).

There are significant fiscal differences between the early Baby Boomers (1946–55) and those born between 1956 and 1964, who are less affluent, in part because of economic recessions. The latter Baby Boomer females also juggle more caring and occupational roles than the earlier cohort because of the increasing involvement of women in paid work alongside family commitments. One US study comparing women of the pre-World War II cohort of 1931–43, with the Baby Boomers (1946–64), and the Baby Bust cohort of 1965–70 also found that, although the youngest cohort had greater access to higher education, higher-status careers and less family pressures against working than the preceding two cohorts, both the Baby Boom and Baby Bust cohorts felt they had less control over their environment than the earlier cohort. This may suggest the negative effects of attempting to juggle work and family commitments simultaneously (Carr, 2004), or possibly demonstrate the oldest cohort harboured lower general expectations about environmental control than the other cohorts and thus rated their control higher. Recent newspaper articles also suggest Baby Boomers are financially worse off than their parents, anxious about their families' security and overwhelmed by fears of ageing (A. Hill, 2007). Many would like to retire early but, because of pension schemes collapsing, poor annuity rates and stock market performance (Glasgow, 2003) (and the current credit crisis exacerbating these), are unable to. By 2020 a third of UK workers, 10 million, will be 50 or over compared with 7 million in 2002 and 5.4 million in 1992.

If rising unemployment impacts on already ageist attitudes extant within the workplace, their prospects may be poor. A US study also found Baby Boomers' health is worse than that of adults twenty years ago, attributing this mostly to stress because of time pressure and poor eating habits (Mochas, 2007).

Certainly stress is paramount in Hislop and Arber's (2003) study of the gendered nature of sleep disruption amongst middle-aged women, where their sleep needs have become compromized by the family and work pressures. Midlifers' parents are living longer and may require care. Their children leave home on average at 25 and many are burdened with large student debts and trying to save for deposits on houses, which parents try to help with (R. Bennett, 2008). Due to the UK's long-hours work culture, over 25 per cent of workers put in over forty-eight paid hours per week, but working time is also impacted upon by domestic work and care activities in conjunction with inadequate state provision of childcare services in comparison with other European countries. While many households are dual-career families, this has not been matched by an equalization of men's domestic work. So, although men worked the longest paid hours at both the manual-worker end of the spectrum, where they have to work more hours for adequate income, and the higher professional end where overtime is expected as the norm, women are profoundly affected by 'time famine' and sleep deficit due to onerous care and work commitments (Chatitheochari and Arber, 2009).

Flexible working arrangements accommodating those with young children are also failing middle-aged women who care for elderly relatives. One study found that, of the female employees aged 47–59 studied, 50 per cent had such caring responsibilities but felt employers were unaccommodating (Ward, 2005). Men in manual jobs also confront vocational challenges when physical decline in middle age means they are unable to maintain their previous levels of strenuous labour (Gilbert and Constantine, 2005). They therefore may find themselves increasingly in competition with younger, stronger, faster workers in a climate where the availability of manual jobs is decreasing due to technological innovations and their frequent redeployment to cheaper countries.

Family relationships and friendships

Regarding family and friendships, much has been covered in previous chapters such as the rise of single households, gay couples and 'off-time' or non-normative childbearing. However, later childbearing, sometimes aided by reproductive treatment, although now more common, can impact negatively, particularly on the mothers. With

79, mostly midlife, couples, who had conceived with donor eggs as a second option, many women felt they were failures or felt subjectively older because of their inability to use their own eggs. They either blamed themselves for their own infertility and not trying to have children when younger or castigated the medical profession for giving them insufficient information to make informed choices earlier. Some also felt discriminated against and stigmatized because of their age, in terms of being denied the full range of fertility treatment or the possibility of adoption (Friese et al., 2006). Many felt discomfort surrounded by much younger mothers and were concerned other parents would view them negatively or as the grandparents, some mothers attempting to look and dress younger to compensate. However, on the positive side, the couples also felt that they were sufficiently mature, responsible and financially solvent to ensure their children were their first priority. Friese et al. (2007) argue that this stigma and discomfort are likely to reduce as the older mother becomes more normalized. This discourse of blame, is, nonetheless, still exacerbated by ongoing negative media representations which label single and older women, and gay people who use new reproductive technologies as 'irresponsible', selfish and messing with 'nature' (e.g. Bunting, 2004b). Rarely are criticisms laid at the door of older men, even those in their sixties, seventies and eighties, such as media personalities, including John Simpson, Des O'Connor, Paul McCartney and Rod Stewart, who conceive children with their natural sperm.

The notion of this generation as a pivot or sandwich generation trying to manage its own needs whilst squeezed from both sides by the demands and needs of younger children, adult children and ageing parents also appears to have resonance, although there is a strongly gendered component to this. Research from New Zealand shows significant support is transmitted from midlife parents to young adult children (although this is lower with widowed or separated parents), in the form of financial, emotional and practical support. A US study shows significant support is offered to ageing parents, although in both studies women were more likely to provide emotional and practical support rather than financial support (Hillcoat-Nalletamby and Dharmalingam, 2003; Ganns and Silverstein, 2006). If these pressures are combined with women's steadily increasing domestic work after the birth of a first child and subsequent children, in comparison to their male partners' decreasing contributions (Baxter et al., 2008), they suggest midlife women may be experiencing considerable time famine and stress with their multiple roles and burdens, and a new term 'the swollen nest' has subsequently emerged. Such work–life conflict is particularly onerous for middle-aged British women. Many work full-time and have fewer opportunities for flexible working, exit and re-entry, and slowly withdrawing from the labour market than women and men in the Nordic countries (Ginn and Fast, 2006).

Numbers of single households are also increasing and, although younger single women are often seen to be 'in between' relationships before committing themselves and older women as widows, middle-aged women tend to be stigmatized by labels such as 'spinster', with its connotations of infertility, unattractiveness, loneliness and desperation. This is despite the fact they may be divorced, separated, widowed, in between relationships themselves, or childless and without a relationship through choice. In Simpson's (2006) study of never-married women, single for at least five years, close relationships with family and friends were common, countering arguments that intimacy and fulfilment are only found in sexual relationships. The women, however, were sensitive about others' negative perceptions and resented assumptions that, because they were single, they should inevitably care for relatives. They did note some disadvantages such as sometimes not having anyone to go on holiday with or not always being invited out socially because of lack of partnership status. Some had very casual relationships with men but did not regard these as real partnerships. Smith (1999) argues the word 'single' denies the complexity and diversity of single women's lives, 40 per cent of whom were living without a partner in the 1990s. A study of identity and re-partnering after separation also found the transition from conjugal marital relationships to notions of 'pure' love changed attitudes towards new partners. These tended to be viewed in terms of 'risk' and possible repeated failure alongside pride about and a desire to retain newly found independence, although 75 per cent aspired to living with someone in five years' time (Lampard and Peggs, 2007)

Very little research has been conducted on gay and lesbian relationships through the life course and perceptions of ageing (Boxer, 1997), although the homosexual/heterosexual dichotomy is fictive and sexuality is far more fluid than this in terms of both practices and identity (Green and Grant, 2008), rendering longitudinal research fraught with conceptual and methodological problems. Some of those gay in midlife married previously and identified as heterosexual, others may have previously been gay but in midlife became involved in a heterosexual relationship. Other groups may resist labels or live a seemingly heterosexual life interspersed with secretive same-sex encounters. However, despite these definitional and methodological problems, all those who now identity as gay or bisexual or are in same-sex relationships now will probably have experienced some discrimination, as well as living through increasing civil rights extensions to gay people, and institutional intolerance and personal hostility are still facts of life for many gay people.

Weeks et al. (2001) argue 'families of choice' are those that gay people choose (heterosexuals could too), and that the gay couples may regard as fictive kin those who are unconnected via marriage or blood relationships. The notion of family of choice or family of origin as being divisive was, however, found to be a false dichotomy by Smart (2007) in her analysis of gay 'marriages' prior to civil partnerships, involving mostly midlife couples. Smart stressed the gargantuan efforts gay couples made to include both biological family and friends at their ceremonies and to enable everyone to feel comfortable. However, great diversity and complexity regarding 'families of choice' were identified. Some couples were greatly admired and supported by biological family but 'coldshouldered' by friends, and with others, friends were closer than their distant and sometimes estranged biological relatives, with a final group combining the two.

Giddens (1991, 1992) argues lesbian relationships may be the blueprint through which the pure relationship can be recognized through *confluent love*. This is deep and meaningful, unconstrained by traditional gender and social expectations and can create its own meanings, structure and morals, but may not endure. However, A. R. Wilson (2007) argues that Giddens fails to account for the privilege and institutional supports available for heterosexual relationships, noting state recognition via civil partnership and other legislative changes is relatively recent. Gay relationships may also offer different possibilities. For example, many gay men are in committed and meaningful, but not necessarily monogamous, relationships. These often commence with a sexual encounter and then progress to intimacy and romance, in comparison to lesbian and heterosexual relationships which tend to flow in the opposite direction (Hostetler and Cohl, 1997). The spectre and reality of HIV/AIDS has also impacted on some midife gay men's understandings of their relationships and mortality, and changed the meanings they attribute to these. Some midlife women's entrance into lesbianism may have also been influenced by their commitment to radical separatist feminism in the 1970s and 1980s and to rather dated and arguably fallacious views that one could not be both a feminist woman and heterosexual as this was seen as colluding with the enemy, 'men'. Younger lesbians are much less likely to engage in same-sex sexual relationships for such reasons.

Regarding friendship, a US study found that male friendships in middle age were stronger and better sustained than previously as men became less competitive, calmer and were more able to befriend women just as friends, although a few commented on not having enough 'real' friends of either sex (Greif, 2008). They also used new technologies such as Twitter to join up with men who had similar interests to them. In contrast women were reported as working harder at their friendships, sustaining them through their twenties and thirties, so often still had the same friends in middle age.

Conclusion

This chapter has explored and analysed sociological and psychological perspectives on middle age. Psychology tends to concentrate on physical and cognitive changes, showing that, although some inevitable decline occurs in both spheres, it is generally of little significance, with the exception of the menopause which halts female reproduction and midlifers' increasing likelihood of being affected by certain physical conditions and diseases. When cognition and intelligence are examined, although there are declines in fluid and analytical intelligence, in other forms of intelligence there may be noticeable increases. Overall intelligence also remains high until the sixties, with compensatory strategies being used to minimize or neutralize declines. In relation to psychosocial changes, although traditional stage theorists conceptualized middle age as a time of crisis, contemporary evidence is conflicting. It suggests that, although midlife involves significant stress and self-reflection, it is frequently also a time of stability, confidence, competence and increasing marital satisfaction, when people tend to become slightly more agreeable, self-aware and less defensive and neurotic.

Sociology criticizes overstated claims of decline and crisis and midlife's increasing medicalization but ironically shows that midlife is currently experienced as a complex, challenging time by many. Midlife women have difficulty with viewing themselves and their appearance favourably when society only sees young women who are beautiful as having value, and the jobs of some older women seem to depend more on their age and appearance than on occupational competence. Some women are consequently resorting to expensive and often dangerous anti-ageing procedures. In relation to sport, midlife is a time when peak performance reduces and attitudes and expectations of what can physically be realistically achieved must be lowered, which may cause great psychological disruption, particularly for committed athletes. The current generation of midlifers also experience multiple time and situational pressures. They often work long hours in responsible jobs, supporting not only young but also adult children and elderly relatives, who may require a variety of financial, emotional and physical assistance and maintenance, hence the term 'the sandwich generation'. Such pressures are exacerbated by the current economic recession, rapidly rising unemployment and the collapse or reduced value of many company pension schemes. This occurs alongside ambivalent media depictions in which Baby Boomers are seen, on the one hand, as innovative and political but, on the other, as selfish, indulgent and a future drain on societal resources. Sociology also shows how different historical and socio-economic circumstances can considerably shape the experiences of two cohorts born not far apart. Changes in family structures and practices, such as increasing late motherhood, single living and the more visible emergence of lesbian and gay couples, have also created different relationships. Unfortunately, continued discrimination and prejudicial viewpoints show attitudes still lag significantly behind innovative and rights-based medical and legal changes for these groups.

Reflection and discussion questions

Does the term 'the midlife crisis' have any contemporary relevance?

What key physical, cognitive and psychosocial changes occur during middle adulthood?

How might social class, gender, race/ethnicity, sexual orientation and disability impact upon how midlife is experienced?

Recommended reading

Willis and Schaie's (2002) US textbook on middle age is a key psychological text and Lachman's (2004) journal article is a clear and accessible review of the contemporary psychological literature. There is negligible sociological literature that deals specifically with midlife, but Phillipson et al.'s (2008) journal article on conflicting views of the Baby Boomer generation is a good review and analysis of the literature surrounding the generation who are currently inhabiting middle age.

Old Age

Introduction

Old age in modern post-industrial societies is generally judged on our chronological age, extending from about 60 to 120 years, the known upper limit of our species. Transitions into old age are denoted by bureaucratic or institutional markers such as compulsory age of retirement, pension entitlements and concessionary travel passes and TV licences, as well as requirements such as having to renew your driving licence every three years after the age of 70. Being old is also unequivocally associated with physical changes such as greying hair, wrinkles, reduced mobility and impaired sensory and cognitive functioning. Even road signs represent old age negatively as an elderly hunchback female figure with a walking stick. Consequently stereotypes which depict older people as unproductive, a burden, unattractive and dependent, are prominent and persuasive. Terminology used to describe the elderly is predominantly negative and terms such as 'old biddy', 'spinster', 'wrinkly', 'dirty old man' and 'second childhood' are common parlance.

In other societies people may be unaware of their chronological age, and other criteria such as vigour, social activity or generation, whereby an aunt may be accorded more social seniority than her niece, even if she is chronologically younger (Keith, 1990), may be more important. Though anthropological reviews have shown that many older people retain status and active involvement in their communities in old age, this is less likely if there are resource problems and with nomadic tribes (Fry, 1985; Tour, 1989). One native American tribe reveres its elders when food is plentiful but uses them as a living larder during famines (Philp, 2008). Negative social and economic changes leading to the breakdown of extended families have also reduced the status and support elderly people receive in some traditional communities, with the Ik people of Uganda developing extreme hostility towards their elderly, resenting any food or medical supplies outsiders brought for them and viewing them as symbolically dead

(Turnbull, 1989). Old age is also culturally relative with a person in their seventies entering into the Chinese parliament being likely to be viewed warily by older peers because of beliefs that they will be prey to a youthful propensity to 'hotheadedness' (Durkin, 1995).

Understandings of old age have traditionally been dominated by medical and biological perceptions, with the development of a substrata of medicine called geriatrics concentrating solely on the pathologies associated with old age and thereby representing it as a time of illness, serious decline and dependency. Social gerontology has recently attempted to counter this viewpoint by examining healthy subjects from a life span viewpoint, emphasizing how old age as problematic is socially constructed. Negative depictions of elderly people must also be located within our global, largely capitalist world in which the profit motive is imperative and those viewed economically unproductive – for example, some children, the profoundly disabled and the elderly – are accorded lower societal value. However, children are treated as investments because of their growing productive potential, but elderly people's economic productivity – although many still do paid, informal caring or voluntary work during old age – will inevitably decline.

Because old age in Western societies encompasses such a wide age spread and because social division effects accumulate throughout the life course – meaning that income or social inequalities related to gender, ethnicity or poverty, for example, will be at their most prominent in old age – elderly people are a very heterogeneous group. They defy easy categorization and frequently negate the stereotypes. Theorists now differentiate between a third age of relative independence, activity and good health, seen mostly to occur between 60 and 75–80, and a fourth age where there is increasing intellectual and physical decline and dependency (Laslett, 1989). Other writers use the terms 'the young old', similar to Laslett's third age, 'the middle old' – a transitional period between dependency and independence where individuals' health and physical and mental functions start to deteriorate – and 'the old old', who are very dependent and have numerous difficulties (Zarrit, 1996).

Those over 80 years old are, according to research, far more likely to be or become more dependent and to suffer from a variety of degenerative age-related diseases such as dementia, cancer and heart conditions, two-thirds of people over 85 suffering from long-term illness or disability (Office for National Statistics, 2008), although many older people confound chronological assumptions. Ageing is also affected not only by genetics and accumulated advantage or disadvantages related to social divisions but by early nutritional experiences, including those in the womb. People's lifestyles and 'habits' throughout life, including their education, physical activity levels, alcohol consumption, whether they smoke, social and kinship networks and overall satisfaction with life, are, however, heavily influenced by cultural norms and structural inequalities, as is perceived individual choice.

From a comparative examination of developmental psychology, life span psychology and sociological texts which deal exclusively or partially with old age, there appears to be less binarism and dichotomy inherent in them when they analyse old age than with other life stages. Although the traditional patterns of psychology being more concerned with biological and cognitive changes and the relationship between the two, and sociology stressing the primacy of the socio-economic and political and cultural contexts are still evident, there is more overlap, agreement and reciprocity between the two disciplines when examining old age. For example, in both Bee's (1994) and Berger's (2005) books on life span psychology, although they consider different biological theories of ageing, they also emphasize the social context. Ageism is placed at the start of the chapter for Berger, and Bee also acknowledges that social factors such as health and disability are important. In Vincent's book on the sociology of old age (2003), he considers the various biological theories of ageing but, significantly, they come towards the end of the book, immediately preceded by a statement about the impact of the social and structured inequalities on the physical.

This unexpected congruence between disciplines occurs in psychology perhaps because ageism is more apparent with the old than with children, and because of the influence of gerontology and its focus on ageism and healthy populations. Psychology is also beginning to reject the previous 'deficit and loss' one-dimensional view of old age and replace it with a more positive, multifaceted and multidirectional view (Baltes and Graf, 1996), although Durkin (1995: 643) amusingly criticizes the patronizing way older people are presented in life span texts as still being able to have sex 'with dignity'. In sociology the importance of ambivalent embodiment and physical decline in old age and the inevitability of death during this period may have encouraged the inclusion of biological perspectives. However, in both sociology and psychology, old age is a comparatively unpopular topic and accorded less attention than other life span stages such as childhood and adolescence. This could be linked to the marginalization of old people in academia, as well as more generally. Durkin (1995), in his generally excellent book on developmental social psychology, subtitled 'from infancy to old age', devotes only 24 out of 655 pages to middle and late adulthood. A content analysis of US undergraduate sociology textbooks on marriage and the family also found on average only 3.6 per cent of the total space in the books was devoted to the elderly, and they were frequently only incorporated in chapters concerned with late-life ageing (Stolley and Hill, 1996). Phillipson (1997), in a review of the research literature on old age, similarly remarked that the sociology of old age was an underdeveloped area. One also has only to glance at the array of books on child development or the sociology of childhood in any university library and compare them with how many books are stocked on middle or late adulthood to hypothesize that, traditionally, old age has not been a favoured or well-researched area within social science.

Old age, ageism and ageing are extremely important areas for contemporary study not least because of the exponentially greying population in Western nations, i.e. the numbers of elderly people are rapidly increasing in proportion to those of different ages. This has been caused by the bulge of the Baby Boomer generation and falling birth rates (until recent fertility increases), alongside improved environmental conditions and medical advances leading to increased longevity for large sections of the population. Between 2010 and 2040 when most of the Baby Boomer generation (born 1946–64), now middle-aged and older, will have died, the number of elderly will increase further but after this time period it will start to drop. In 2005, the UK population over 65 was 9.6 million out of a total of 59.8 million (then 16 per cent of the population), estimated to rise to 15 million in 2031 (Help the Aged, 2006). Currently, 12,276,600 people in the UK are over 60 and they constitute one-fifth of the population (Office for National Statistics, 2009). By 2021 it is estimated the number of people over 65 will be greater than that of under-16s (Self, 2008). The fastest-growing age group are the over-80s (National Statistics Online, 2008). The Audit Commission (2008) projected that this age group will almost double in size, rising from 2.4 million in 2009 to approximately 4.3 million in 2029, although demographic predictions must be treated cautiously as they are often used to exaggerate potential crises related to political agendas (Vincent et al., 2006). Life expectancy is now calculated to be an average of 77.2 years for men, and for women 85.2 years, in the UK (Office for National Statistics, 2008). In North America the fastest-growing segment of the population are 85 and over (Robine et al., 2007) and China became an ageing society in 1999 with 153 million people (11.6 per cent of the population) then over 60 and projected estimates of 400 million by 2037 (Dan Zhang, 2008). Overall in the developing countries, the UN (2002) predicted that by 2050 those over 60 will constitute a third of the population, and in less-developed countries, 20 per cent (Bond et al., 2007).

In contrast, only about 100 years ago, due to poor environmental conditions and diet, the ravage of infectious diseases and, for women, the risks associated with repeated childbirth, it was unusual for people to survive to old age. However, those surviving had a similar upper-end life span to the elderly alive now. So the life span potential of people appears to not to have extended – it is the proportion of people reaching old age in comparison to previous birth cohorts or generations, and their ratio in the population as a whole, which have increased. Science has already manufactured increased life expectancy through improved environmental health, the control of infectious diseases and medical technology, offering a few more years of life through techniques such as fitting a heart pacemaker or dialysis in the Western countries. It has therefore been argued that, unless there is some sophisticated modification of humans' genetic potential, life span will not increase further to any significant extent (Vincent, 2003). However, we still appear to be fixated on extending old age and preserving youth through various potions and medications. In a section on ageing in Wikipedia, a free internet encyclopaedia which anyone can contribute to and which is therefore not a very reliable source of knowledge, several substances, some of which have been tested on animals but not humans, were listed which have been shown to slow or reverse ageing. These include Reseveratol, a chemical compound in red grapes, a combination of the food supplements acetyl–L-carnatine and alphalipoic acid, a drug called Rapamycin and walnuts (http://en.wikipedia.org.wiki/Ageing), although it is not recommended any readers consume these substances.

This chapter will examine sociological and psychological understandings of old age and, while recognizing that both disciplines seem to cover biological and social issues, although according different import to them, will tend to analyse biological, cognitive and psychosocial development and decline from a psychological angle, and social factors and the impact of historical and social transitions from a sociological perspective.

Old age and psychology

Theories of Ageing

There are a number of different theories hypothesizing how and why we age and speculating to what extent maximum life spans could be enhanced (or even if it is desirable to extend life substantially, because of both resource and existential issues), but no one theory is definitive. It could also be deemed ageist to examine ageing in a chapter on old age, as we age throughout our life and in each stage of the life course there are gains related to ageing as well as losses.

For example, young children lose fantasy play as they become more cognitively expert (Baltes and Graf, 1996), adolescents experience significant pruning of redundant neural pathways as other growth processes in the brain occur (Thornton, 2008) and the ability to learn a foreign language proficiently reduces significantly by adulthood (W. Klein, 1996). However, given that ageing processes have a cumulative effect throughout life and as, particularly with the 'old old', there appear to be some irreversible losses and reductions, both cognitively and physically (although these were previously exaggerated), theories of ageing will be examined here.

Ageing can occur in two ways, which are generally combined. As explained before, primary or intrinsic ageing refers to inevitable genetically programmed ageing, which varies in different individuals. This has been linked in evolutionary terms to older people's lower value. Secondary or extrinsic ageing refers to the cumulative impact unfavourable lifestyles or environments may have on the ageing process. Although the risk of diseases such as cancer and heart conditions increases genetically with old age, this may be exacerbated by secondary ageing. The three main theories explaining ageing are (i) 'wear and tear', (ii) 'genetic ageing' (both relating to ageing of the entire body), and (iii) 'cellular ageing', which focuses on ageing at the level of the cell. The first theory hypothesizes that the body simply wears out after repeated use and exposure to pathogens and diseases, a machine metaphor. In potential support of this theory, competitive athletes generally manifest significant physical problems by middle adulthood; childless women have greater longevity than childbearing females; people who are overweight die earlier, possibly because of the extra energy required to sustain them; and modern medical technology frequently repairs worn-out body parts such as organs, hips and knees (K. Berger, 2005), although other factors may account for these outcomes. Against this theory are the facts that humans are not machines and the body frequently repairs itself, and activity is beneficial overall for us, inactivity often leading to illness. Therefore, although this theory may explain some parts of the ageing process, it is not a satisfactory comprehensive theory (Austad, 2001).

The second theory relates to genetic ageing and the notion of a maximum life span with individual variation. Genetic adaptation may be important here as, although we have a genetic propensity to certain diseases, many – such as dementia, Type 2 diabetes and cancer – disproportionately manifest themselves during midlife or old age when we are less likely to be producing or caring for children. The third theory, cellular ageing, claims ageing is genetically determined, with the 'Hayflick Limit' suggesting there is a limited number of times cells can be duplicated because minor errors accumulate in replication over time. Other cellular ageing theories relate to increased oxygen free radicals – highly unstable cells, which can produce cellular dysfunction and ultimately cause diseases such as cancer and arteriosclerosis. Since many parts of the immune system weaken over time, it has also been hypothesized that this takes place at a cellular level, either the weakened cells exacerbating ageing or leaving the individual more prone to disease (Effros, 2001). However, when examining ageing, variation between individuals actually increases in old age, contrary to what psychologists originally expected.

Physical Changes during Late Adulthood

Although primary ageing is exacerbated by secondary ageing, a number of physical changes are good markers of age but do not affect health. Appearance changes, with the skin becoming drier, thinner and less elastic, blood vessels more visible and age spots appearing on the skin's surface, with pockets of fat accumulating underneath. Hair pigment turns grey, ultimately to white, and hair on the body thins. However, old age is ultimately associated with an increasing weakening of the body, a dulling of the senses and an overall slowing down. So, for example, an older person may take longer to tie their shoelaces or their reaction time to a potential hazard when driving may be slower, older people having more accidents per mile driven than younger people, although huge individual variations exist.

With age, people become slightly shorter as vertebra settle together and fat distribution relocates, collecting in the torso and lower face. Muscular, bone and overall weight losses ensue with associated reductions in muscle flexibility, strength and increased stiffness, although some compensation can be achieved through activities such as walking and weight training (Rice and Cunningham, 2002). Sensory losses also occur with taste, vision and hearing. Although poor eyesight can generally be corrected with glasses, and cataracts and glaucoma occur more in the elderly and are often operable, macular degeneration – retinal deterioration for which there is no cure – affects one in six Americans over 80 (O'Neill et al., 2001) and ultimately causes blindness. At 65, 40 per cent of individuals have difficulty hearing normal conversation (K. Berger, 2005), exacerbated by background noise, although hearing aids and medical interventions may partially compensate. Individuals with sensory loss also need to learn new habits to compensate, and those who live or work with older people, such as health and social care professionals, need to learn ways of optimum communication.

The vital organs – cardiovascular, respiratory, digestive and renal/

urinary – also become less effective and slower, and organ failure is a major cause of death in old age. Disease, however, in mitigation, advances at slower rates than in younger years, and many people at autopsy who had died of other causes also had slow-growth cancers. Although cancer in itself is a leading cause of death for the elderly, it falls behind heart disease, strokes, diabetes and arteriosclerosis in death rates. Sleep disorders are also more likely to occur with the elderly finding it harder to fall asleep, experiencing less deep sleep, waking up more frequently and experiencing tiredness during the day and taking 'naps'. Although some are prescribed sleeping tablets which have significant side-effects or self-medicate through alcohol, it has been suggested that accepting that the change is normal and some minor adjustment to routines are all that is required for many (K. Berger, 2005).

When minimal secondary ageing is present, what is presented as the ideal in terms of ageing is *compression of morbidity*. This occurs whereby, after a long and healthy life, the time spent ill or disabled is compressed into a short period of time, rather than the person suffering years of debility, and the 'average incapacity free life expectancy' has risen faster than average life expectancy overall. The credibility of shortening the period between chronic morbidity and death therefore represents a radical departure from the idea chronic disability and disease characterize old age. Older people normally adjust to getting old and it does not impact upon their self if they are emotionally content and the health challenges faced are manageable on a daily basis (Gibson, 1992; Hendry and Kloep, 2002). The Amsterdam longitudinal ageing study showed positive functioning in conjunction with poor health is more likely if one has close social relationships, a partner, feels independent and has self-esteem (Penninx et al., 1998). Subjective feelings of wellbeing are also more important for sustained health and longevity than objective medical diagnoses (Hendry and Kloep, 2002).

Cognitive Changes

Many early studies of cognition in old age were overwhelmingly negative, because cross-sectional studies examining, for example, intelligence appeared to demonstrate lower intelligence in older as opposed to younger persons. However, they did not take into account factors such as that older people may have received less education and faced different life challenges from younger people, and the culture-, age- and class-bound nature of IQ tests (Hendry and Kloep, 2002), as well as the impact of adjusting to rapidly and progressively changing post-industrial technological societies. They therefore were methodologically flawed and the majority of older people function well enough to live independently and without significant support for all or most of their lives. Although older people's information processing becomes progressively slower and less accurate with age, it has been argued the brain restructures itself to cope with the demand as effectively as possible (Labouvie-Vief, 1982). Nevertheless, in advanced old age, when significant mental and physical difficulties may set in, normally at 80 or over, considerable challenges and major stress may be experienced. However, changing or modifying one's goals or patterns, such as devoting one's energy to a small group of friends rather than retaining a wide range of acquaintances alongside a hectic social life, or comparing oneself to one's peers rather than energetic young people is an effective way of maintaining self-esteem and satisfaction.

Psychological and neurological studies have shown that, in some areas, there is inevitable deterioration, which, although possessing improvement potential, will not, even after signicant training, reach anywhere near the levels of young adults who have only received minimal training in the activities being tested (Baltes and Kliegl, 1992). When difficult tasks are set, involving multiple dimensions, older adults fare even worse due to declines in effective working and short-term memory and problems with process and recall. Therefore, although there is a lot of *development reserve capacity* in old age, sometimes known as *plasticity*, which can lead to significant compensation or adjustment, there are age-related limits to how far it will stretch. The key deterioration noted is in fluid intelligence, which involves learning new ways to solve tasks or being presented with unfamiliar problems that are irresolvable using previous strategies. However, with crystallized intelligence, which involves utilizing the cognitive skills and accumulated knowledge we already have, there is not necessarily deterioration, and research has shown improvement for some in old age on skills such as reading, writing, comprehension and language. Furthermore, with particular groups, such as academics, or those nominated as wise, there is not necessarily a decline even in fluid intelligence until around 80. This may suggest higher fluid intelligence can be retained if the skills are continually refreshed and used during old age and/or were intensively used prior to old age (Shimamura et al., 1995; Baltes and Staudinger 1993). However, another study conversely found that academics declined even more on fluid intelligence than blue-collar workers during a five-year period (Christensen et al., 1997) but this may have been because their previous levels were so high or because of a dramatic change in lifestyle after retirement.

Schaie's longitudinal study on age and overall intelligence shows, among the individuals studied, aged between 60 and 80, some retained stability on performance, others deteriorated and some actually increased their performance (1996). In an almost representative study of 70- to 105-year-old Germans, looking at both 'self' and 'intelligence', significant interindividual variability was noted (Smith and Baltes, 1993). Interestingly, in this particular study of ageing in Berlin, virtually no association between subjective wellbeing and intellectual functioning existed, although vision and hearing were powerful predictors for overall intellectual functioning (Lindenberger and Baltes, 1994). Physical activity has also been found to sharpen one's cognitive facilities in old age (Whitbourne et al., 2008).

Psychologists sometimes use the concept *selective compensation with optimization* to describe how many people – particularly elderly ones – cope well with declining abilities through innovation (Freund and Baltes, 2002). This strategy can de deployed by children and younger adults too. Selection involves choosing activities which you know you can perform well on and then usefully searching for and activating novel ways of orchestrating them to the best of your abilities, despite being aware of your shortcomings or deficits. One study discovered how elderly typists, although compromised in their motor processing skills (affecting the speed they could physically type at), could type as fast as younger typists by reading the script farther ahead (Salthouse, 1984). Baltes and Graf (1996) also give the interesting exemplar of an 80-year-old virtuoso concert pianist, Rubinstein, whose coping strategies comprised of reducing his repertoire (*selection*), spending more time than before practising his pieces (*optimization*) and slowing down his playing before fast sections of the piece in order to give the illusion of a faster tempo than he was actually producing (*compensation*).

Creativity, although an elusive concept and not always easy to judge/measure does not always decrease with old age, as demonstrated by Michelangelo painting the frescoes in the Sistine Chapel at 75, and Verdi composing the opera *Falstaff* when he was 80. Some people discover untapped creative potential after they retire and are freed from work and family commitments, and develop, for example, new artistic skills (K. Berger, 2005). It has also been suggested older people become wiser in old age to counteract the negative views of cognitive decline (Labouvie-Vief, 1992).Wisdom is a complex concept to define, operationalize and measure, but may involve significant insight and judgement, particularly in relation to complex and unclear human matters. However, in a longitudinal study of 814 people from adolescence to old age, there was little evidence wisdom was the province of the old although, for some, humour, perspective and altruism appeared to increase (Vaillant, 2002).

Certain illnesses or diseases affecting cognition are more prevalent in old age, particularly affecting those over 80. An analysis of thirteen studies from different countries found the incidence of Alzheimer's rose from 1 in 100 at age 65 to 1 in 5 at over-85 (Ritchie et al., 1992), with other studies suggesting even higher rates. Alzheimer's disease is the most common form of dementia worldwide, and Alzheimer's subjects participating in performance improvement cognition tests, unlike other older participants, did not benefit at all (Baltes and Graf, 1996). Alzheimer's initially commences with absentmindedness, forgetting where one has just been or people's names, and is often confused with normal ageing, but being unable to recall a common word is a key indicator. Confusion then worsens, as does concentration and short-term memory, and words become misused. One's personality changes and previous traits such as volatility often become enhanced. Memory loss then degenerates further to the stage where a person may go out half-dressed, forget they have lit a fire and lose the ability to recognize familiar people. Eventually people express no emotions, are inactive, and death generally comes ten to fifteen years after commencement (Fromholt and Bruhn, 1998), although for many the symptoms are not identified at an early stage. Other dementias result from strokes or may be linked with Parkinson's disease, which causes increased tremors and shakes, both conditions becoming more prevalent during old age. Positively psychiatric illnesses such as schizophrenia, anxiety and bipolar disorder are less common, although the research on depression is conflicting and inconclusive, with some suggestions it rises substantially after the age of 70–75. Conversely, in a study involving 4,000 adults, aged 65+, which looked at a number of influential factors such as financial and emotional support and health status, Blazer et al. (1991) concluded that, if confounding variables are controlled, the elderly are less likely to become depressed than people at other ages. However, depression and dementia may be conflated, with depression following a significant bereavement sometimes producing devastating dementia-like symptoms (Kasi-Godley et al., 1998).

Old Age and Social and Personality Changes

Psychologists tend to concentrate on changes in social and occupational roles/positions in old age and their impact on personality and identity. Erikson's final psychosocial challenge is that of *integrity versus despair*. This involves preparing for and accepting the reality of death, and a review or summing up of one's life thus far. It results in either satisfaction with one's accomplishments, be they occupational, social or familial, or a desperate feeling one has not achieved everything one intended and there is insufficient time left to do so. Erikson also asserted the search for identity was lifelong and is challenged in late adulthood because of potentially deteriorating health, appearance and loss of an occupational role (Whitbourne, 2001), all of which are often central to a positive identity. However, many older people's values, personalities, attitudes and outlook on life remain stable. There is a need to retain a firm but flexible view of identity, one danger being refusal to alter previous self-concepts, such as identity based on looks or occupation or fitness, necessitating running 10 miles a day or frequent plastic surgery. The other risk is, alternatively, adopting a completely new identity, which may adhere to negative stereotypes of elderly people as passive and vulnerable, and involve submerging personality and self in the process.

There are a number of stratification theories which explain changes in old age. The oldest theory, *disengagement theory* (Cummings and Henry, 1961), is a role-stripping theory. It contends elderly people and mainstream society mutually withdraw socially and psychologically from each other and this is beneficial for both parties as it frees up opportunities for younger people and alleviates older people's responsibilities. Disengagement theory has been criticized because of its functionalist and ageist assumptions and the implicit focus it places on economically productive potential. It additionally assumes disengagement is a mutual process, but psychologists often argue that, if people do withdraw, it is generally unwillingly because they are marginalized and excluded (Rosow, 1985). It has also been argued disengagement theory can be used to justify policies which exclude or ghettoize older people (Estes et al., 2001), such as establishing segregated accommodation (D. Tanner and Harris, 2008). Research shows the more active and engaged in hobbies and interests older people are, the greater longevity and life satisfaction they have, although a lifelong passion for dangerous sports may have to be substituted for other more sedate activities like bungee jumping! Older people therefore need to substitute relinquished roles and identities, such as occupational ones, with others to avoid a reduced sense of identity and enhance self-esteem (Stuart-Hamilton, 2006). In accordance, *socioemotional selectivity theory* posits that, when older people perceive their future as open-ended, they frequently concentrate on knowledge acquisition and wider social engagement, but if faced with perceived inevitable decline and death, they assume an emotion-related focus with the greatest potential of positive gratification (Fung and Carstensen, 2004).

Negative stratification by gender and ethnicity combined with age stratification may also lead to multiple discrimination, often called *double* or *triple jeopardy* (Cruikshank, 2003). However, some characteristics which may, for example, have disadvantaged women when they were younger, such as socialization into nurturant roles, mean they are more likely to be both sensitive to others and independent in old age and thus to possess the skills to make new acquaintances.

Another core psychological theory is *continuity theory* which emphasizes how, in response to changing systems, contexts and individual states, individuals adapt but the core of their personality and interests show continuity. So a healthy retired ex-head teacher who has always been religious, altruistic and interested in justice may still do voluntary teaching or be on the school's board of governors. They may also become a part-time magistrate or support vulnerable people in their local church or community. Retired people may also occupy themselves with tasks at home such as redecorating and maintaining their house in a pristine condition, the hours of housework done also increasing post retirement. Although most elderly people choose to stay in their home, health needs and downsizing may lead to moving to purpose-built or sheltered accommodation. In the USA and Australia there has been a rise in retirement communities, purpose-built settings exclusively for the elderly which cater for their perceived social and changing health needs within one location. There is also a trend for people to retire to warmer climes or spend extended holidays there, with some British people retiring to live in Spain and Italy, Benidorm being one popular British destination and many elderly Americans choosing the sunshine states such as Florida. However, this inevitably depends upon fiscal, capital and reciprocal health and pension arrangements between the countries, as well as the currency exchange rate.

Losing a spouse or a long-term partner is also an inevitable part of old age for 50 per cent of those partnered. With heterosexual couples, in the USA and the UK, it is more common for men to marry women a few years younger and because women on average live longer, they are in the USA likely to outlive their husbands, often quite considerably. But widows tend to adapt better than widowers, who are often very dependent on their wives for both companionship and a range of other support, and widows are voluntarily less likely to remarry (K. Berger, 2005). The widowed and divorced are often lonelier than those never married. The more partners lost and the more recent the loss, the lonelier one is likely to be (Peters and Liefbroer, 1997), although the size of social networks prior to the loss is an important mediator. Perhaps surprisingly, older people's satisfaction with life is more linked to the quality and quantity of their friendships than contact with younger family (Lawton et al., 1999). This may be because even though the older generation often provide familial support, for example through caring for grandchildren, some feel their opinions are ignored or rejected, or they self-censor to prevent conflict (Bengston, 2001). Others who receive support from younger kin may feel guilty and indebted. Those who are childless, either involuntarily or through choice, seem no less satisfied with their lives than others. In one study, when asked to list regrets, childlessness was placed half-way down or lower by most participants (Jeffries and Konnert, 2002). For the frail elderly who experience major problems with daily living, of those who are not in residential care, the majority are cared for by a relative, most often a spouse, daughter or daughter-in-law.

Old age and sociology

Like psychologists, sociologists recognize that during old age most elderly people are likely to suffer at least some cognitive and physical decline and are more at risk of certain illnesses and diseases. However, sociologists place a lot more emphasis than psychologists on the heterogeneity of old age and how diversity and inequality throughout life may increasingly affect it – known as *cumulative advantage/disadvantage* (Dannefer and Miklowski, 2006) – examining how what may seem to be very personal events are profoundly influenced by the social (Phillipson, 1997). Although there is no legal definition of old age (Brammer, 2007), it is a social construction and therefore a relative concept, but one that is often construed negatively by both society generally and older people themselves. This is despite the fact older people's ages can be seen to vary from 65 to 90+, with similar variation in almost every attribute or characteristic they possess. Nevertheless, both insidious and ingrained negative attitudes result in considerable *ageism* – the systematic stereotyping of and discrimination against individuals on the basis of their age. Older people rarely label themselves as elderly because of this, and completely disassociate themselves from their mirror image, seeing the person inside as very different and unconnected with their actual and reflected appearance, a phenomenon known as the 'mask of ageing' (mentioned in the previous chapter) (Featherstone and Wernick, 1994).

Ageism

Examples of ageism are both individual and structural. Some forms of ageism range from *subtle ageism* which involves treating the elderly as a homogeneous group, to *compassionate ageism* which is paternalistic but benevolent in intent, thought preferable to direct discrimination and overt hostility. Examples of ageism range from using terms like 'old dear' to refer to elderly ladies, talking in a patronizing, infantilistic manner to the elderly, sending ageist supposedly humorous birthday cards, through to assuming that, if an elderly person (but not a younger person) forgets a word or trips, this is automatically because they are elderly and their senses and limbs are failing. *Institutional ageism* includes enforced retirement at a certain age, although employers now have a duty to *consider* requests to work beyond retirement age (Employment Equality (Age) Regulations, 2006). A recent Age Concern study (2007) found ageism was the most pervasive form of discrimination in the UK, affecting 29 per cent of adults. Butler (1987) found old people were perceived by others as senile, rigid and possessing outdated views on morality and rendundant skills. Correspondingly, another Age Concern survey (2005) reported one in three respondents believed the over-70s are incompetent and incapable. Even in TV and film older people are more likely than younger age groups to be exploited for the purposes of humour via stereotypes of physical, cognitive and sexual impotency (Zebrowitz and Montepare, 2000).

It could also be argued that the level the national pension is paid at is ageist as it puts many elderly people 'on the breadline' and is not in line with the average national wage (Blytheway, 1995). In the UK, 600,000 pensioners now rely on means-tested benefits and are living below the poverty line (Walker and Foster, 2006). Many benefits are paid at a lower level than in other European countries (Naegel and Walker, 2007) and, at the beginning of the twenty-first century, a quarter of all old people were entitled to some income support because their own income was so minimal (Vincent, 2003). The Department for Work and Pensions additionally estimated that, between 2000 and 2001, between 24 per cent and 32 per cent of pensioners entitled to the Minimum Income Guarantee did not claim it, either because they were unaware of their rights, because the forms were too complex or because they felt claiming stigmatized them (Price, 2006; Age Concern, 2005). Minimal income reinforces the stereotype that poverty is a natural consequence of old age, well illustrated by the discounts and concessions that are offered to pensioners on a regular basis. These create the view that the elderly are naturally dependent and a burden on the state, whereas, if they were paid a sufficient pension, such discounts, which could be seen as a patronizing optional 'kindness', would be unnecessary.

The medicalization of old age has also led to medical ageism which assumes inaccurately that old age and ill health are intrinsically interlinked. Nevertheless, many health care practices have also been shown to be ageist, through not offering breast screening, despite clinical need, for cancer, or support with giving up smoking, to the over-65s (Timonen, 2008). Depression is often untreated or rarely directed to specialist mental health care, only 15 per cent of elderly people receiving any treatment at all, in comparison with much higher proportions of younger adults with depression and anxiety (Equalities Review Panel, 2007). Elderly people received into casualty are also far less likely to be subject to 'aggressive' and sustained resuscitation attempts than younger people, intimating their lives are accorded lower value (Timmermans, 1999). Patients over 65 also have a lower probability of referral to cardiac rehabilitation programmes (Harries et al., 2007). Furthermore, older patients admitted into hospital with trauma or fracture are more likely to have their operations delayed, with younger people's needs taking preference (British Geriatrics Society, 2007), and six out of ten older people are additionally at risk of becoming malnourished or their condition worsening whilst in hospital (Age Concern, 2007). Such practices are exacerbated through, for example, the professional socialization of nursing students into seeing working with elderly patients as dull and routine (McLafferty and Morrison, 2004). The development of managerialism and the rise of care management within Social Services departments, and restricted budgets, have also been experienced by social workers as controlling and leading to poorer social work practice with elderly service users (Lymberry, 2004). A recent newspaper headline, furthermore, reported that some elderly care homes were refusing to take patients with dementia unless they had feeding tubes fitted, a process that is mostly unnecessary, carries risks and deprives people of the enjoyment and social interaction involved with eating and drinking (Bosely, 2010).

Older people themselves are sensitive to negative stereotypes and may self-internalize them. A study testing younger adults and older adults on memory abilities found those older adults who were implicitly primed with negative stereotypes about older people did worse than older adults who were not and younger adults who also received the same priming (Levy, 1996). Younger people may also implicitly assume old people are far less able to cope than they actually are and may unknowingly convey this in their interactions, known as 'ambiguous normative guidance' (Johnson, 1999), which leads elderly people to regard themselves as others do and ultimately to a diminishment in their skills. In one study, whilst few elderly people had experienced outright aggression or hostility, most had been treated negatively in some ways, occasionally positively, and were accustomed to various external parties scrutinizing their vulnerability (Minichiello et al., 2000). Elder abuse is also common, whether it be sexual, financial, physical or emotional. Current estimates suggest between 1 and 2 million people (2–10 per cent of those aged 65-plus) have been injured, exploited or mistreated by a family member or caregiver they depended on for care and protection (Thobaben, 2008). The fact these alarming statistics are rarely reported suggests again an implicit, institutionalized ageism and that the abuse of elderly people is seen as less serious than child abuse.

Structured Dependency Theory and the Civilizing Process

Although sociologists refer to and are generally critical – as are contemporary psychologists – of early theories of ageing such as disengagement theory, sociology advances a more structural theory, *the political economy perspective*, sometimes known as *structured or enforced dependency theory* (Townsend, 2006) to understand the position of elderly people and ageism's impact. This theory demonstrates ageism is not an individualized issue by showing how external structures and forces, such as global capitalism and a statutory retirement age actually force people into poverty by preventing them from working. For many the state pension, which in 2008 was £90.70, is their only source of income (Pollock, 2008). Although six out of ten households have additional occupational or private pensions, these only contribute a tiny supplement (Baldock, 2000). There is also evidence that elderly people, particularly those living alone, are subject to much unseen poverty and often choose between paying heating bills and buying food, which is particularly dangerous in the winter because of the risk of hypothermia (Bradshaw, 2008). Even those who have been able to make additional financial provision for themselves through private pension funds are currently at risk because of their falling value (Cebulla et al., 2007), and the recent collapse of many banks and fiscal institutions may further exacerbate this. Although the political economy perspective appears to have relevance in contemporary society, Elias suggested that negative attitudes towards the elderly may also be based upon the way in which our society has, since mediaeval times, become less tolerant of those unprepared or unable to exercise bodily and emotional restraint in public. Elias (1994) argues this civilizing process has become, throughout history, embedded in our personalities, shaming those who are unable to, for example, control their dribbling or urinary functions – namely, the elderly with physical and mental difficulties and younger people with a disability, both of whom, Elias claims, in contemporary societies often incite revulsion from others.

Social Cues to Old Age and Variations in Experience According to Cohort and Generation

Vincent (2003) shows how various social cues signal a person is becoming older, and these often also have direct impacts upon their life.

These may include *bodily reminders* such as recognition of becoming less fit or slower; *generational reminders* such as seeing your parents become frail and die, or being the oldest member of the family or the last living member of particular social groups; and *contextual reminders* in relation to work, social life and home, such as being the oldest person at work, becoming distanced from the lives and experiences of your students if you are a lecturer, or expecting or watching friends suffer from life-threatening illnesses.

The cohort and generation you emanate from will also have profound effects on how you experience old age, and even cohorts born within a few years of each other may have vastly divergent experiences through the life course as well as in old age. Cribier (1989) analysed two longitudinal, representative studies of people who initially drew their pensions in Paris in 1972 and 1984. The First World War divided the dates of the two cohorts and led to greater educational opportunities for the younger cohort, which impacted on enhanced employment opportunities. Those in the younger cohort had more children and had them closer together than the older cohort, possibly because they were the first recipients of income support and social housing. The younger cohort were more likely to have parents alive still but less likely to want to live with them, associated with the decline in the extended family. They were more prone to be affluent than the older cohort and to retire earlier and live in more desirable areas. Although only eleven years apart, because of profound social, economic and familial changes, these cohorts had very different experiences throughout life and during their old age.

With those from the Caribbean and South Asia, there are also significant differences between many of the early, first-generation immigrants who came to Britain between the 1940s and 1960s, who are now mostly elderly, and their British-born children and families. Many first-generation immigrants view themselves as *denizens* – temporary visitors to Britain and essentially outsiders, despite the fact most will never return to their birth countries because their younger families live here. They are also far less vocal about racism and their rights despite being subject to considerable racism for many years after they arrived. This initially included much verbal and physical abuse, 'colour bars' – such as exclusion from hotels, public houses, shops and clubs which had notices on the door with phrases inscribed upon them such as 'no blacks, no Irish and no gypsies' – overcrowding, poverty and being located in the most undesirable low-paid jobs (read Andrea Levy's novel *Small Island* for an evocative description). Their children all speak English, regard themselves as British citizens and Britain as their home, and are much more political about refusing to accept racial aggression, low-paid jobs, inferior education or being identified as foreigners or 'invitees in a host country' (Small and Solomos, 2007: 252; Hussain and Bagguley, 2005).

Old Age and Social Divisions

Age can be seen as a social division in the same way as gender, race/ethnicity and sexuality are, although it differs though because it only affects you during a certain time period and you have to navigate your way through it without past experience and knowledge. You may yourself also have been guilty of ageism at a younger age. Ageism combines with other social divisions and sociologists tend to use the same language as psychologists, *double* or *triple jeopardy*, to describe multiple oppressions which may include ageism, sexism or racism and the interactions between them. For example, elderly women are not immune from the pressure on all women to look a certain way and exude beauty, vitality and youthfulness. Hence one sees a string of affluent but ageing actresses and media personalities such as Cher, Jackie Collins, Dolly Parton, Sharon Osborne and Joan Rivers resorting to extensive and recurrent plastic surgery to mimic the look of a younger woman. Conversely, women who are labelled 'mutton dressed as lamb', rather than 'growing old gracefully' are ridiculed for not acting or dressing their age (Fairhurst, 1998). A paradox exists here because women are surrounded by images of youthful beauty, yet if they are judged as emulating it unsuccessfully they are denigrated. 'Growing old gracefully' would, according to society, be admitting one was not attractive or sexually desirable, so the concept itself is not alluring and the participants in Fairhurst's study talked about the importance of smartness and moderation in dress and appearance.

Older women today, like older men, are also affected by the idea of the body as a lifelong reflective project we can mould and influence through sport, make-up, body building, dieting and surgery, but when that becomes harder and harder to do because of visible ageing and physical decline, then this potentially leads to existential anxiety about death as well as self-devaluation. Women are also disadvantaged financially when older, known as *the feminization of poverty* in old age. They are more likely than men to have taken time out of the work force to care for children, to have accepted lower-paid and part-time jobs, and to outlive their male partners. Consequently, labour market disadvantages throughout life translate into lower income in old age, with only 38 per cent of women having a private occupational pension compared with 64 per cent of men (EOC, 2001). Women are also more likely to live alone and end their days in residential care than older men (Arber, 2006; Bond et al., 2007).

Although little research exists on elderly men and ageing, a special edition on this topic in one journal illuminates this neglected area. Drawing from both her own and others' research, van den Hoonaard's (2007) editorial argues ageing and the death of a partner is profoundly problematic for older men and challenges their previous constructions of masculinity. Consequently, the older widowed men she interviewed often referred to themselves as bachelors, resisting a widower identity with its connotations of possible loss, grief and loneliness. Furthermore, these older men often symbolically re-masculinized and reconstructed tasks they would have previously seen as feminine, but now had to do, such as cooking and cleaning, in technological and scientific ways. Some, for example, talked of the technology of vacuuming and cooking as a necessary activity for feeding 'fuel' to the body, thereby conceptualizing their body as a machine. Other research articles in this editorial show how older men fight against or deny their declining strength and society's view of them as unproductive, often reasserting their masculinity by demeaning women and femininity in comparison to themselves, refusing to show overt emotion and highlighting their previous career or sporting achievements.

With the ethnic-minority women interviewed as part of an Economic and Social Research Council (ESRC) project which included British Muslim, Dominican, African-Caribbean and Irish women, mostly in their sixties, although many had low incomes and health problems, they were very positive about their lives, and work and leisure were experienced as empowering, and often religious or community activities as a source of companionship and social inclusion (Wray, 2003). Because of cumulative disadvantage throughout life, including poor educational and employment opportunities, disabled people are likely to be subjected to poverty in old age because many will not have been able to accumulate sufficient savings or pensions to elevate their standard of living (Hyde, 2006).

Sexuality in old age is often characterized as either non-existent or heterosexual and male, female sexuality being frequently invisibilized. Even then, older male sexuality is still depicted as unattractive and predatory, with terms like 'dirty old man' being commonly used. These suggest older men are lecherous and obsessed with younger women or have the inclination to have sex but are impotent or seek it in inappropriate ways (Waltz, 2002). However, there are exceptions, with some older men, namely those with financial acumen or ageing film stars, being seen as distinguished and desirable. Although the marketing of Viagra as a cure-all for male impotence may appear to have shattered the stigma around admitting to sexual problems, the perceived attitude of the GP, the internalization of the asexual stereotype and the belief sex was a taboo subject and that younger people should receive treatment first, were major barriers to asking for help with sexual problems for older men (Gott and Hinchliff, 2003).

One study of the sexual behaviour of people with dementia in a residential home found heterosexual behaviour was more tolerated than homosexual behaviour, even when heterosexual advances were directed towards staff and the homosexual behaviour in question only involved two men holding hands (Archibald, 1998). Another study found psychiatrists were more likely to take a sexual history from middle-aged men than from older men with the same symptoms and, if a diagnosis of sexual dysfunction was given, younger men would tend to be referred for sexual therapy whereas older men were more likely to be referred to generic community psychiatric nurses (Bourman and Arcelus, 2001).

Heath (2002) asserts that, in residential care, same-sex partners are commonly restricted in relation to visiting rights because they are not legally deemed as 'family', and that older gay men are excluded and self-exclude from the gay 'community', which tends to be centred on the nightclubbing scene and focused on youth, looks and vitality. They are often silent about their sexuality because they were brought up in an era in which homosexuality was seen as deviant and criminalized. Because of combined and potent discriminatory attitudes about homosexuality, race/ethnicity and age, certain groups are also less likely to be considered at higher risk of HIV/AIDS than others, although 10 per cent of cases are in the over-50s and one group at significant risk are older ethnic/racial-minority males who have sex with other men (Jimenez, 2003).

Social class and socioeconomic status also impact significantly on one's experience of old age. The notion of the third age as a time for casting off work responsibilities and enjoying one's leisure and life to the full may not be realistic for the old from working-class backgrounds, where for some men a life of hard physical work may have taken its toll and, for both sexes, limited income may mean they have to continue to work and cannot afford a fit, leisurely old age. A recent statistical study calculating whether increased life expectancy at middle age has added quality of life to those from all socioeconomic groupings, focused on the younger old from 50 to 70 years old. It found the difference in quality of life between the professional and managerial group and the lowest occupational grouping was of such a size it compared with that due to having a long-standing limiting illness (Blane et al., 2007) and was exacerbated in old age. This calls into question the possibility of the third age for all, although at least half of all social class groupings are able to enjoy a third age lifestyle. However, this lifestyle is strongly linked not only with possessing a sizeable occupational pension but also to social networks, health and area of residence, which become more important when faced with increasing difficulties in old age (Deeming and Keen, 2002). Life expectancy also remains strongly determined by environment and geographical variation, with life expectancy being 81 years for men in East Dorset but only 69.1 years in Glasgow (Office for National Statistics, 2004).

The Demographic Time Bomb

With the advent of a rapidly ageing or greying population and the numbers of the oldest old or frail old becoming significant in many Western countries, concerns have been raised about the financial ability of nations to care for their elderly. Sometimes these have been phrased in a benevolent manner. At other times, great hostility has been shown to older people and they have been represented as a burden in terms of their health and social care needs and a threat to the younger generations' financial security, with old people on pensions being seen as no better than social security claimants (G. Wilson, 2000). A recent Age Concern public survey (2007) found 32 per cent of respondents believed the increasing numbers of elderly people in the UK would have a detrimental impact on life for everyone compared to 15 per cent who felt a positive effect would result, although 64 per cent felt older people had contributed more to the system than they were extracting, compared to 16 per cent who felt otherwise. Vincent (2006) has argued that the media and politicians have amplified the problem to such an extent that coverage has become alarmist and taken on the shape of a moral panic. This attitude has moved from national level to a global context, with financial institutions such as the World Bank and World Trade Organization contributing to this manufactured construction of a crisis and subsequent scaremongering (Estes et al., 2001). This is particularly prevalent in the USA as the President's Council on Bioethics demonstrates: 'The coming of the mass geriatric society will affect every dimension of human and social life . . . in the extreme there is the unwholesome possibility of "a war between the generations", as people insist on securing their own advantage with little regard for intergenerational good and with no organized voice to speak up for the rising generations' (COB, 2005: 11).

But is the concern about the needs of older people becoming unmanageable and a burden justifiable in any way, or is this panic-mongering another form of ageist discrimination manifesting itself? According to the European Commission, utilizing Eurostat population projections and raising care costs in line with economic growth, care expenditure is likely to double in cost between 2000 and 2050 (Commas-Herrera et al., 2006). However, in the UK, the mixed economy of care and local authorities' (LAs') discretionary rationing through the 'Fair Access to Care' eligibility criteria have created a situation where low-level preventative needs are unmet and the LA only responds in a crisis situation, arguably increasing care costs at a later date. There is no doubt that some elderly people, namely largely proportions of the frail or 'old old', may need significant care, but what is not taken into account is older people's paid and unpaid contributions to society. Older people have contributed to their national state pensions throughout their working lives and many have also paid into occupational or private pensions. When elderly people enter residential care, whatever assets they may possess, such as a house, are also used to pay for this, although how fair this is remains debatable.

Many older people offer informal care to other elderly and disabled people in their communities. One study estimated unpaid carers in the UK saved the economy £87 billion per year, which exceeds the NHS budget of £81.67 billion; and that, out of 6 million unpaid carers, over 2 million were over 50 years of age and 24 per cent were over 75 (Buckner and Yeandle, 2007). According to 2010 published rates, the most carers paid by the state could receive was £53.90 per week for a minimum of 35 hours (a maximum rate of £1.54 per hour). They are therefore paid approximately a quarter of the minimum wage for full-time workers over 22, who could earn £203 for a 35-hour week. Many third-generation older people (aged 55–75) are also likely to be the providers of care to their adult children and grandchildren (Grundy, 2005). According to the Audit Commission report *Don't Stop Me Now: Preparing for an Ageing Population* (2008), 60 per cent of childcare provision is supplied by grandparents, saving the country an estimated £4 billion per year. It has therefore been suggested that, rather than intergenerational conflict emerging, more reciprocal intergenerational relationships are being formed, with parents more likely to offer care to their own parent if they in turn are prepared to offer care to grandchildren (Bengston and Putney, 2006; Grundy, 2005). However, a recent Equality and Human Rights Commission (EHRC) report asserts grandparents in low-income families risk financial hardship if they relinquish paid work or reduce their hours in order to provide such free childcare. The government's dual aims of increasing the number of both lone parents and older people doing paid work, therefore, seem to be working against each other (Griggs, 2010).

Elderly people are also increasingly offering their services to voluntary organizations, which can benefit the lives of others as well as enhance their own status and psychological/social wellbeing (Biggs, 2006; Erlinghagen and Hank, 2006). Many older people want to continue paid work, either par-ttime or full-time, into their old age, and when B&Q opened a store staffed entirely by older people absenteeism decreased by 39 per cent, staff turnover became less and profits went up by 18 per cent. Furthermore, there is the financial power of the 'grey' pound, with some elderly people, particularly the more affluent, becoming active consumers (Bond and Cabrero, 2007; Blaikie, 2006). They feed into the economy through purchasing holidays and buying consumer goods which may include new computer technologies, the term 'silver surfers' being coined to describe computer-literate elderly people.

How do we repay older people for their contribution to society throughout life and in old age? We represent them as a burden, as dependent, as unproductive, and as draining our national resources. When and if they enter residential care, we staff such institutions with low-status, poorly paid and negligibly trained staff. As previously stated, negative representations can become internalized by older people and lead to psychological ill health and decreases in their capacities. Even if older people are dependent in some ways, so are we all, and a modicum of dependency does not mean you cannot be productive for society in other ways. The manufactured *crisis* of the ageing population or the pension crisis has also been in the interests of, and generated by, specific financial elites who are concerned with profit-making from pension schemes and whose greed and financial mismanagement have led to many collapsing (Vincent, 2006). The issue is not, as it has been presented, solely about generational inequality and a younger generation supporting the older generation, worrying they will not receive an equivalent pension (Johnson, 1995). It is also about social justice and exploitation and how the state plays a role in reproducing unacceptably high levels of wealth and power in certain groups (Vincent, 2006).

If a less short-termist, wider and more balanced view of redistribution was taken and older populations were not represented as unproductive burdens, then the issue need not necessarily be framed as a crisis. It is interesting, as Vincent points out, that there is rarely similar concern expressed about issues such as the long-term costs of safely disposing of nuclear or other waste or of global warming, much of which has been generated by profit-making capitalist industries, which evade bearing the brunt of the long-term costs they generate.

Conclusion

This chapter has examined old age from sociological and psychological perspectives, although there is much interdisciplinary overlap.

In the introduction, the negative representations and connotations surrounding old age in Western societies were introduced and compared with how old age is represented differently in diverse cultures and during other time periods. Western understandings of old age were contextualized within a medical-model geriatric perspective that conceptualized old age as synonymous with disease, decline and ultimately death. Old age was also located within the confines of global capitalism, in which those seen as unproductive and needy are demeaned and negated. The recent delineations between a third and fourth age were also introduced and the heterogeneity of older people was stressed. The importance of understanding old age in post-industrial societies was also asserted because of the presence of and increase in ageing or greying populations. In the section on psychology, competing theories of ageing were examined, and physical changes during late adulthood, their implications and possible compensations to losses were described and analysed. Cognitive changes were also evaluated, as were diseases that become prominent in old age and are associated with serious cognitive decline, such as Alzheimer's disease. Erikson's final psychosocial stage of integrity versus despair was considered and different psychological theories about old age, withdrawal and activity were investigated, alongside social changes relating to friends and family in old age.

In the section on sociology, how ageism operates and impacts on older people's behaviour and self-concept was investigated, with a particular emphasis on pensions and income support in old age, alongside health care provision. Sociological theories of old age such as the structured dependency theory and Elias' notion of the civilizing process, were also analysed to try to better understand ageism and older people's position within contemporary society. How older people recognize socially they are aging, and the different life experiences cohorts and generations not far apart can have, were then examined. How ageism interacts with other social divisions such as social class, gender and sexuality was then explored to show how cumulative disadvantage throughout the life course can further be impacted upon by old age and ageism. Finally, the common perception of old people as a financial burden or as representing a demographic time bomb was critically investigated and found to be lacking. This was not only because many old people are independent and productive throughout their old age, but also because constructions of older people as a burden have been generated by particular financial elites. These have vested interests in accruing profit from pensions and other insurance schemes and do not take into account a long-term or social justice viewpoint.

Reflection and discussion questions

Is old age always a time of significant decline, disability and illness?

In what ways are we an ageist society in respect of older people?

How might representations and experiences of old age differ across culture and history?

Recommended reading

Life span development texts have useful and comprehensive sections on old age although most are North American and therefore largely incorporate US statistics and research studies. UK sociological books worth referring to include Vincent's (2003) key introductory text and both Bond et al.'s (2007) and Vincent et al.'s (2006) edited texts. Pertinent journals include *Ageing and Society*, *Psychology and Aging*, the *Journal of Aging Studies* and the *Journal of Gerontology*.

CHAPTER
08
Death, Dying, Grief and Loss

Death is the one final inevitability in our lives, even more inescapable than paying taxes, and we are the only species who has any understanding of death and knows they will die. Our ancestors accepted death as an everyday communal part of life and were psychologically and physically very close to it, but we confront death today far less frequently, publicly or personally. In our often urbanized, fragmented and impersonal Western societies, religion, the family and the community now play a much smaller role in explaining and handling death than in previous eras. Improved environmental conditions and medical technology have led to greater longevity. People often die in hospital or, when someone dies unexpectedly, the body is immediately removed to the funeral directors or coroners. This institutionalized medicalization and bureaucratization of death shields us from most aspects of it, alongside its less obvious occurrence. We consequently often find death threatening and an affront to the emphasis we place on youth, vitality, beauty and the value of the individual. The positing of bereavement grief as potentially deviant or pathological, furthermore, leaves many people fearful about how they will or should react when someone close to them dies.

Psychology and sociology examine different aspects related to death and dying. Psychology engages primarily with the emotional experience of the dying or bereaved individual whereas sociology concentrates on the social and historical contexts and their impact on how death is represented and responded to. Psychological theories relating to grief and loss, however, do not pertain exclusively to bereavement. One may grieve during a relationship breakdown or after a shift from a valued way of life to one potentially less valued, but here bereavement acts as a key exemplar of grief and loss theories. This chapter initially appraises traditional and contemporary psychological perspectives, followed by the sociological 'take', later synthesizing them to present a more coherent, interdisciplinary understanding of grief, loss, death and dying.

Bereavement and psychology

Traditional psychological theories of grief and loss were initially linear and stage or phase focused. They treated grief processes as if they were universal across all contexts, historical time periods, cultures and people. They therefore ignored social factors and individual variation, focusing on observable processes and patterns, shortcomings which have been attributed to psychology's positivist paradigm and privileging of quantitative methods (C. Valentine, 2006). More recent theories are less linear and more context aware, although the emphasis on variation is still limited. The older traditional theories are also often the ones taught uncritically to health and welfare students and expounded by the mass media. Initially in this section the mainstream traditional theories will be analysed and then later developments addressed. Mainstream theories originally emanated from Bowlby's theories on grief and loss which primarily addressed the mother/child relationship and children's subsequent social and psychological functioning (Bowlby, 1990). These theories are largely intra-psychic and deal with separation anxiety and the emotional processes which allow the living successfully to separate psychologically from those deceased.

Mainstream Psychological Theories

Kubler Ross' (1969) exposition of how individuals adjust to a prognosis of terminal illness, through the stages of denial, then anger, negotiation or bargaining, depression/resignation and finally acceptance, with hope persisting throughout, is probably the most well-known stage theory of grief. Her book was based loosely on clinical observations and conversations with dying patients and clinicians, stemming from her empathizing with the isolation dying people experienced. She viewed impending death as 'the biggest crisis people had to face', which necessitated developing coping and defence mechanisms (1969: 21). Her theory was later extended to explain the stages of grief for those bereaved as well as those who are dying. Kastenbaum (1998), however, claims there is no evidence to confirm all dying or bereaved people go through all or even any of the five stages or that they normally follow a particular order, although, to be fair to Kubler Ross, she has to some extent been misinterpreted as she did not stipulate all individuals necessarily went through every stage or that the process was always linear (C. Valentine, 2006). Kastenbaum also criticizes the theory for being overly prescriptive as people may be labelled inadequate or 'stuck' if they don't progress through all stages sequentially, asserting Kubler Ross neglects both the holism of a person's life and the impact the environment has, in favour of focusing on particular preordained stages.

Parkes (1972), also a popular stage theorist, deals with stages involving distress and impaired functioning which then progress to psychological recovery and resolution. Parkes' four chronological stages proceed from an initial stage involving shock, numbness or disbelief to a secondary stage where grief, anger, searching, guilt or sadness are paramount. Despair constitutes the third stage, and acceptance or adjustment the final stage. Worden (1991) focuses more on the active accomplishment of certain tasks to resolve bereavement grief. These include accepting the reality of the loss, 'working through' the grief, adjusting to life without the dead person and then being able to relocate them to a different and less central place. Although Worden (1991) recognizes the complexity involved, acknowledging the possibility of movement back and forth between stages, the implication in his early work is that grief resolution is essentially forward-moving and linear. However, when focusing later on child grief, Worden (1996) is more attuned to the individuality and fluidity of grief. This later work has been heralded as a paradigmatic shift away from the earlier traditional linear phase theories (Rothaupt and Becker, 2007). Worden, furthermore, emphasizes the importance of the relationship concerned, and how grieving differs according to whether the relationship was close, distant, conflictual or ambivalent and whether the death was anticipated, unexpected, suicide, a murder, or a 'natural' or unnatural death.

Recent Challenges and Modifications

There have been recent challenges regarding the claim that recovery and moving on means separating oneself off from the deceased and one's previous relationship with them. Some theorists now argue that, either consciously or unconsciously, taking on interests and characteristics of the dead person is a healthy not a pathological grief reaction (Corr, 1989/1999; C. A. Walter, 2003; T. Walter, 1999). Maintaining continuing bonds with the dead person is also beginning to be seen as acceptable and normal. Empirical validation for this emanates from studies of parents whose children have died (Rando, 1986), of the partners of men who died from AIDS (Richards, Acree and Folkman, 1999) and of older widows (Hallam, Hockey and Howarth, 1999). T. Walter (1999) proposes a biographical model of grief, in which he argues that, because of the dissolution of extended and close family networks, linked to increasing geographical mobility in a modernist society, people may only have a partial knowledge of the dead person's life. They therefore may grieve by seeking out others who knew the person well and questioning them and listening to their accounts. Recent theorists have also challenged stage theorists' claims that people never really accept a prognosis of death or recover from a serious bereavement. They suggest terms like 'coping' and 'managing' may be more realistic than those suggesting full resolution or recovery (Rothaupt and Becker, 2007).

One revisionist view of grieving asserts there are themes that may occur post bereavement but many can occur at once. These therefore are not necessarily stage based but each may have a common trajectory. According to Jacobs et al. (1986), depression, separation anxiety and distress could all be experienced simultaneously but distress is likely to be initially very high but drop drastically within a month and then slowly to very low levels over the next five months. Despair and depression are likely to start low, reach a peak at five months and then slowly drop. Separation anxiety starts at a moderate level, rises to high levels within the first two months and then declines to a lowish level at six months. Furthermore, Bowlby's (1990) view – that if individuals do not grieve at the time, they will suffer later, and if there is immediate distress, there will be a good outcome – is not borne out by the research. This shows, conversely, *absent grief*, where little or no distress is expressed at the time or much later, is remarkably common, and delayed grief very rare, and that extreme distress at the time may still engender problems many years later. In Wortman and Silver's 1990 study of spouses, absent grief was noted in 24 per cent of their sample, but in other studies they reviewed the proportion rose as high as 77 per cent. Research with parents whose children have died, conversely, indicates most experience profound long-term loss, impacting significantly on their lives and relationships (Riches and Dawson, 2000).

Social factors and personality differences, including kinship and peer support and age, ethnicity and gender, have also recently featured as important factors in psychological accounts. For example, Martin and Doka (2000) assert the existence of two different gendered grieving styles but claim neither is necessarily superior to the other. *Affective grieving* entails deep and overt expressions of distress and the search for support and validation and is associated with more feminine patterns of grief. *Cognitive grieving* in contrast is more associated with acceptable forms of 'unemotional' masculine behaviour. It focuses on active and instrumental ways of coping, achieved, for example, through organizing funeral arrangements or engaging in new activities or seeking companions. Different research studies have to some extent corroborated this gendered theory but not as fully as one might expect (Riches and Dawson, 2000; Murphy et al., 2002). Stroebe and Schut (1999) also present a more sophisticated challenge to earlier linear models by developing a dual process model. This takes into account both the grieving process and how the bereaved person copes with associated changes, suggesting people fluctuate back and forth between feelings of loss and actively rebuilding their lives, at times denying their loss and at other times confronting it.

Traditional stage or phase theories, because of their Western, linear and normative prescriptions, have also led to grief judged as delayed, lengthy, emotionally debilitating or 'masked' subsequently being labelled as abnormal, pathological or complicated (Corr, 1998/1999; Greenstreet, 2004). There is a danger that grief which does not follow expected patterns may become medicalized as a psychiatric disorder (Lichtental et al., 2004), without a corresponding understanding of the importance of the cultural or socioeconomic context. Arthur Kleinman, a physician and an anthropologist, insightfully points out that what may be seen as a normal emotional response to bereavement in some social contexts, such as grief lasting up to two years, could now, according to the *Diagnostic and Statistical Manual of Mental Disorders*, 4th edition (DSM-IV), be seen as a depressive disorder after two months (Kleinman, 2004).

Kleinman also suggests some depressive disorders may conversely not be diagnosed as such because of gender, age, social class and cultural differences. Chinese immigrants in the USA express depression in culturally coded ways, not through sadness but through boredom, general discomfort, dizziness, the experience of pain and extreme tiredness. Despite DSM-IV, presenting depression as the only recognized psychiatric complication of abnormal grief, an absence of consensus exists because recent research has uncovered different symptomatology to that associated with depression and anxiety (Dodd et al., 2005). This includes distinctive EEG sleep patterns, and relationships to the bereaved which include obsessive preoccupation, symptoms such as emotional numbness and an avoidance of situations that remind the person of the bereaved. These seem more akin to post-traumatic stress disorder than to depression (Prigerson et al., 1999). In Japan, and where Buddhist and Shinto religions are practised, in contrast to Western British traditions, contact with the deceased is encouraged (Rothaupt and Becker, 2007). In Japan fear of the dead is also unusual, and Klass and Gross (1999: 549) cite the example of a Japanese businessman who whilst watching a production of Shakespeare's play *Hamlet*, could not understand why Hamlet was fearful of the spectre of his dead father.

Disenfranchised Grief

Doka's (1989) concept of *disenfranchised grief*, integrating multi-disciplinary viewpoints, is a prime example of how dangerous these socially unaware stage theories can be if taken literally, as they may in effect 'blame the victim'. Doka asserts some bereavements are more recognized and socially supported than others, and that the grief, the loss or the death can be disenfranchised. Deaths associated with significant stigma or not easily understood, such as those due to AIDS, suicide or assisted suicide, Doka termed 'disenfranchised deaths'. The moral context is also important, and hence a woman grieving over a termination may be treated less sympathetically than one who has spontaneously miscarried. Grief may, furthermore, be disenfranchised if the relationship is not known about by others or seen as insignificant. This could occur with unrequited love, the death of a child's pet, or an adult with learning disabilities losing a parent or carer.

People viewed as unable to grieve, particularly those not seen as fully sentient, such as the young and old, and people with dementia, may also be excluded from partaking in normal grieving rituals or may sometimes not even be informed of the death. Same-sex partnership bereavement may be disenfranchised because of actual or feared discrimination and prejudice, the possibility of being 'in the closet' or only partially open about the relationship, and internalized homophobia. This is exacerbated by the historical criminalization and psychiatrization of gay relationships, alongside recurrent media demonization emanating from right-wing journalists, politicians and religious leaders (Green and Grant, 2008). The combination of two taboo subjects, sexuality and death, furthermore renders the areas especially difficult for both gay people and professionals to navigate and discuss (Bevan and Thompson, 2003). Therefore, although psychological theories of grief and mourning related primarily to bereavement have become more complex and less linear and prescriptive in recent years, they still largely ignore many key social factors or factor them in as additional peripheral facets without understanding their central importance. Modern Western perceptions of bereavement are also still largely conceptualized in terms of the early theories. Kubler Ross' acceptance stage, for example, is mirrored in a leaflet, 'Facing Death', targeted at bereaved individuals: 'Not that you will always have to be gloomy; once you have faced facts and expressed feelings of grief to which they give rise, you will find you are ready to enjoy the next stage of your life' (Parkes, 1988: 3). The next section will therefore examine sociological constructions of death and dying which place the historical, social and cultural context at the forefront and elevate the importance of structural divisions and inequalities.

The sociology of death and dying

The sociology of death and dying became a productive subdiscipline in the 1990s, although, long before this, founding sociologists were writing about death (T. Walter, 2008). Engels, an early materialist sociologist, documented how an exploitative capitalism committed 'social murder' by crippling and killing the working classes. Engels cited statistics from a Liverpool Commission showing that average longevity in 1840 for the upper classes was thirty-five years, for business men and craftsmen twenty-two years, and for those working in the factories and 'in service' fifteen years (1843/1969). Durkheim (1915) discussed Aboriginal funerary rites and how death threatens group solidarity in close communities and encourages collective sentiments, as well as showing how in larger, more developed societies different rates of suicide were strongly influenced by societal factors such as religion and community integration (Durkheim, 1897/2002). For P. Berger (1969), social order was instituted to stave off the meaninglessness and fear surrounding death. Weber (1930) traced how the development of capitalism could be linked to the Protestant Calvinists' belief in a predestined favoured afterlife, hard work and frugality indicating you could potentially be one of the chosen ones. The contemporary sociology of death and dying has also been strongly influenced by other disciplines such as anthropology, and Ariès' pioneering historical analysis of changing attitudes towards death in Western civilizations (1974) was the precursor to many modern studies.

The next section examines historical changes in attitudes and behaviour towards death in the West, as well as giving cross-cultural exemplars to illustrate the different ways in which death and dying can be socially constructed. The impact that medical technology, a preoccupation with health, vitality and youth and improved environmental conditions have on how we experience and view death will be analysed, as will current views that death is a taboo subject and the fact that we are largely sequestered from it. Notions of what a good death and a bad death are will be critically examined, and how social divisions might impact on longevity, ways of dying and grief processes will also be analysed. Contemporary issues such as euthanasia and the institution of the hospice movement will additionally be discussed.

Historical and Cross-cultural Understandings of Death

Ariès (1974) documents five distinct death epochs in Western history over the last millennium. The epoch of *tame death* involved a period where death was not feared. It was accepted as a part of the collective continuum of life in which the dying person had some control and died at home with family and friends present, including children. The *death of self* emerged in the late mediaeval period after the Black Death, alongside increasing individualism. Human beings were seen to express their true and individual selves in the process of dying, although death was still a communal event presided over largely by the Catholic Church (Mellor and Shilling, 1997). Macabre iconography accompanied this period, such as pictures of rotting corpses with maggots and snakes entwined around them. With the rise of science and rational thought, weakened religious influence and the primacy placed on the individual in the 1700s and 1800s, *remote and imminent death* followed. Death was seen to represent a break with life rather than being part of it, and therefore as lonely and isolating.

In the nineteenth century, *death of the other* occurred, and the focus shifted from the death of oneself to that of significant others, along-side a romanticization of death in novels. Dying people, such as those suffering from tuberculosis, were depicted in paintings as beautiful and alluring but also pale, ethereal figures. During this period a belief in the afterlife and the possibility of being reunited with the deceased became popular. Although early Christian doctrine held that one could expect paradise in an afterlife just by being a Christian, by the fifteenth century judgement was made at the time of death and on every living move one had made. It was thus well established by the nineteenth century. In the Victorian era post-mortem photography was also very popular, in which dead people were dressed up in their best clothes and photographs were taken of them for their loved ones to keep, a practice we might find distasteful today. Ariès' final epoch of *invisible death* equates to contemporary Western society. This form of death is lonely and isolating and the dead person tends to die in a hospital where their death is invisibilized and screened away from others. Elias (1985) argues that how we treat death is consonant with the *civilizing process* in which increasing restraint is progressively exercised over both bodily functions and extreme emotional feelings throughout our historical evolution. Therefore, the dying and dead are currently mostly shrouded to limit the expression of deep and public emotion, except in specific, approved situations such as funerals.

In terms of cross-cultural comparison, there are stark differences in how death is seen and responded to. The Merina in Madagascar, for example, regard the life course as a continual process of gradual dying and therefore all members of the community are preparing for death, not just the terminally ill (Bloch, 1988: 13). The Khasi in India hold three funeral ceremonies. Initially the deceased is cremated and the bones buried in an individual grave. After several other relatives have died, they are then all exhumed and buried in a mass grave.

Many years after this, they are moved to a community grave accompanied by an elaborate ceremony. Arhem (1988) sees this process as a journey both for the dead to the graves of their ancestors and for the living, with the first ceremony allowing grieving by kin and friends and the final one involving ritual community acknowledgment. Every society, however, does develop some kind of funeral rites, and means of disposing of bodies, and symbolically differentiates between the living and the dead, although in some cultures the dead are seen to have great influence over the living. The dying process may be either a private or a public affair and cultures can be *death accepting, death denying* or *death defying*, or a combination of these orientations. Death may signal the end of existence or transitioning to another state. For Buddhists and Hindus, what is feared is not dying itself but the painful ordeal of possible rebirth. Death and dead bodies can also be regarded as sacred or profane. The Yolngu, Aboriginal Australians, view dead bodies as unclean pollutants which must undergo ritual cleansing, whereas traditional Hindus embalmed and preserved the body to ensure the wellbeing of the soul.

Many books treat Western, European or Anglophone societies as if all understandings and practices are the same, which is problematic. For example, in Britain most coffins are closed but in Ireland it is customary for the coffin to remain open, revealing the dead body in a cosmeticized, clothed state. In the USA, capitalist commodification of death has occurred whereby monopolistic funeral directors exploit and emotionally manipulate the vulnerable recently bereaved. They encourage them to pay for lavish funerals they cannot afford on the basis that this is what the dead person would have wanted. In England, although funeral directors advertise in local newspapers, it is the relatives who initiate first contact. In England, it is also now common practice to inform terminally ill patients of their prognosis, but this is proscribed in Japan because of the cultural belief it robs the person of all hope.

Death and Dying in Western Modernity – Denial, Defiance or Acceptance?

Currently across Europe and the USA there are rapidly ageing or greying populations and, with the elderly fast becoming the largest group in society, death will soon become more noticeable than at present. In most high-income countries, it is predominantly the elderly who face death, at age 75 or older. In middle-income countries such as Latin America, death occurs often decades earlier. In the low-income countries such as Africa, it is children who die, 50 per cent of them before the age of 10 (Macionis and Plummer, 2002), a situation very much akin to the UK's in earlier epochs. In 1900 in England the key causes of adult death were tuberculosis, cholera, pneumonia, diarrhoea and related diseases. Today, 70 per cent of all deaths are a consequence of heart attacks, strokes and cancer. Many are associated with ageing, but the so-called 'diseases of affluence', related to fatty foods, sedentary living, alcohol consumption and obesity may play a part (S. Hunt, 2005). Ironically, these diseases are most likely to affect adversely those individuals who have low social status and are disadvantaged and poor, for whom cigarettes or alcohol may be the only pleasurable activities they indulge in amidst lives of overwhelming stress, insecurity, violence and uncertainty (Marmot, 2004).

Today, 60 per cent of deaths occur in hospital, 25 per cent at home and 3.5 per cent in hospices (Victor, 2000). This echoes the relocation of death from the private sphere to the increasingly impersonal and bureaucratized institutional spaces of funeral directors, coroners and morgues, alongside the focus doctors place on 'taming death' (Machin, 1998). Medics traditionally have been trained to preserve life at all costs, which can mitigate against embracing and enhancing the quality of emotional life left for dying patients (Kastenbaum, 1998; Rich, 2003). This suggests that the hypothesis that death is privatized, taboo, invisible and sequestered may be right (O'Gorman, 1998; Ariès, 1974; Giddens, 1991). After all, rarely is anyone aware someone in the community has died today unless they see a funeral procession or read the obituaries in the local paper.

Early research exposed considerable reluctance to deal transparently and honestly with death and dying issues. Kubler Ross (1969) encountered significant institutional and individual resistance when conducting her research with dying people. Glaser and Strauss (1965), in their landmark study of awareness contexts in a cancer ward, found at the time that medical professionals rarely informed patients they were dying. This led to either (i) a *closed context* in which patients were unaware; (ii) a *suspected awareness* where they tried to elicit information and confirmation; (iii) a *mutual pretence* in which both sides were aware but pretended otherwise; or (iv) an *open awareness* where the patient knew their prognosis and professionals and family were prepared to discuss it. Sudnow's (1967) ethnographic study of a US hospital, furthermore, found hospital staff experienced great difficulty in handling deaths and consequently routinized and impersonalized the process. They 'protected' visitors and other patients from the reality of people dying by strategies such as screening the dying person's bed, moving dying patients into side rooms and moving the bodies at particular times such as during the night.

Arguably, such studies have influenced a change in contemporary medical and nursing practice (Exely, 2004). These include the rise of palliative care and the hospice movement through which those dying are helped to have as peaceful, dignified and pain-free a death as possible, with family and friends participating (Rokach et al., 2007). Despite this, very few people die in hospices and most who do are cancer patients. Recent studies have led to some consternation by revealing some hospice care has become more routinized and that *dirty deaths* may occur, whereby certain patients are relegated to the less visible back regions because of the bodily decay, pain and odour associated with some long and lingering deaths (Lawton, 1998). Those who are older or disabled (Bevan and Thompson, 2003), who are working class or who have dementia or other terminal diseases with less clear trajectories than cancer, are also less likely to access hospice care (Holloway, 2007). They are more likely to experience *disadvantaged dying*, ending their lives alone in a strange hospital bed. Recent policy initiatives such as the DOH End of Life Strategy (2008), Dignity in Care and the Liverpool Care Pathway (LCP) have all attempted to redress the disparity between the patients' wishes and the treatment they receive, including dying at home if they wish. It remains to be seen how successful these strategies will be as they ideally require an open awareness context embraced by all and adequate resource allocation. The LCP has also been criticized for not being activated until too near death (Ladd, 2007), although it offers a structured approach to deciding about issues such as nutrition, social contact, resuscitation and funeral arrangements.

Representations and understandings of death also appear to be contradictory. Death is a constant presence in the media, but only in a distanced manner and in relation to certain deaths caused by war, disasters or terrorism, and those of high-profile media personalities such as rock stars, politicians and the royal family. However, Walter et al. (1995) argue certain deaths allow the 'public invigilation of private emotion' whereby the death of a distant person such as Princess Diana elicits an unexpected outpouring of public grief, behind which lies individuals' own possibly previously unexpressed and unacknowledged private grief. Additionally, it has been argued that rapacious and vampiric endeavours by reporters to 'catch' newsworthy deaths represent a pornography of death (Gorer, 1965). Documentaries and films conversely cover issues associated with death, such as voluntary euthanasia ('A Short Trip to Switzerland', BBC1 – 15.01.2009) and dementia (*Iris*, a film) with seriousness and openness. A recent US television series, *Six Feet Under*, also dealt with the trials and tribulations of a family-run firm of funeral directors, giving viewers greater understandings of the inner workings of such institutions. This media coverage has led to death being seen as 'publicly present' and 'privately absent', although *virtual grief* could occur when we become so accustomed to viewing mediatized traumatic death depictions, we are unexpectedly devastated when we confront death first-hand. The contemporary emergence of the bereavement counsellor might suggest greater acceptance of death, but the encounter between client and counsellor is likely to be a privatized hidden affair and support only accessed or offered when a bereaved person is experiencing significant problems.

We still continually use euphemisms to talk abut death, such as 'passed over', 'sleeping' and 'at peace'. Crematoriums and funeral homes are replete with camouflaging façades like flowers, but the bodies which traditionally would have been in the home are now 'kept out of sight in a clanking garage-like morgue whose slightly putrid smell is not completely masked by detergent' (Widgery, 1993: 18). Terms like 'terminal illness' have also been replaced by more uncertain terms like 'life limiting' or 'life threatening' illness, which make death seem more uncertain, although some people live many years with terminal illnesses like cancer or HIV/AIDS. Similarly, 'death' terms are often used to express conquest and desperate need, such 'as we killed that team dead in the last game' and ' I could murder a drink.' Davies (1997), however, argues some ways of handling death, such as euthanasia, cremation and cosmeticization (to erase all signs of distress, pain or decomposition) may not, as often assumed, represent a denial of, but a triumphing over, death and the decaying body.

Therefore, although death in the media is a constant, and the rise of the hospice movement, bereavement counsellors and palliative care suggests a more open acceptance, conversely the way individuals and institutions often still approach death in a routinized, bureaucratic and medicalized manner and the way in which open expressions of grief are often proscribed, illustrate that we still largely avoid and invisibilize death. So do we therefore still live in a death-denying society where the subject is taboo or has society substantially changed in the last few decades? Most dying people are still routinely transported to hospital (Cockerham, 1991) where their biological needs may be met but their emotional needs rarely are (Fennell et al., 1988). Furthermore, if Orcutt's (1977) theory of 'closure of communication', whereby both family and patient are aware of the diagnosis but conspire to protect the other by refusing to discuss the situation, is still relevant, then we must concede to some extent we are death denying.

Yet other elements of our behaviour, such as the eternal search for immortality through a spiritual belief in ghosts, a recourse to clairvoyants and spiritualists or deploying medical or technological strategies such as cloning, genetic engineering and cryonics, support the notion we are a death-defying society. Cryonics involves the deep freezing of one's body, or for the less affluent one's head, in the hope we can be restored back to life later. This technique was made famous by the Woody Allen film *Sleeper* and by media dissemination of the report that Walt Disney, the famous cartoon and film maker, was kept in suspended animation. The constant recourse by predominantly the rich and famous to various forms of delusionary youth-inducing plastic surgery would also suggest we are both death denying and death defying. Immortality, near-death experiences and reincarnation are also a recurrent theme in films from the 1980s onwards, such as *Interview with a Vampire*, *Ghost*, *Stir of Echoes*, *Flatliners* and *Final Destination*. The current plethora of vampire-focused films and TV series emerging in the last couple of years, in the USA and UK, including *The Vampire Diaries*, *Moonlight*, *Twilight*, *Daybreakers*, *True Blood*, *Sanctuary* and *Being Human*, to name a few, suggest this preoccupation is not diminishing. It therefore appears that our society has mixed, ambivalent views about death and dying in different situations and can be construed to be both death denying and defying, and occasionally death accepting. Our constant, perhaps unconscious or semi-conscious, preoccupation and obsession with death, albeit often digested in an abstract mediatized or sensational manner, also suggest it is never far from our thoughts and fears. Oregon's Death with Dignity Act, which was the first legislation passed on physician-assisted suicide decided by a public vote, highlights, however, adults' willingness to debate death issues openly if given the opportunity (Humphry, 1999).

Different Modes of Death and Dying and Ethical Considerations

The nature and manner of deaths today differ from earlier times when many people died much earlier, quicker and of natural causes. We have proceeded from an era of premature deaths, where the majority of the population died as children or young adults, often from infectious diseases, to one where, debatably, many deaths could be seen as 'post mature', such as those of the frail old with advanced dementia, who have little quality of life. In most Western countries, with the exception of Switzerland, the city of Amsterdam and the state of Oregon in the USA, euthanasia or assisted suicide is outlawed. Yet, conversely, there are a small but growing group of chronically ill and disabled children in Western countries whose lives were saved by the interventions of modern medicine, but who are now housebound and so technology-dependent that their parents have difficulty in differentiating between their roles as parents and as nurses (Kirk et al., 2005). We also have situations where even medical professionals do not want to intervene actively with life-saving treatment, for example with profoundly disabled babies, because they evaluate that the child's life will be so untenable due to ongoing, severe pain and profound disability. With Charlotte Wyatt, who was born in 2003 with permanent brain, lung and kidney damage, the parents successfully challenged in court the medical decision not to actively intervene medically to resuscitate. They subsequently divorced and now rarely visit the child, who exists for much of the time with little, if any, quality of life on a hospital ward. The last newspaper citations spoke of the difficulties in finding a part-time foster family for Charlotte (Yeoman, 2006).

These situations present a multiplicity of contradictions and ethical dilemmas. Should we allow anyone to choose to end their life prematurely? If so, should this only be terminally ill people and what safeguards should be in place? Is it acceptable to allow adults who have gone from an active life to being paralysed from the neck down – such as the young rugby player, Daniel James – actively to end their life if they feel it is not worth living (S. Stewart, 2008)? What about people who choose to end their lives whilst sane because the majority of their life has been blighted by traumatizing and untreatable mental illness? This is a difficult situation, particularly in relation to 'living wills', because even terminally ill people with depression are more likely to change their mind about voluntary euthanasia than terminally ill people without depression (Kelly and McLoughlin, 2002). What about cases involving religious beliefs, and/or where one life has to be sacrificed to save another before both lives are lost? This occurred with the Maltese conjoined twins, Mary and Josie Attard, born in 2000 (Bosely, 2008). The medics had to go to court for permission to separate them as the parents refused consent because of their Catholic beliefs.

Should we save all premature and profoundly disabled babies regardless of their anticipated future disability, even if they will suffer a lifetime of severe pain? Some profoundly disabled people enjoy life to the full, despite the pain and difficulties they encounter. Others in a similar medical situation may castigate medical science and wish they had never been saved. However, before we make decisions about whose life is worth living or saving, or whether euthanasia or withdrawing life-saving intervention in any situation is morally acceptable, ideally adequate resources must be available to enable people to live as good a life as they possibly can. If this is not the precursor to any discussion, then seriously ill or disabled people may feel they are a burden, or family members may feel the responsibility of caring with insufficient resources is untenable, and therefore pressurized decisions may be made. Nevertheless, we do not live in an ideal world and realistically decisions must always take into account available resources and necessary prioritization.

The way we see and categorize certain deaths has been the province of sociologists and demographers. They illustrate we not only distance ourselves from deaths through medicalizing them and measuring them in terms of 'death by' causes, or natural or unnatural causes, but through viewing certain deaths as 'dirty' or disadvantaged, timely or untimely, good, bad or heroic. *The good death* is said to be one where there is dignity, bravery and symptom control (McNamara et al., 1995). This is in contrast to *the bad death* where there may be loss of personhood, as in dementia, or where symptom control is unsuccessful, or where the person and their illness may be stigmatized and demonized as in deaths from HIV/AIDS in the late 1980s and early 1990s. *Social death* is a term used to describe deaths where the person has disengaged physically and mentally before the actual physical death occurs, or alternatively where dying people are treated by hospital staff or relatives as if already dead and denied conversation or feeding, or their death is talked about in their presence (Sweeting and Gilhooly, 1997). Seale (1990) also refers to *heroic deaths*, such as a soldier dying whilst fighting for his country.

Death in our modern society is also more likely to be slow rather than sudden because infectious diseases are now largely under control. People often die slowly from degenerative diseases and have their lives medically prolonged. For example, someone in an intensive treatment hospital unit may be brain-dead – although debates are ongoing as to what actually constitutes brain death – but will not be technically pronounced dead until after the life-support machines are switched off and their vital organs cease functioning. This may be done slowly for their relatives' benefit so it mimics the path of a slow natural death rather than a painful sudden one.

Social Differences, Divisions and Inequalities

Attitudes towards life are also influenced by death. Even in our modernist Western societies, people may proclaim we should 'eat, drink and be merry' because we may be dead tomorrow. Alternatively, others may become obsessively preoccupied with their own potential longevity and bodily preservation. One school of thought, on the basis of research with rats, advocates semi-starvation through caloric restriction, claiming this lifestyle will lead to a longer (but not necessarily a more enjoyable) life. In the contemporary UK, individuals are, however, given significant responsibility for their own health preservation, with some health professionals and politicians appointing themselves moral arbiters and resource gatekeepers. The recent horrific case of two paramedics, recorded accidentally by phone, refusing to attempt to resuscitate a dying man and laughing about the state of his house as he lay there dying is a prime example (Jones, 2008). However, politicians and prominent medics frequently admonish those who smoke, drink or are obese as unworthy of medical intervention. Rarely are pronouncements made about how structural inequalities related to, for example, combinations of poverty, gender and ethnicity and low social status impact on one's health and lifestyles (Marmot, 2004). Such acknowledgment might counter the weighty but context-devoid responsibility placed on the individual. The following paragraphs illustrate how social differences, more notably social and structural divisions and their related inequalities throughout life, may lead to further inequalities in relation to death and dying.

Few empirical studies have been conducted with dying people within either psychology or sociology, and those conducted mostly focus on white middle-class, middle-aged people with cancer (Exely, 2004; T. Walter, 2008). Their findings or theories, therefore, can scarcely be seen as representative of the UK, let alone globally relevant or sensitive. Consequently, we need to understand whether working-class people have ways of expressing grief and organizing for death that are different from those of middle-class families and, if so, what they are. T. Walter (2008) is sharply critical of UK sociologists for ignoring material inequalities and disadvantaged dying, as well as working-class and ethnically different ways of coping with death. This is despite numerous statistical studies showing high adult and infant morbidity and mortality rates are profoundly influenced by poverty and social class (Townsend and Davidson, 1981; Acheson, 1998), as well as gender and ethnicity: 'Researchers, like Western societies at large, have ignored their own elderly, their own poor, the poor half of the world and those made stateless by exile or war, all of whom experience death and loss disproportionately often' (T. Walter, 2008: 328).

Even studies of capital punishment in the USA show death-row inmates are far more likely to come from black and/or poor families, against whom jurors are often inadvertently prejudiced (Fleury-Steiner, 2004). Furthermore, they are also frequently the state-sponsored adult products of inadequate child protection, domestic violence, juvenile justice and drug and alcohol programmes which fail(ed) to protect children from chronic child abuse, neglect and poverty or later to diagnose and treat the resultant severe psychological conditions (Beck, Britto and Andrews, 2007).

If children are used as a prime example, for decades they were banned from funerals 'for their own protection' (Riches and Dawson, 2000) and adults were duplicitous with them about death and dying. However, attitudes are slowly beginning to change and children now seem more common at funerals. In mediaeval times, in contrast, children were not only in close physical and psychological contact with death but learned to accept it by visiting ancestors' graves on All Souls' Day. They offered cakes to the dead, welcoming them out of their cold graves into the warmth of family and friends' homes (Mellor and Shilling, 1997). That said, on the negative side, children during this period were threatened with 'eternal damnation' by their parents if they did not behave. In accordance with the views of sociology of childhood, children are actors and agents, and what little research has been conducted with children shows they possess an awareness of and sensitivity to death. One pioneering study of dying children in a cancer ward found most deployed inventive strategies to ascertain their prognosis and protected their families from their knowledge of their imminent death (Bluebond-Langner, 1978). Another study found children as young as 7 could understand death involved irreversibility, non-functionality and universality (Speece and Brent, 1987).

Nevertheless, children's comprehension may depend as much on their exposure to, and familiarity with, death as on their developmental stage or age. One study found that elderly adults with learning disabilities, presumably because of greater exposure, had a better understanding of death than comparable younger adults (Dodd, Dowling and Hollins, 2005). An English study involving 179 children aged 9–10 revealed children's unexpected openness about cancer and its relationship to death. The children used monstrous, invasive imagery to depict cancerous bodies, focusing on individual risk factors such as smoking, poor diet and inactivity. They also acknowledged environmental influences such as pollution, toxic waste and the sun, but seemed completely unaware of structural factors such as poverty. Somewhat contradictorily, given their emphasis on individual behavioural factors, the children perceived those who died as blameless, having experienced untimely, unjust deaths (Williams and Bendelow, 1998). Most studies have, however, been conducted with white middle-class children, neglecting gender, social class, ethnicity and the environment (Bevan and Thompson, 2003). The few studies examined here, though, suggest children want to engage with death openly, despite Ariès' 'veil of silence' metaphor.

Since the UK has a rapidly ageing population, there is a need for greater knowledge about death and dying pathways, and grief and loss related to the elderly and their families, as well as a fuller understanding of how gender and sexism, racism and ethnicity, social class and poverty might impact on both grief and death. How might older people react to multiple deaths and their friends dying around them in rapid succession? Might these cumulative deaths create bereavement overload in the sense that one death occurs after another, before people have had sufficient time to grieve over the first one (Corr et al., 1997)? A similar situation was noted with gay men and HIV/AIDS in the late 1980s and 1990s, when the 'gay community' that homosexual men might have expected to receive support from was so demoralized it was unable to provide any. There was also evidence of different styles of grieving and coping emerging in response to successive HIV/AIDS deaths (see Green and Grant, 2008). Such differences need to be studied with other communities where similar death trajectories occur, or where unexpected natural and unnatural disasters make it difficult or impossible to partake in 'normal' grieving rituals.

There is much anthropological work on bereavement rituals in small rural, premodern societies but little work conducted in the UK with ethnically diverse groups. How might relatively recent immigrants or even third-generation immigrants understand death and dying, and adopt, reject or modify British traditions in respect of their cultural heritage? Students and practitioners need to be culturally competent when dealing with dying and bereaved people but little literature exists to help them. Firth (1997) gives the example of a nurse who moved a Hindu patient back into his bed because she feared him getting cold but the family had sat him up near the window in accordance with a spiritual belief that requires them to be near nature. We should conduct more research on refugees and asylum seekers who might have lost family in violent political uprisings or genocides and find themselves in an alien country, isolated, misunderstood and possibly subject to racism. Alternatively, if gendercide (the active killing of newborn baby girls or their indirect murder through sex-selective terminations or neglect and malnutrition) is common in countries such as India and China because females are so devalued there (Green and Taylor, 2010), might this continue to occur in the UK with recent immigrants, as occurs with genital circumcision, despite its illegality here?

Additionally, might our current economic recession, in which unemployment is rising and a long-working-hours and casualized labour culture exists, merit reviewing studies examining the social epidemiology of 'karoshi'. Karoshi is a Japanese term for death through overwork, coined in the 1990s because of the disproportionate number of apparently healthy young Japanese workers who died unexpectedly in their twenties or thirties, ostensibly because of heart-related illnesses. However, such deaths were also clearly linked to extreme work-related pressure, little control over work and inordinately long working hours (Scott, 2000).

Furthermore, there should be more research conducted with groups previously subject to paternalism and protectionism, such as disabled people and children and stigmatized and marginalized groups. How might the debated existence of 'Englishness' addtionally impact on how we experience and talk about deaths and how others comprehend our behaviour? The English often manage difficult social interactions through the deployment of irony, humour and distraction tactics such as talking about the weather. Fox (2004) asserts that modesty and reserve are integral to British behaviour, hence the colloquial term 'stiff upper lip'. Observers from other countries, foreign nationals working here or recent immigrants could wrongly misinterpret these reserved, satirical and sometimes avoidant behaviours as indicating a lack of depth or insensitivity, but if they apply to English behaviour generally then they may apply to how we view and treat death and perhaps this should be studied too.

Conclusion

Death across all time periods, countries and cultures raises uncomfortable existential and ontological questions. These are particularly evident in a secularized postmodern, individualistic society where people treat their bodies and lives as ongoing individual projects, whose purpose and meaning become threatened by death. Those with a religious faith appear to confront death with more acceptance and less fear than agnostics and atheists (Ladd, 2007). Practices such as organ donation could also be seen to be forging a continuum between death and new life for those who are not religious. At the same time, the global trade in organ sales suggests those in poorer countries are exploited and endanger their own health to save the lives of rich Westerners.

Psychology in the main deals with the emotions and processes of grief individualistically with little reference to the social context. Conversely, sociology tends to over-privilege the social at the expense of acknowledging human emotion, even if human emotions themselves are profoundly infused with the social. Craib, a social theorist, a psychoanalyst and at the time (1994) a cancer survivor, admonishes sociologists for prioritizing macro institutional contexts without looking at the huge importance of feelings when confronted with possible bereavement or one's own death. Other sociologists also assert that sociologists are frequently in denial themselves about death, at the same time as they ironically assert we are a death-denying or death-defying society. This is because of their refusal to confront the associated human emotions or study how our awareness of death might motivate our behaviour throughout life (Willmott, 2000). Ironically, although psychology concentrates on individuals, it homogenizes them because of its emphasis on universal theories which largely ignore social factors, inequalities and geographical and cultural variation. Sociology, also, has for the most part ignored inequalities and differences within Western culture in relation to death and dying, and left unstudied the multiplicities of cultures that can exist with one 'dominant' society and their different ways of experiencing and organizing for death and dying, making more reference to differences within other societies and earlier historical times.

The task for both sociologists of death and dying and psychologists of grief and loss is to try and work together in an interdisciplinary manner to produce more comparative and holistic research around the subject, embracing the individual experience, the social context and subcultural differences and inequalities. As T. Walter (2008) points out insightfully, there are no comparative texts on the sociology of dying, so students are unable to understand whether all, any, or parts of their texts apply to other countries. For those studying or working with dying or bereaved people and their families, this chapter offers a short overview and analysis of general themes and issues. If one is working with particular groups of individuals such as asylum seekers or children, or located in a particular setting, such as a hospice or home for people with learning disabilities, it is recommended that further research is consulted, although as this chapter indicates there are huge gaps in the research which have yet to be filled.

Reflection and discussion questions

Critically evaluate traditional, mainstream psychological theories pertaining to bereavement grief *and* analyse more contemporary modifications and explanations.

Contrast and compare different historical and cross-cultural constructions of death and dying.

To what extent would you agree with the claim that death and dying are taboo subjects in contemporary society?

Recommended reading

Rothaupt and Becker's (2007) article is an excellent review of early and contemporary Western psychological bereavement theory, and Corr's (1998/1999) article elucidates and extends Doka's concept of disenfranchised grief. Seale's (1998) text is a comprehensive and insightful sociological analysis of death and dying, and Holloway (2007) links death and dying specifically to health and social care. Useful journals also include *Omega – The Journal of Death and Dying*, *Mortality* and *Death Studies*.

Conclusion

This book initially separately explains and analyses, and then contrasts and compares, key sociological and psychological literature pertaining to the life course, integrating and synthesizing the findings and theories of the two disciplines as far as possible in the conclusion at the end of each chapter. It does so in a way particularly relevant to researchers, students and practitioners within the health, social care and education fields and those studying mixed social science, non-vocational, degrees. The book is deliberately structured in a fairly traditional, chronological, age-related manner, dealing with childhood initially and then finishing with chapters on old age and death and dying in order to offer maximum coherence and cohesiveness. This structure also reflects the fact that the notion of chronological age is so deeply entrenched in modern Western societies; it is often the prima facie standard against which any other perceptions of age or ageing, such as biological or self- or other-perceived age, can be understood through or by. Ironically, in the most recent editorial of *Advances in Life Course Research*, the journal is referred to as 'coming of age' and becoming 'adult' (Billari, 2009: 83). Although the word 'adult' is located in inverted commas, its deployment to convey maturity suggests how deeply embedded in understandings and language chronological age is. Chronological age is, additionally, frequently drawn on in psychometrics, as a benchmark against which variables, such as personality, cognition and intelligence, are calculated. However, the chronological structure of the book importantly enables these often taken for granted age periods, spans or categories, such as childhood, adolescence or middle age (and certain characteristics frequently deterministically associated with them), to be rigorously evaluated and their shortcomings exposed.

For example, psychological and 'common sense' notions of the child as unequivocally deficient, dependent and an incomplete model of finished adult humanity have been challenged in the book and exposed as problematic by various childhood sociologists and critical psychologists. Through their analysis of a variety of social, cultural, political and historical constructions of children, these academics reveal the profound influence of the social and historical. They illustrate how the social, rather than an isolated biology per se, profoundly influences children's knowledge, competence, autonomy and identity, through our treatment and expectations of them and the associated, linked way that social, educational and political structures are organized and function. We have also seen how in contemporary Western society, adults' apparently paternalistic, protective and benevolent (although simultaneously often stringently controlling) behaviour towards children, ultimately disadvantages them. It frequently restricts and constrains their initiative and autonomy to such an extent many children are no longer able cumulatively to build up a repertoire of strategies to deal with risky and uncertain situations. They may, therefore, metaphorically become prisoners within their own homes or, as is the case with many middle-class children, always be escorted, observed or have their activities channelled outside the home by adults. Children can also be found to take on board second-hand the mantel of adult fears surrounding how dangerous contemporary society has become for them, with negligible autonomous experience of 'outside' society to compare these fears with. These features and experiences have led to an unnecessarily and arguably problematic extended childhood emerging for many, and much infantilizing of children, even those currently inhabiting middle and late childhood. Such dependency induction can even be extended to encompass some young adults, hence the contemporary, colloquial term, 'helicopter parenting'.

Within every chapter, characteristics and experiences assumed to be age-related have been critically evaluated. For the most part, these characteristics are over-defined, over-generalized and sometimes entirely the result of a cohort effect completely unrelated to chronological age, two examples being the now largely redundant concepts of gender role crossover and the empty nest syndrome in middle age. It is clear from evaluating the psychological and biological literature that chronological age, nevertheless, is still at times important. Most children do behave and think differently from adults in some respects, regardless of culture, and their moral and intellectual understanding and reasoning shifts throughout childhood and into adulthood in a manner that is generally viewed as progressive by psychologists. Despite this, such changes in thought and behaviour are rarely as linear, unidirectional, discontinuous or biologically preordained as was assumed by some of the early psychologists. However, Elder's longitudinal life course work on children of the Great Depression did find that children's age, whether or not that is conceptualized in terms of developmental stage, had a significant effect on how well they coped with lack of stability and deleterious circumstances. Children's and adults' cognitive, attachment and personality styles and values are also profoundly influenced by the society and culture they inhabit and by historical precedents and residues too. This illuminates the danger stemming from most psychological research, until relatively recently, having been Western-based and culturally naive.

Cultures, therefore, which are more collectivist and less oriented towards individual achievement, may, as a result, be ethnocentrically or eurocentrically judged as inferior to Western cultures if their inhabitants reach certain stages slower than their Western counterparts or never attain them – for example Piaget's final stage of logical and abstract thought. Methodological problems relating to studying different cultures by and through Western research techniques and standards, and applying Western logic and concepts – such as intelligence or healthy attachment – also invoke difficult questions about how research should be conducted with dissimilar cultures, what questions should be posed, and how any subsequent findings or results should be interpreted and disseminated. The unthought-through adultcentric nature of much research is, in addition, problematic for the study of children and also elderly people, who both tend to have been typecast as dependent, vulnerable and possessing limited capacity and competence.

The manner in which individuals approach problems, perceive and respond to criticism and forge their identities also varies to some extent chronologically. Erikson's notion of identity achievement is highly resonant, particularly in Western cultures, for middle-class adolescents and young people, but less applicable to poor, working-class and disadvantaged youth and those resident in low-resource/income countries. There, conversely, however, do seem to be some universal, cross-cultural similarities in some selective early attachment behaviours, how individuals of different ages approach problems in relation to defence mechanisms and how, as one ages, one appears to become more mellow, less confrontational and less directly defensive or easily angered.

The recent individualized, destandardized or 'yo-yoization' hypotheses of contemporary life courses, put forward by postmodernist thinkers, suggest considerable choice for all individuals and the ability to change or restructure many life experiences previously viewed as chronologically unalterable. Institutional age-defined structuring such as that related to schooling and careers, biologically imposed age-related restrictions regarding 'natural' reproduction, particularly pertinent to middle-aged women, and the far-reaching and cumulative impact of social divisions, such as social class, gender, race/ethnicity and disability, in opposition to these claims, strongly suggest there is not as much choice or flexibility for everyone as some assume. Social divisions and inequalities impact greatly on identity and the choices and the opportunities one has throughout life. The advantages and disadvantages related to, and arising from, such social divisions, furthermore, accrue and accumulate over the life course, resulting in a significantly more affluent, comfortable and healthy old age for some than for others, and significant differences in morbidity, mortality and life expectancy.

There are also vast, but recent, generational and cohort disparities in transitions into and the markers associated with, for example, young adulthood or old age. Young adulthood was previously delineated by markers such as spatial, economic and emotional independence from family of origin, full-time employment, and marriage and childbearing, but is currently becoming increasingly difficult to demarcate chronologically through these increasingly irrelevant markers. It has consequently been suggested that new markers, such as taking full responsibility for one's actions, autonomous thought and relational factors, such as caring for others, may be more relevant today in terms of characterizing adulthood. Old age is also seen as extending, in tandem with rapidly increasing average life expectancy, and has been subdivided by some theorists into distinct subcategories such as the 'young old', 'middle old' and 'old old', or the third and fourth age in old age. Laslett (1989), for example, likened the third age to an autonomous, affluent and comfortable middle age, and represented the fourth age as a later time period in which the individual becomes increasingly prone to long-term disability and health problems and may require considerable support. Laslett, however, unfortunately failed to attend sufficiently to the impact of factors such as social class and poverty on old age and ageing, and these omissions considerably weaken the universal, or even full Western, applicability of his theory.

Therefore, although chronological, age-related understandings are sometimes important, they should *not* be taken on board in a definitive, reductionist and asocial manner, as has often been the case in the past. Furthermore, they rarely tell us a great deal about what a person and their life are actually like. Our understandings of age and the way we perceive, label and stereotype people of different ages, clumsily clumping together or homogenizing vastly different people and often a wide spread of ages, abilities and experiences under one category or label, such as 'childhood' or 'middle age', seems, therefore, to be problematic. There currently appear to be potentially very significant differences between 'emergent' young adulthood, when adults often have few responsibilities and greater choices, and later young adulthood. During late young adulthood, early choices made about career and family may limit and constrain one's activities, although lower social class and poverty, combined with little familial or partner support and young parenthood, would additionally seem to close down opportunities, even earlier, for single adolescent mothers.

There also appear to be differences between early and late middle age as in the latter any 'natural' childbearing becomes ruled out for women, there is less possibility of progressing further up one's occupational ladder, even if this is aspired to, and individuals generally become more reflective and retrospective, focusing more on time lived and time left to live than previously. Social division and cohort and social generational effects, influenced by both historical and contemporary changes, can also impact seriously on one's life during a particular age stage. Therefore, one's social class or gender, the impact of social movements and/or the advent of mass consumption and new technology may render the life experiences, values and lifestyles of two cohorts, born only a few years apart, immeasurably different. Due to the advent of new reproductive technology, the increasing acceptability of solo living, same-sex partnerships and reconstituted families, and the increasing likelihood of later parenthood, one middle-aged or even older couple may have young children whilst another may have grown-up children and even grandchildren. Other middle-aged people may be voluntarily single or childless or may have significant caring responsibilities for ageing relatives. The financial and living situations of individuals and couples of similar age will also vary significantly according to their social class and other factors, and their values may be profoundly different.

The generation now mostly inhabiting middle age, commonly referred to as the Baby Boomers or bulgers (so named because of the increase in conceptions after World War II when the men returned home from the war) are likely to have very divergent experiences during middle age in comparison to the next generation to enter middle age (currently inhabiting young adulthood). This latter generation seem to be less socially and politically aware than the boomers in a social justice sense, more educated, and more fatalistic and individualistic in their 'living for the present' behaviour and values. They demonstrate greater proficiency with, and debatably at the same time over-dependence on, a range of new technologies, as well as being more materialistic and consumption-driven than the current middle-aged (and older) Baby Boomers. How these characteristics, alongside currently unknown possible future changes in society, and within the economy, might impact upon these young adults' impending midlife experiences remains yet to be seen and studied.

One's self-perceived age, actual behaviour, life experiences and historical precedents, consequently, seem, increasingly, to have more import than objective, chronological age. Age categories or spans such as 'adolescence' and 'old age', furthermore, are frequently insufficiently nuanced or analytical enough to incorporate the experiences of everyone who might fall within that category, either at one period in time or across time or cultures. Referring to someone as old, adolescent or middle-aged also labels, de-individualizes and stereotypes people according to only one aspect – age – therefore often imposing socially constructed expectations and limitations on them. These often affect their perceptions and consequently their behaviour and self-concept in occasionally positive but, most often, negative ways. Older people and children, for example, may become increasingly less able and more dependent and helpless when they are repeatedly treated and labelled as such and much research reinforces these self-fulfilling prophecies.

In terms of future directions for research, this book strongly suggests prospective research and study on life courses needs to be increasingly interdisciplinary and trans-disciplinary and to bridge sociological, psychological and natural science perspectives and viewpoints to have full relevance. Physical changes throughout the life course do unequivocally have effects (albeit often unclear or confusing effects) upon individual psychological states and functioning and vice versa, and historical precedents and social factors are also extremely important, profoundly interacting with and influencing biology and psychology. Because of this, biological, psychological and sociological research on the life course needs to be conducted in a collaborative spirit. Such collaborative research will not be easy to achieve and any subsequent findings or conclusions will not always be simple to understand or apply, not least because psychological and biological states (notwithstanding the influence the social has on these) often decouple and interact in complex, multifaceted and difficult-to-decipher ways, producing confounding and unclear results or findings. Negotiating through these webs, will, however, lead to much more in-depth and sophisticated understandings of the life course in all of its many guises. Consequently, as accessible longitudinal studies proliferate, alongside improvements in analytical techniques and both planned comparative studies and comparative analyses enabled by 'natural' experiments increase, all of which indicate the profound importance of context, the insights which could be reaped from this life course research endeavour have the potential to be both profound and far reaching.

Bibliography

Aarsand, P. A. (2007) 'Computer and Video Games in Family Life: The Digital Divide as a Resource in Intergenerational Interactions', *Childhood*, 14(2): 234–56

Aasve, A., Billari, F. C. and Picarreta, R. (2007) 'Strings of Adulthood: A Sequence Analysis of British Women's Work–Family Trajectories', *European Journal of Population*, 23: 369–88

Abercrombie, N. (2004) *Sociology*, Cambridge: Polity

Abrams, F. (2007) 'Bad Hair Pay', *The Guardian*, 18.09.07, Education Guardian P1

Abrams, M. (1959) *The Teenage Consumer*, London: Press Exchange

Acheson, D. (1998) *Independent Inquiry into Health Inequalities: The Acheson Report*, London: Stationery Office:

Adam, B. (1990) *Time and Social Theory*, Cambridge: Polity Press

Adams, S. (1991) 'Qualitative Age Differences in Memory for Text: A Life Span Developmental Perspective', *Psychology and Aging*, 6: 323–36

Affolter, F. and Bischofberger, W. (2000) *Nonverbal Perceptual and Cognitive Processes in Children with Language Disorders: Towards a New Framework*, Mahwah, NJ: Lawrence Erlbaum

Age Concern (2005) *How Ageist is Britain?* Age Concern Reports, www.AgeConcern. org.uk (accessed on 17.11.2008)

Age Concern (2008a) *Ageism in Britain 2006*, Age Concern Reports, www. AgeConcern.org.uk (accessed on 17.11.2008)

Age Concern (2008b) available from www.ageconcern.org.uk/ageconcern/htbh-problem.asp (accessed on 17.11.2008)

Age Concern England (2007) *Age of Equality: Outlawing Age Discrimination Beyond the Workplace*, Age Concern Reports, www.AgeConcern.org.uk (accessed on 17.11.2008)

Ainsworth, M. D. S., Blehar, M. C., Waters, E. and Wall, S. (1978) *Patterns of Attachment: A Psychological Study of the Strange Situation*, Mahwah, NJ: Erlbaum

Alibhai Brown, Y. (2001) *Mixed Feelings: The Complex Lives of Mixed Race Britons*, London: The Women's Press

Allan, G. and Crow, G. (2001) *Families, Households and Society*, London: Palgrave

Allan, G. and Jones, G. (eds.) (2000) *Social Relations and the Life Course*, Basingstoke: Palgrave

Allender, S., Cowburn, G. and Foster, C. (2006) 'Understanding Participation in Sport and Physical Activity among Children and Adults: A Review of Qualitative Studies', *Health Education Research*, 21(6): 826–35

Arber, S. (2006) 'Gender and Later Life: Change, Choice and Constraints', in J. A. Vincent., C. R. Phillipson and M. Downs (eds.), *The Futures of Old Age*, London: Sage

Archibald, C. (1998) 'Sexuality, Dementia and Residential Care: Manager's Report and Response', *Health and Social Care in the Community*, 6(2): 761–70

Arhem, K. (1988) 'Into the Realm of the Sacred: An Interpretation of Khasi Funerary Ritual', in S. Cederroth; C. Corlin and J. Lindstrom (eds.), *On the Meaning of Death: Essays on Mortuary Rituals and Eschatological Beliefs*, Uppsala: Almqvist and Wiksell Tryckeri

Ariès, P. (1960) *Centuries of Childhood*, Harmondsworth: Penguin

Ariès, P. (1974) *Western Attitudes towards Death*, Baltimore, MD: John Hopkins University Press

Arlin, P. (1984) 'Adolescent and Adult Thought', in M. L. Commons, F. A. Richards and C. Armon (eds.), *Beyond Formal Operations: Adolescent and Adult Cognitive Development*. New York: Praeger

Armstrong, L. (2007) 'Age Old Dilemmas', *The Times*, 18.07.2007

Arnett, J. (1999) 'Adolescent Storm and Stress', *American Psychologist*, 54(5): 317–26

Arnett, J. (2000) 'Emerging Adulthood: A Theory of Development from the Late Teens through The Twenties', *American Psychologist*, 50(5): 469–80

Aronson, P. (2008) 'The Markers and Meaning of Growing Up: Contemporary Young Women's Transition from Adolescence to Adulthood', *Gender and Society*, 22(1): 56–82

Asthana, A. (2008) 'Generation Y: They Don't Live for Work . . . They Work to Live', *The Observer*, 25.04.2008

Ashworth, P. (1997) 'The Variety of Qualitative Research, Part One: Introduction to the Problem', *Nurse Education Today*, 17(3): 215–18

Audit Commission (2008) *Don't Stop Me Now: Preparing for an Ageing Population*, www.audit-commission.gov.uk (accessed 31.11.2008)

Austad, S. N. (2001) 'Concepts and Theories of Aging', in E. J. Masuro and S. N. Austad (eds.), *Handbook of the Biology of Aging*, 5th edition, San Diego, CA: Academic Press

Avis, N. (1999) 'Women's Health at Midlife', in S. L. Willis and J. D. Reid (eds.), *Life in the Middle*, San Diego, CA: Academic Press

Babb, P., Bucher, H., Church, J. and Zealey, L. (2006) *Social Trends: Office for National Statistics*, London: Palgrave Macmillan

Back, L. (1996) *New Ethnicities and Urban Culture: Racism and Multiculture in Young Lives*, London: UCL Press

Bacon, H. and Richardson, S. (2001) 'Attachment Theory and Child Abuse: An Overview of the Literature for Practitioners', *Child Abuse Review*, 10: 377–97

Baechler, J. (1979) *Suicides*, Oxford: Blackwell

Baillargeon, R., Spelke, E. S. and Wasserman, S. (1985) 'Object Permanence in Five Month Old Infants', *Cognition*, 20: 191–208

Ball, S. J. (2003) *Class Strategies in the Educational Market: The Middle Classes and Social Advantage*, London: RoutledgeFalmer

Baldock, J. (2000) 'Old Age', in R. Dallos and E. McLaughlin (eds.), *Social Problems and the Family*, Milton Keynes: The Open University

Baltes, P. B. (1987) 'Theoretical Propositions of Life-Span Developmental Psychology: On the Dynamics between Growth and Decline', *Developmental Psychology*, 23: 611–26

Baltes, P. B. and Graf, P. (1996) 'Psychological Aspects of Aging: Facts and Frontiers', in D. Magnusson (ed.), *The Lifespan Development of Individuals*, Cambridge: Cambridge University Press

Baltes, P. B. and Kliegl, R. (1992) 'Further Testing of Limits of Cognitive Plasticity:

Negative Age Differences in a Mnemonic Skill are Robust', *Developmental Psychology*, 28: 121–5

Baltes, P. B. and Staudinger, U. M. (1993) 'The Search for a Psychology of Wisdom', *Current Directions in Psychological Science*, 2: 75–80

Baltes, P. B., Reuter-Lorenz, P.A. and Rosler, F. (eds.) (2006) *Lifespan Development and the Brain: The Perspective of Biocultural Co-constructivism*, Cambridge: Cambridge University Press

Baltes, P. B., Staudinger, U. M. and Lindenberger, U. (1999) 'Lifespan Psychology: Theory and Application to Intellectual Functioning', *Annual Review of Psychology*, 50: 471–507

Bandura, A (1977) *Social Learning Theory*, Upper Saddle River, NJ: Prentice Hall

Barr, D. and McCann, P. (2005) 'No-man's Land', *Times Online*, 12.12.2005

Barrett, A. E. (2005) 'Gendered Experiences in Midlife', *Journal of Aging Studies*, 19: 168–83

Barron, D. N. and West, E. (2007) 'The Emotional Costs of Caring Incurred by Men and Women in the British Labour Market', *Social Science and Medicine*, 65: 2160–71

Bauer, I., Wrosch, K. and Jobin, J. (2008) 'I'm Better Off than Most People: The Role of Social Comparisons in Young Adulthood and Old Age', *Psychology and Aging*, 23(4): 800–11

Bauer, P. J. and Dow, G. (1994) 'Episodic Memory in 16 and 20 Month Old Children: Specifics Are Generalised but Not Forgotten', *Developmental Psychology*, 30: 43–417

Bauman, Z. (1990) *Thinking Sociologically*, Oxford: Basil Blackwell

Bauman, Z. (2001) *The Individualized Society*, Cambridge: Polity

Baxter, J., Hewitt, B. and Haynes, M. (2008) 'Life Course Transitions and Housework: Marriage, Parenthood and Time on Housework', *Journal of Marriage and Family*, 70: 259–72

Bayley, N. (1966) 'Learning in Adulthood: The Role of Intelligence', in H. J. Klausmeier and C. W. Harris (eds.), *Analysis of Concept Learning*, New York: Academic Press

Beck, U. (1992) *Risk Society: Towards a New Modernity*, London: Sage

Beck, U. (2000) The *Brave New World of Work*, Cambridge: Polity

Beck, E., Britto, S. and Andrews, A. (2007) *In the Shadow of Death*, New York: Oxford University Press

Beckett, A. (2009) 'Back to the Dark Ages', *The Guardian*, 17.04.09, G2: 6–11

Beckett, C. (2002) *Human Growth and Development*, London: Sage

Bee, H. (1994) *Lifespan Development*, New York: HarperCollins

Bengston, P. L and Putney, N. M. (2006) 'Future Conflicts across Generations and Cohorts', in J. A. Vincent., C. R. Phillipson. and M. Downs (eds.), *The Futures of Old Age*, London: Sage

Bengston, V. L. (2001) 'Beyond the Nuclear Family: The Increasing Importance of Multigenerational Relationships in American Society: The 1989 Burgess Award Lecture', *Journal of Marriage and the Family*, 63(1): 1–16

Bennett, A. (1999) 'Subcultures or Neo-Tribes? Rethinking the Relationship between Youth, Style and Musical Taste', *Sociology*, 33: 599–617

Bennett, R (2008) 'Middle-Aged People Are Being Overwhelmed by Their Family Responsibilities?' *The Times*, 10.12.2008

Berger, K. (2005) *The Developing Person through the Life Span*, 6th edition, New York: Worth

Berger, P. (1963) *Invitation to Sociology*, London: Penguin

Berger, P. (1969) *The Social Reality of Religion*, London: Faber

Berry, J. W., Portinga, Y. H. and Pandey, J. (eds.) (2002) *Handbook of Cross-Cultural Psychology*, 2nd edition, Boston: Allyn and Bacon

Beteille, A. (1996) 'Sociology and Common Sense', *Economic and Political Weekly*, 31 (September 1996): 2361–5

Bevan, D. and Thompson, N. (2003) 'The Social Basis of Loss and Grief', *Journal of Social Work*, 3(2): 179–94

Biggart, A., Cairns, D., Machado Pais, J., Pappamikail, Bendit, R. and Hein, K. (2003) *Families and Transitions in Europe: Survey Report of Young Adults in Education and Training Institutions*, Executive Summary, June 2003, EUR20796, Luxembourg: European Commission

Biggs, S. (2006) 'Ageing Selves and Others: Distinctiveness and Uniformity in the Struggle for Intergenerational Solidarity', in J. A. Vincent., C. R. Phillipson and M. Downs (eds.), *The Futures of Old Age*, London: Sage

Billari, F. C. (2009) 'Editorial: The Life Course is Coming of Age', *Advances In Life Course Research*, 14: 83–6

Blackburn, S. (2001) *Being Good*, Oxford: Oxford University Press

Blacker, T. (2006) 'A Generation Still Trying to Grow Up', *The Independent*, 07.02.2006

Blackman, S. (2005) 'Youth Subcultural Theory: A Critical Engagement with the Concept, its Origins and Politics, From the Chicago School to Postmodernism', *Journal of Youth Studies*, 8(1): 1–21

Blaikie, A. (2006) 'Visions of Later Life: Golden Cohort to Generation Z', in J. A. Vincent., C. R. Phillipson and M. Downs (eds.), *The Futures of Old Age*, London: Sage

Blanchard-Fields, F. (1999) 'Social Schematicity and Causal Attributions' in T. M. Heiss and F. Blanchard-Fields (eds.), *Social Cognition and Aging*, San Diego, CA: Academic Press

Blanchard-Fields, F. and Coats, A. H. (2008) 'The Experience of Anger and Sadness in Everyday Problems Impacts Age Differences in Emotion Regulation', *Developmental Psychology*, 44(6): 1547–56

Blane, D., Netuvelli, G. and Bartley, M. (2007) 'Does Quality of Life at Older Ages Vary with Socio-Economic Position?' *Sociology*, 41(4): 717–26

Blatterer, H. (2007) 'Adulthood: The Contemporary Redefinition of a Social Category', *Sociological Research Online*, 12(4), www.socresearchonline.org.uk/12/4/3.html

Blazer, D., Burchett, B., Service, C. and George, L. K. (1991) 'The Association of Age and Depression among the Elderly: An Epidemiologic Exploration', *Journal of Gerontology*, 46: 210–15

Bloch, M. (1988) 'Death and the Concept of a Person', in S. Cederroth, C. Corlin and J. Lindstrom (eds.), *On the Meaning of Death: Essays on Mortuary Rituals and Eschatological Beliefs*, Uppsala: Almqvist and Wiksell Tryckeri

Bluebond-Langner, M. (1978) *The Private Worlds of Dying Children*, Princetown: Princetown University Press

Blytheway, B. (1995) *Ageism*, Bristol: The Open University

Bogin, B. (1999) *Patterns of Human Growth*, 2nd edition, New York: Cambridge University Press

Bolzan, N. (2005) '"To Know Them is To Love them" but Instead Fear and Loathing: Community Perceptions of Young People', in J. Mason and T. Fattore (eds.), *Children Taken Seriously: Theory, Policy and Practice*, London: Jessica Kingsley

Bond, J. and Cabrero, S. (2007) 'Health and Dependency in Later Life', in J. Bond., F. Dittman-Kohli., S. Peace and G. J. Westerhof (eds.), *Ageing in Society*, 3rd edition, London: Sage

Bond, J., Dittman-Kohli, F., Peace, S. and Westerhof, G. J. (eds.) (2007) *Ageing in Society*, 3rd edition, London: Sage

Bose, M. (2003) 'Race and Class in the Post Industrial Economy', in M. Bose., D. Muggleton and R. Weinziert (eds.), *The Post Sub-Cultural Reader*, Oxford: Berg

Bosely, S. (2007a) 'British Children: Poor, At Greater Risk and More Insecure', *The Guardian (14.02.07)*

Bosely, S. (2007b) 'The Truth about HRT', *The Guardian*, 06.06.2007

Bosely, S. (2008) 'One in 200,000 Medical Miracles', *The Guardian*, 4.12.2008

Bosely, S. (2010) 'Care Homes Forcing Elderly to Have Feeding Tubes Fitted', *The Guardian*, 06.01.2010

Bosely, S. and Saner, E. (2009) 'Britain is Bulging', *The Guardian*, 29.08.09

Bottero, W. (2000) 'Review Article: Gender and the Labour Market at the Turn of the Century: Complexity, Ambiguity and Change', *Work, Employment and Society*, 14(4): 781–91

Bould, S. (2003) 'Neighbourhoods and Inequality: The Possibility for Successful Transition to Adulthood', *Sociological Studies of Children and Youth*, 9: 49–66

Bourdieu, P. (1984) *Distinction: A Social Critique of the Judgment of Taste*, London: Routledge

Bourman, W. and Arcelus, J. (2001) 'Are Psychiatrists Guilty of "Ageism" When it Comes to Taking a Sexual History?' *International Journal of Geriatric Psychiatry*, 16(1): 27–31

Bower, T., Broughton, J. and Moore, M. (1970) 'Infant Responses to Approaching Objects: An Indication of Response to Distal Variables', *Perception and Psychophysics*, 8: 51–3

Bower, T. and Wishart, J.G. (1972) 'The Effects of Motor Skill on Object Permanence', *Cognition*, 1: 165–72

Bowlby, J. (1969) *Attachment and Loss, Vol. 1: Attachment*, New York: Basic Books

Bowlby, J. (1973) *Attachment and Loss, Vol. 2: Separation*, New York: Basic Books

Bowlby, J. (1980) *Attachment and Loss, Vol. 3: Loss, Sadness and Depression*, New York: Basic Books

Bowlby, J. (1990) *Attachment and Loss, Vol. 3: Loss, Sadness and Depression*, London: Penguin

Boxer, A. M. (1997) 'Gay, Lesbian and Bisexual Aging into the Twenty-First Century: An Overview and Introduction', *Journal of Lesbian, Gay and Bisexual Identity*, 2(3/4): 187–97

Bradshaw, J. (2008) 'Who is Fuel Poor?' *Poverty*, 131: 8–11

Brammer, A. (2007) *Social Work Law*, 2nd edition, Harlow: Pearson Education

Brannen, J. (2003) 'Towards a Typology of Intergenerational Relations: Continuities and Change in Families', *Sociological Research Online*, 8(2): www.socresonline.org.uk/8/2/brannen.html

Brannen, J. (2006) 'Cultures of Intergenerational Transmission in Four-Generation Families', *The Sociological Review*, 54(1): 133–54

Brannen, J. and Nilsen, A. (2005) 'Individualisation, Choice and Structure: A Discussion of Current Trends in Sociological Analysis', *The Sociological Review*, 53(3): 413–28

Braungart, R. and Braungart, M. M. (1986) 'Life Course and Generational Politics', *Annual Review of Sociology*, 1: 205–31

Breggin, P. (2001) *Talking Back to Ritalin: What Doctors Aren't Telling You about Stimulants and ADHD*, Cambridge: Perseus Press

Brim, O. G. (ed.) (1992) *Ambition: How We Manage Success and Failure Throughout Our Lives*, New York: Basic Books

Brislin, R. W. and Yoshida, T. (1994) *Improving Intercultural Interactions: Modules for Cross Cultural Training Programmes*, Thousand Oaks, CA: Sage

British Geriatrics Society (2007) *The Human Rights of Older People in Health Care: Call for Evidence. Submission by the BGS to the UK Parliament, Joint Committee on Human Rights*, www.bgs.org.uk/Publications/.../psn_human_rights.htm

Bronfenbrenner, U. (1979) *The Ecology of Human Development*, Cambridge, MA: Harvard University Press

Brown, P. and Hesketh, A. (with Williams, S.) (2004) *The Mismanagement of Talent: Employability and Jobs in the Knowledge Economy*, Oxford: Oxford University Press

Brownlie, J. and Anderson, S. (2006) 'Beyond Anti Smacking: Rethinking Parent–Child Relations', *Childhood*, 13(4): 479–98

Bruce, S. (1999) *Sociology: A Very Short Introduction*, Oxford: Oxford University Press

Brunsma, D. L. and Rockquemore, K. A. (2002) 'What Does "Black" Mean? Exploring The Epistemological Stranglehold of Racial Categorization', *Critical Sociology*, 28(1): 101–21

Bryant, P. (1990) 'Empirical Evidence for Causes in Development', in B. Butterworth and P. Bryant (eds.), *Causes of Development: Interdisciplinary Perspectives*, London: Lawrence Erlbaum

Bryman, A. (2004) *Social Research Methods*, Oxford: Oxford University Press

Bryman, A., Blytheway, B., Allatt, P. and Keil, T. (eds.) (1987) *Rethinking the Life Cycle*, London: Macmillan

Buck, N. and Scott, J. (1994) 'Households and Family Change', in N. Buck., J. Gershuny and J. Scott (eds.), *Changing Households: The British Household Panel Survey 1990–1999*, Colchester, ESRC Centre of Micro Social Change, University of Essex

Buckingham, D. (2001) *After the Death of Childhood: Growing Up in the Age of Electronic Media*, Cambridge: Polity

Buckingham, D. (2002) 'The Electronic Generation: Children and New Media', in L. Lievrouw and S. Livingstone (eds.), *Handbook of New Media*, London: Sage

Buckingham, D. and Bragg, S. (2005) 'Opting in to (and out of) Childhood: Young People, Sex and the Media', in J. Qvortrup (ed.), *Studies in Modern Childhood: Society, Agency, Culture*, Basingstoke: Palgrave

Buckner, L. and Yeandle, K. (2007) *Valuing Carers: Calculating the Value of Unpaid Care*, London: Carers UK available from www.carersuk.org/Policyandpractice/Research/Profileofcaring/1201108437/ValuingcarersFINAL. [pdf accessed 12.11.2008]

Bukowski, W. M., Newcomb, A. F. and Hartup, W. W. (1996) *The Company They Keep: Friendship in Childhood and Adolescence*, New York: Cambridge University Press

Bumpass, L. L. and Aquilino, W. S. (eds.) (1995) *A Social Map of Midlife: Family and Work over the Middle Life Course*, Vero Beach, FL: Macarthur Foundation

Bunting, M. (2004a) *Willing Slaves: How the Overwork Culture is Ruining Our Lives*, London: HarperCollins

Bunting, M. (2004b) 'Messing with Life', *The Guardian*, 02.02.2004

Burman, E. (1994) *Deconstructing Developmental Psychology*, London: Routledge

Burton, L. M. and Bengston, V. L. (1985) 'Black Grandmothers: Issues of Timing and Continuity of Roles', in V. L. Bengston and J. F. Robertson (eds.), *Grandparenthood*, Beverley Hills, CA: Sage

Buss, D. M. (1999) *Evolutionary Psychology: The New Science of the Mind*, Needham Heights, MA: Allyn Bacon

Butler, R. (1987) 'Ageism', in *The Encyclopaedia of Aging*, New York: Springer

Bynner, J. (2002) 'Youth Transitions in Comparative Context', *Journal of Youth Studies*, 4(1): 5–14

Bywater, M. (2006) 'Baby Boomers and the Illusion of Perpetual Youth', *New Statesman*, 30.10.2006

Cacioppo, J. Y., Bermston, G. G., Sheridan, J. F. and McClintock, M. K. (2000) 'Multilevel Integrative Analysis of Human Behavior: Social Neuroscience and the Complementing Nature of Social and Biological Approaches', *Psychological Bulletin*, 126(6): 829–43

Calasanti, T. (2007) 'Bodacious Berry, Potency Wood and the Aging Monster: Gender and Age Relations in Anti-Aging Ads', *Social Forces*, 86(1): 335–55

Carr, D. (2004) 'Psychological Wellbeing across Three Cohorts: A Response to Shifting Work–Family Opportunities', in O. G. Brim, C. D. Ryffer and R. Kessler (eds.), *How Healthy Are We? A National Study of Wellbeing in Midlife*, Chicago: University of Chicago Press

Carstensen, L., Fung, H. H. and Charles, S. T. (2003) 'Socioemotional Selectivity Theory and the Regulation of Emotion in the Second Half of Life', *Motivation and Emotion*, 21: 103–23

Cartner-Morley, J. (2007) 'All in The Head', *The Guardian*, 11.07.2007

Carvel, J. (2009a) 'Crunch Hitting Youngest and Oldest Workers Hardest – Report Says', *The Guardian*, 19.02.09

Carvel, J. (2009b) 'Young Adults Delay Leaving Family Home', *The Guardian*, 15.04.2009

Cate, R. A. and John, O. P. (2007) 'Testing Models of Structure and Development of Future Time Perspective: Maintaining a Focus on Opportunities in Middle Age' *Psychology and Aging*, 22(1): 186–201

Cebulla, A., Butt, S. and Lyon, N. (2007) 'Working Beyond the State Pension Age in the United Kingdom: The Role of Working Time Flexibility and Effects in the Home', *Ageing and Society*, 27(6): 849–67

Cerulo, K. A. (2009) 'Nonhumans in Social Interaction', *Annual Review of Sociology*, 35: 531–52

Charles, N. and Davies, C. A. (2008) 'My Family and Other Animals: Pets as Kin' *Sociological Research Online*, 13(5), www.socresonline.org.uk/13/5/4.html

Charles, S. T. and Carstensen, L. (2008) 'Unpleasant Situations Elicit Different Emotional Responses in Younger and Older Adults', *Psychology and Aging*, 23(3): 495–504

Chatitheochari, S. and Arber, S. (2009) 'Lack of Sleep, Work and the Long Hours Culture: Evidence from the UK Time Use Survey', *Work, Employment and Society*, 32(30): 30–48

Chayko, M. (2002) *Connecting: How We Form Social Bonds and Communities in the Internet Age*, New York: State University of New York Press

Cheng, S., Olsen, W. Southerton, D. and Warde, A. (2007) 'The Changing Practice of Eating: Evidence from UK Time Diaries, 1975 and 2000', *The British Journal of Sociology*, 5(1): 39–61

Child Poverty Action Group (CPAG) (2001) *An End in Sight? Tackling Child Poverty in the UK: Background Briefing and Summary*, London: CPAG

Child Poverty in Perspective: An Overview of Child Wellbeing in Rich Countries (2007), UNICEF Innocenti Research Centre Florence, UNICEF

Chiriboga, D. A. (1989) 'Mental Health at the Midpoint: Crisis, Challenge or Relief?' in S. Hunter and M. Sundel (eds.), *Midlife Myths: Issues, Findings and Practice Implications*, Newbury Park, CA: Sage

Chomsky, N. (1988) *Language and the Problems of Knowledge*, Cambridge, MA: MIT Press

Christensen, H., Henderson, A., Griffiths, K. and Levings, C. (1997) 'Does Ageing Inevitably Lead to Declines in Cognitive Performance? A Longitudinal Study of Elite Academics', *Personality and Individual Differences*, 23(1): 67–78

Christensen, P. (1993) 'The Social Construction of Help among Danish Children', *Sociology of Health and Illness*, 15(4): 488–502

Christian, M. (2000) *Multiracial Identity: An International Perspective*, London: Macmillan

Cockerham, W.C. (1991) *This Ageing Society*, New Jersey: Prentice Hall

Cohen, P. (1997) *Rethinking the Youth Question*, London: Macmillan Press

Colby, A., Kohlberg, L., Gibbs, J. and Lieberman, M. (1983) 'A Longitudinal Study of Moral Development', *Monographs for the Society for Research in Child Development*, 48 (1–2, Serial 200)

Cole, M., Cole, S. R. and Lightfoot, C. (2005) *The Development of Children*, 5th edition, New York: Worth

Coleman, J. and Hendry, L. (1999) *The Nature of Adolescence*, 3rd edition, London: Routledge

Coles, B. (1995) *Youth and Social Policy: Youth, Citizenship and Young Careers*, London: UCL Press

Collinson, P. (2009) 'Truth about Our Kidult Generation', *The Guardian*, 18.04.09, Money Section: P4

Collishaw, S., Vaughan, B., Goodman, R. and Pickles, A. (2004) 'Time Trends in Adolescent Mental Health', *Journal of Child Psychology and Psychiatry*, 43: 1350–62

Commas-Herrera, A., Wittenberg, R., Costa-Font, J., et al. (2006) 'Future Long Term Care Expenditure in Germany, Spain, Italy and the United Kingdom', *Ageing and Society*, 26(2): 285–302

Conway, M. A. and Holmes, A. (2004) 'Psychosocial Stages and the Accessibility of Autobiographical Memories across the Lifecourse', *Journal of Personality*, 72: 461–80

Cooke, G. (2008) 'Effacing the Face: Botox and the Anarchivic Archive', *Body and Society*, 14(2): 23–38

Cooke, P. and Ellis, R. (2004) 'Exploitation, Protection and Empowerment of People with Learning Disabilities', in M. Lymbery and S. Butler (eds.), *Social Work Ideals and Practice Realities*, Basingstoke: Palgrave Macmillan

Cooley, C. H. (1902) *Human Nature and the Social Order*, New York: Scribner's

Coppock, V. (2005) '"Mad", "Bad" or "Misunderstood"?' in H. Hendrick (ed.), *Child Welfare and Social Policy: A Reader*, Bristol: Policy Press

Corby, B. (2004) 'The Mistreatment of Young People', in J. Roche., S. Tucker, R. Thomson and R. Flynn (eds.), *Youth in Society*, 2nd edition, London: Sage / Oxford University Press

Corr, C. A. (1998/1999) 'Enhancing the Concept of Disenfranchised Grief', *Omega: The Journal of Death and Dying*, 38(1): 1–20

Corr, C. A., McNabe, C. M and Corr, D. M (1997) *Death and Dying: Life and Living*, 2nd edition, Pacific Grove, CA: Brooks/Cole

Corsaro, W. (1997) *The Sociology of Childhood*, California: Pine Forge (2nd edition, 2005)

Côté, J. (2000) *Arrested Adulthood: The Changing Nature of Maturity and Identity*, New York: New York University Press

Côté, J. and Bynner, J. (2008) 'Changes in the Transition to Adulthood in the UK and Canada: The Role of Structure and Agency in Emerging Adulthood', *Journal of Youth Studies*, 11(3): 251–68

Coward, R. (1999) '8 Children', *The Guardian*, 20.02.1999

Craib, I. (1994) *The Importance of Disappointment*, London: Routledge

Cramer, D. (1998) *Close Relationships: The Study of Love and Friendship*, New York: Oxford University Press

Cramer, P. (2008) 'Identification and the Development of Competence: A 44 Year Longitudinal Study from Late Adolescence to Late Middle Age', *Psychology and Aging*, 23(2): 410–21

Crawford, K. and Walker, J. (2007) *Social Work and Human Development*, Exeter: Learning Matters

Cribier, F. (1989) 'Changes in Life Course and Retirement In Recent Years: The Example of Two Cohorts of Parisians', in L. Johnson (ed.), *Workers vs. Pensioners*, Manchester: Manchester University Press

Crittenden, P. M. and Ainsworth, M. (1989) 'Child Maltreatment and Attachment Theory', in D. Cicchetti and V. Carlson (eds.), *Child Maltreatment: Theory and Research on the Causes and Consequences of Child Abuse and Neglect*, New York: Cambridge University Press

Crittenden, P. M. and Clausen, A.H. (2002) *The Organization of Attachment Relationships: Maturation, Culture and Context*, Cambridge: Cambridge University Press

Croghan, R., Griffin, C., Hunter, J. and Phoenix, A. (2006) 'Style Failure: Consumption, Identity and Social Exclusion', *Journal of Youth Studies*, 94: 463–78

Cross, W. E. (1971) 'Towards a Psychology of Black Liberation: The Negro-To-Black Conversion Experience', *Black World*, 20(9): 13–27

Cruikshank, M. (2003) *Learning to Be Old: Gender, Culture and Aging*, Lanham, MD: Rowman and Littlefield

Cummings, E. and Henry, W. (1961) *Growing Old: The Process of Disengagement*, New York: Basic Books

Cunningham, H. (2006) *The Invention of Childhood*, London: BBC Books

Cunningham, S. and Tomlinson, J. (2005) '"Starve Them Out": Does Every Child Really Matter? A Commentary On Section 9 of the Asylum and Immigration (Treatment of Claimants) Act 2004', *Critical Social Policy*, 25: 353–75

Curtis, P. (2008) 'Free School Meal Pupils Lose Out in Race for Top A-Levels', *The Guardian*, 23.11.2008

D'Souza, C. (2007) 'My Name is Christa. I'm an Age-orexic', *The Observer*, 13.05.2007

Dafermos, M. and Marvakis, A. (2006) 'Critiques in Psychology: Critical Psychology', *Annual Review of Critical Psychology*, 5: 1.20

Dan Zhang, Counselor (2008) 'Preventing Neglect and Abuse in a Rapidly Ageing Society', Briefing to the United Nations, New York, May 2008, www.china-un.org/eng/xwt459174, accessed 16.11.2008

Dannefer, D. and Miklowski, C. (2006) 'Developments in the Life Course', in J. A. Vincent., C. R. Phillipson and M. Downs (eds.), *The Futures of Old Age*, London: Sage

Davenport, G. (1994) *An Introduction to Child Development*, 2nd edition, London: Collins Educational

Davies, D. J. (1997) *Death, Ritual and Belief: The Rhetoric of Funerary Beliefs*, London: Cassell

Davis, S. N. (2007) 'Gender Ideology Construction from Adolescence to Young Adulthood', *Social Science Research*, 36: 1021–41

De Vries, F. (1969) 'Constancy of Genetic Identity in the Years Three to Six', *Monographs of the Society for Research in Child Development*, 34(127)

Deeming, C. and Keen, J. (2002) 'Paying for Old Age: Can People on Lower Incomes Afford Domiciliary Care Costs?' *Social Policy and Administration*, 36: 465–81

Denscombe, M. (1998) *The Good Research Guide*, Buckingham: Open University Press

Denzin, N. (1989) *Interpretive Interactionism*, Applied Social Research Methods Series, 16, Newbury Park, CA: Sage

Dermott, E. (2006) 'What's Parenthood Got to Do With it? Men's Hours of Paid Work', *The British Journal of Sociology*, 37(4): 619–34

Dickson, E. J. (2009) 'We've Locked Up Children in Jail and in Our Homes', *The Independent*, 15.08.2009

Dinero, R. E., Conger, R .D., Shaver, P. R., Widama, K. F. and Larsen-Rife, D. (2008) 'Influence of Family of Origin and Adult Romantic Partners on Romantic Attachment Security', *Journal of Family Psychology*, 22(4): 622–32

Dodd, P., Dowling, S. and Hollins, S. (2005) 'A Review of the Emotional, Psychiatric and Behavioural Responses to Bereavement in People with Intellectual Disabilities', *Journal of Intellectual Disability Research*, 49(7): 537–43

Doka, K. (1989) *Disenfranchised Grief: Recognising Hidden Sorrow*, Lexington, MA: Lexington Books

Donaldson, M. (1978) *Children's Minds*, London: Fontana

Donnellan, B. M. and Lucas, R. E. (2008) 'Age Differences in the Big Five Across the Life Span: Evidence from Two National Samples', *Psychology and Aging*, 23(3): 558–56

Donnelly, E., Burgess, E., Anderson, S., Davis, R. and Dillard, J. (2001) 'Involuntary Celibacy: A Life Course Analysis', *The Journal of Sex Research*, 38 (May): 159

Doucet, A. (2006) '"Estrogen–Filled Worlds": Fathers as Primary Caregivers and Embodiment', The *Sociological Review*, 54(4): 696–716

Du Bois-Reymond, M. (1998) '"I Don't Want to Commit Myself Yet": Young People's Life Concepts', *Journal of Youth Studies*, 1(1): 63–7

Duggan, S., O'Brien, M. and Krone, J. (2001) 'Young Adults' Immediate and Delayed Reactions to Stimulated Marital Conflict: Implications for Intergenerational Patterns of Violence in Intimate Relationships', *Journal of Consulting and Clinical Psychology*, 69(1): 13–24

Dunn, J. (1988) *The Beginnings of Social Understanding*, Cambridge, MA: Harvard University Press

Dunn, J. and Deater-Deckard, K. (2001) *Children's Views of Their Changing Families*, York: Joseph Rowntree

Durkheim, E. (1897/2002) *Suicide: A Study in Sociology*, London: Routledge

Durkheim, E. (1915) *The Elementary Forms of the Religious Life*, London: Unwin

Durkheim, E. (1961) *Moral Education*, Glencoe: The Free Press

Durkheim, E. (1982) 'Childhood', in C. Jenks (ed.), *The Sociology of Childhood: Essential Readings*, London: Batsford

Durkin, K. (1995) *Developmental Social Psychology: From Infancy to Old Age*, Oxford: Blackwell

Edemariam, A. (2010) 'Mark Serwotka: "Call Centres are the New Dark Satanic Mills"', *The Guardian*, 10.04.2010

Edmunds, J. and Turner, B. (2002) *Generations, Culture and Society*, Buckingham: Open University Press

Effros, R. B. (2001) 'Immune System Activity', in E. J. Masuro and S. N. Austad (eds.), *Handbook of the Biology of Aging*, 5th edition, San Diego, CA: Academic Press

Eisenstadt, S. N. (1956) *From Generation to Generation*, New York: Free Press

Elchardus, M. and Smits, W. (2006) 'The Persistence of the Standardized Life Cycle', *Time and Society*, 15(2/3): 303–26

Elder, G. H. (1974) *Children of the Great Depression*, Chicago: University of Chicago Press

Elder, G. H. (1986) 'Military Times and Turning Points in Men's Lives', *Developmental Psychology*, 22: 233–45

Elder, G. H. (1994) 'Time, Human Agency and Social Change: Perspectives on the Life Course', *Social Psychology Quarterly*, 57(1): 4–15

Elder, G. H. (1998) 'The Life Course as Developmental Theory', *Child Development*, 69(1): 1–12

Elias, N. (1985) *The Loneliness of the Dying*, Oxford: Basil Blackwell

Elias, N. (1994) *The Civilizing Process*, Oxford: Blackwell

Ellerman, C. R. and Reed, P. G. (2001) 'Self Transcendence and Depression in Middle-Age Adults', *Western Journal of Nursing Research*, 23(7): 698–713

Elliot, L. (2008) 'Up. Up. Up. Child Poverty, Pensioner Poverty, Inequality', *The Guardian*, 11.06.2008

Employment Equality (Age) Regulations (2006) – statutory instrument 2006 no. 1031, www.opsi.gov.uk/si/si2006/20061031.htm, accessed 19.05.2010

Epstein, D. (1998) *Schooling Sexualities*, Buckingham: Open University Press

Equalities Review Panel (2007) *Fairness and Freedom: The Final Report of the Equalities Review*, London: Crown Copyright

Engels, F. (1843/1969) *The Condition of the Working Class In England*, London: Panther

EOC (2001) *Men and Women: Pensions and Social Security*, London: Equal Opportunities Commission

Erikson, E. (1963) *Childhood and Society*, 2nd edition, New York: Norton

Erikson, E. (1968) *Identity, Youth and Crisis*, New York: Norton

Erikson, E. (1980) *The Life Course Completed*, New York: Norton

Erlinghagen, M. and Hank, K. (2006) 'The Participation of Older Europeans in Volunteer Work', *Ageing and Society*, 26(4): 567–84

Estes, C., Linkins, K.W. and Binney, E. A. (2001) 'Critical Perspectives on Ageing', in C. Estes (and associates), *Social Policy and Aging,* Thousand Oaks CA: Sage

Evans, D. (1994) 'Falling Angels? The Material Construction of Children as Sexual Citizens', *The International Journal of Children's Rights*, 2: 1–33

Eve, M. (2003) 'Is Friendship a Sociological Topic?' *Archives of European Sociology*, 43(3): 386–409

Exely, C. (2004) 'Review Article: The Sociology of Death, Dying and Bereavement', *Sociology of Health and Illness*, 2(1): 110–22

Fairhurst, E. (1998) '"Growing Old Gracefully as Opposed to Mutton Dressed as Lamb": The Social Construction of Recognising Older Women', in S. Nettleton and J. Watson (eds.), *The Body in Everyday Life*, London: Routledge

Fausto-Sterling, A. (2000) 'Beyond Difference: Feminism and Evolutionary Psychology', in H. Rose, S. Rose and C. Jencks (eds.), *Alas Poor Darwin: Arguments against Evolutionary Psychology*, London: Jonathan Cape

Fawcett, B., Featherstone, B. and Goddard, J. (2004) *Contemporary Child Care Policy and Practice*, Basingstoke: Palgrave

Featherstone, M. and Wernick, A. (eds.) (1995) *Images of Ageing: Cultural Representations of Later Life*, London: Routledge

Feeny, J. A. and Noller, P. (1992) 'Attachment Style and Romantic Love: Relationship Dissolution', *Australian Journal of Psychology*, 44: 69–74

Feeny, J. A., Noller, P. and Patty, J. (1993) 'Adolescent Interactions with the Opposite Sex: Influence of Attachment Style and Gender', *Journal of Adolescence*, 16: 169–89

Fehr, B. (1996) *Friendship Processes*, Thousand Oaks, CA: Sage

Feinstein, L., Bynner, J. and Duckworth, K. (2006) 'Young People's Leisure Contexts and Their Relation to Adult Outcomes', *Journal of Youth Studies*, 9(3): 305–27

Fennell, G., Phillipson, C. and Evers, H. (1988) *The Sociology of Old Age*, Milton Keynes: Open University Press:

Fenton, S. and Dermott, E. (2006) 'Fragmented Careers: Winners and Losers in Young Adult Labour Markets', *Work, Employment and Society*, 20(2): 205–21

Finch, J. (1986) *Family Obligations and Social Change*, London: Polity

Firth, S. (1997) *Death, Dying and Bereavement in a British Hindu Community*, Leuven: Peeters

Fishbein, H., Lewis, S. and Keifer, K. (1972) 'Children's Understanding of Spatial Relations: Coordination of Perspectives', *Developmental Psychology*, 7: 21–33

Fiske, J. (1989) *Reading the Popular*, Boston: Unwin Hyman

Fitzgerald, B. (2005) 'An Existential View of Adolescent Development', *Adolescence*, 40 (160): 793–809

Fleury-Steiner, B. (2004) *Jurors' Stories of Death: How America's Death Penalty Invests in Inequality*, Ann Arbor, MI: University of Michigan Press

Flynn, R. J. (1987) 'Massive IQ Gains in 14 Nations: What IQ Tests Really Measure', *Psychological Bulletin*, 1: 171–91

Forsyth, A. and Furlong, A. (2000) *Socioeconomic Disadvantage and Access to Higher Education*, Bristol: Policy Press

Fox, K. (2004) *Watching the English: The Hidden Rules of English Behaviour*, London: Hodder and Stoughton

Fox Harding, L. (2001) *Perspectives in Child Care Policy*, 2nd edition, London: Longman

France, A. (2007) *Understanding Youth in Late Modernity*, Maidenhead: Open University Press

France, A. (2008) 'Risk Factor Analysis and the Youth Question', *Journal of Youth Studies*, 11(1): 1–15

Franklin, B. and Horwath, J. (1996) 'The Murder of Innocence: Newspaper Reporting of the Death of Jamie Bulger', in S. Wagg and J. Pilcher (eds.), *Thatcher's Children*, London: Falmer Press

Freese, J., Allen Li, J. C. and Wade, L. D. (2003) 'The Potential Relevance of Biology to Social Inquiry', *Annual Review of Sociology*, 29: 233–56

Freund, A. M. and Baltes, P. B. (2002) 'The Adaptiveness of Selection, Optimization and Compensation as Strategies of Life management: Evidence from a Preference Study on Proverbs', *Journal of Gerontology: Psychological Sciences*, 57B: 416–34

Freysinger, V. G. (1995) 'The Dialectics of Leisure and Development for Women and Men in Midlife', *Journal of Leisure Research*, 27(1): 61–84

Friedan, B. (1993) *The Fountain of Age*, London: Cape Books

Friese, C., Becker, G. and Nachtigall, R. (2006) 'Rethinking the Biological Clock: Eleventh Hour Moms, Miracle Moms and the Meanings of Age-Related Infertility', *Social Science and Medicine*, 63: 1550–60

Friese, C., Becker, G. and Nachtigall, D. (2008) 'Older Motherhood and the Changing Life Course in the Era of Assisted Reproductive Technologies', *Journal of Aging Studies*, 22: 65–73

Frith, M. (2004) 'Baby Boomers Defiantly Refuse to Grow Old', *The Independent*, 12.07.2004

Fromholt, B. and Bruhn, P. (1998) 'Cognitive Dysfunction and Dementia', in I. H. Nordhus, G. R. VandenBos, S. Berg and P. Fromholt (eds.), *Clinical Geropsychology*, Washington, DC: American Psychological Association

Fry, C. L. (1985) 'Culture, Behavior and Aging in a Comparative Perspective', in J. E. Birren and K. W. Schaie (eds.), *Handbook of the Psychology of Aging*, 2nd edition, New York: Van Nostrand

Fulcher, J. and Scott, J. (2007) *Sociology*, 3rd edition, Oxford: Oxford University Press

Fung, H. and Cartensen, L. L. (2004) 'Motivational Changes in Response to Blocked Goals and Foreshortened Time: Testing Alternatives to Socioemotional Selectivity Theory', *Psychology and Aging*, 19: 66–78

Furedi, F. (2003) 'Children Who Won't Grow Up', *Spiked Online*, www.spiked-online.com/articles/00000006DE8D.htm

Furlong, A. and Cartmel, F. (2007) *Young People and Social Change*, 2nd edition, Maidenhead: Open University Press

Furnham, A. F. (1989) *Lay Theories: Everyday Understanding of Problems in the Social Sciences*, Oxford: Pergamon Press

Furstenberg, F. F., Brooks-Gunn, J. and Morgan, S. P. (1987) *Adolescent Mothers in Later Life*, New York: Cambridge University Press

Ganns, D. and Silverstein, M. (2006) 'Norms of Filial Responsibility for Aging Parents across Time and Generations', *Journal of Marriage and Family*, 68: 961–76

Ganska, H. (2010) 'Cougars Ready to Pounce', *The Sunday Times*, 14.02.2010, pp. 16–17 [Australian newspaper]

Garnett, M. (2007) *From Anger to Apathy: The British Experience Since 1975*, London: Cape

Gentleman, A. (2009) 'Majority of Poor Children Have At Least One Parent in Work, Says Study', *The Guardian*, 18.02.2009

George, L. K. (1993) 'Sociological Perspectives on Life Transitions', *Annual Review of Sociology*, 19: 353–73

Gibson, E. J. and Walk, R. D. (1960) 'The Visual Cliff', *Scientific American*, 202: 64–72

Gibson, H. B. (1992) *The Emotional and Sexual Life of Older People*, London: Chapman and Hall

Giddens, A. (1987) *Social Theory and Modern Sociology*, Oxford: Polity Press

Giddens, A. (1991) *Modernity and Self Identity: Self and Society in the Late Modern*, Cambridge: Polity

Giddens, A. (1992) *The Transformation of Intimacy: Sexuality, Love and Eroticism in Modern Societies*, Cambridge: Polity

Gielen, N. and Markoulis, D. (1994) 'Preference for Principled Moral Reasoning:

A Developmental and Cross Cultural Perspective', in L. Adler, U. Loeb and N. Gielen (eds.), *Cross Cultural Topics in Psychology*, Westport, CT: Praeger Greenwood

Gilbert, R. and Constantine, K. (2005) 'When Strength Can't Last a Lifetime', *Men and Masculinities*, 7(4): 424–33

Gilligan, C. (1977) 'In a Different Voice: Women's Conceptions of Self and of Morality', *Harvard Educational Review*, 47: 481–517

Gilroy, P. (2002) *There Ain't No Black in the Union Jack*, London: Routledge

Ginn, J. and Fast, J. (2006) 'Employment and Social Integration in Midlife: Preferred and Actual Time Use across Welfare Regimes', *Research on Aging*, 28(6): 669–90

Gittins, D. (1998) *The Child in Question*, Basingstoke: Macmillan

Gittins, D. (2004) 'The Historical Construction of Childhood', in M. Kehily (eds.), *An Introduction to Childhood Studies*, Maidenhead: McGraw Hill / Open University Press

Glaser, B. and Strauss, A. (1965) *Awareness of Dying*, Chicago: Aldine

Glasgow, F. (2003) 'Beware of the Baby Boomers as Retirement Time Gets Further Away', *The Independent*, 06.09.2003

Glenn, N. D. (1990) 'Quantitative Research on Marital Quality in the 1980s: A Critical Review', *Journal of Marriage and the Family*, 52: 818–31

Goldacre, B. (2007) 'A Menace to Science', *The Guardian*, 12.02.2007

Goldacre, B. (2008) *Bad Science*, London: Fourth Estate

Goldson, B. (2001) 'The Demonization of Childhood: From the Symbolic to the Institutional', in P. Foley, J. Roche and S. Tucker (eds.), *Children in Society: Contemporary Theory, Policy and Practice*, Basingstoke: Palgrave / Open University Press

Goldson, B. (2002) 'Children, Crime and The State', in B. Goldson., M. Lavalette and J. McKechnie (eds.), *Children, Welfare and The State*, London: Sage

Goodman, R. (2000) *Children of the Japanese State*, Oxford: Oxford University Press

Gordon, D., Levitas, R., Pantazis, D., et al. (2000) *Poverty and Social Exclusion in Britain*, York: Joseph Rowntree Foundation

Gorer, L. (1965) *Death, Grief and Mourning*, London: The Cresset Press

Gornick, J. C. and Meyers, M. K. (2003) 'Welfare Regimes in Relation to Paid Work and Care', in J. Z. Giele and E. Holst (eds.), *Advances In Life Course Research: Changing Life Patterns in Western Industrial Societies*, vol. VIII: 45–68, Oxford: Elsevier

Gott, M. and Hinchliff, S. (2003) 'Barriers to Seeking Treatment for Sexual Problems in Primary Care: A Qualitative Study with Older People', *Family Practice*, 20(6): 690–5

Goulbourne, H. (2001) 'The Socio-political Context of Caribbean Families in the Atlantic World', in H. Goulbourne and M. Chamberlain (eds.), *Caribbean Families in Britain and the Trans-Atlantic World*, London: Macmillan

Gramsci, A. (1971) *Selections from the Prison Notebooks*, London: Lawrence and Wishart

Green, E. and Singleton, C. (2007) 'Mobile Selves: Gender, Ethnicity and Mobile Phones in the Everyday Lives of Young Pakistani-British Men and Women', *Information, Communication and Society*, 10(4): 506–26

Green, L. (1998) 'Caged by Force, Entrapped by Discourse: A Study of the Construction and Control of Children and Their Sexualities within Residential Children's Homes', unpublished Ph.D. thesis, University of Huddersfield

Green, L. (2001) 'Children, Sexual Abuse and the Child Protection System', in

P. Foley, J. Roche and S. Tucker (eds.), *Children in Society: Contemporary Theory, Policy and Practice*, Basingstoke Palgrave / Open University Press

Green, L. (2004) 'Gender and the Social Construction of Identity', in G. Taylor and S. Spencer (eds.), *Social Identity: Multidisciplinary Approaches*, London: Routledge

Green, L. (2006) 'An Unhealthy Neglect? Examining the Relationship between Child Health and Gender in Research and Policy', *Critical Social Policy*, 26: 74–100

Green, L. and Grant, V. (2008) 'Gagged Grief and Beleaguered Bereavements: An Analysis of Multidisciplinary Theory Relating to Same Sex Partnership Bereavement', *Sexualities*, 11(3): 275–300

Green, L. and Taylor, J. (2010) 'Exploring the Relationship between Gender and Child Health: A Comparative Analysis of High and Low Economic Resource Countries', in B. Featherstone, C. A. Hooper, J. Scourfield and J. Taylor (eds.), *Gender and Child Welfare in Society*, Chichester: Wiley

Green, L., Parkin, W. and Hearn, J. (2001) 'Power', in E. Wilson (ed.), *Organizational Behaviour Reassessed: The Impact of Gender*, London: Sage

Greenstreet, W. (2004) 'Why Nurses Need to Understand the Principles of Bereavement Theory', *British Journal of Nursing*, 13(10): 590–3

Greif, G. (2008) *Buddy System*, Oxford: Oxford University Press

Griffin, C. (2001) 'Imagining New Narratives of Youth Research, the "New Europe" and Global Youth Culture', *Childhood*, 8(2): 147–66

Griggs, J. (2010) *Protect, Support, Provide: Examining the Role of Grandparents in Families at Risk of Poverty*, Report Prepared for Grandparents Plus and the EHRC, March 2010, www.equalityhumanrights.com/media-centre/new-report-from-grandparentsplus, accessed 06.03.2010

Groskop, V. (2009) 'I've Felt Like a Boy for a Long Time', *The Guardian*, 29.08.09

Grossman, K. E., Grossman, K., Huber, F. and Wartner, U. (1981) 'German Children's Behaviour towards Their Mother at 12 Months and Their Fathers at 18 Months in Ainsworth's Strange Situation', *International Journal of Behavioral Development*, 4: 157–81

Grotevant, H. D. (1998) 'Adolescent Development in Family Contexts', in W. Damon and N. Eisenberg (eds.), *Handbook of Child Psychology, Vol. 3: Social, Emotional and Personality Development*, 5th edition, New York: Wiley

Grundy, E. (2005) 'Reciprocity in Relationships: Socioeconomic and Health Influence on Intergenerational Exchanges between Third Generation Parents and their Adult Children', *The British Journal of Sociology*, 56(2): 233–55

The Guardian (2009) 'UK Lags behind Most of Europe in Child Wellbeing League', 21.04.2009

Guru, S. (2009) 'Divorce: Obstacles and Opportunities – South Asian Women in Britain', *The Sociological Review*, 57(2): 285–305

Guttmann, D. (1994) *Reclaimed Powers: Men and Women in Later Life*, 2nd edition, Evanston, IL: Northwestern University Press

Haerpfer, C., Wallace, C. and Spannring, R. (2002) *Young People and Politics in Eastern and Western Europe*, Vienna: Reighe Soziologie

Hakim, C. (2003) 'A New Approach to Explaining Fertility Patterns: Preference Theory', *Population and Development Review*, 29(3): 349–74

Hall, G. S. (1904) *Adolescence, Its Psychology and Its Relation to Physiology, Anthropology, Sociology, Sex, Crime, Religion and Education*, New York: Appleton

Hallam, E., Hockey, J. and Howarth, G. (1999) *Beyond the Body: Death and Social Identity*, London: Routledge

Halson, A. (1991) 'Young Women, Sexual Harassment and Heterosexuality: Violence, Power Relations and Mixed Sex Schooling', in P. Abbott and C. Wallace (eds.), *Gender, Power and Sexuality*, London: Macmillan

Hardey, M. (2002) 'Life beyond the Screen: Embodiment and Identity through the Internet', *The Sociological Review*, 50(4): 570–85

Harkin, J. (2006) 'The Baby Boomers are an Inspiration to Us All', *The Independent*, 21.07.2006

Harries, C., Forrest, D., Harvey, N., McClelland, A. and Bowling, A. (2007) 'Which Doctors Are Influenced by A Patient's Age? A Multi-Method Study of Angina Treatment in General Practice, Cardiology and Gerontology', *Quality and Safety in Health Care*, 16: 23–37

Harrison, T. (1995) *Disability: Rights and Wrongs*, Oxford: Lion

Harrup, W. W. (1989) 'Social Relationships and their Developmental Significance', *American Psychologist*, 44: 120–6

Haskey, J. (2005) 'Living Arrangements in Contemporary Britain: Having a Partner Who Lives Elsewhere and Living Apart Together (LAT)', *Population Trends*, 122(Winter): 45

Hatten, W., Vinter, L. and Williams, R. (2002) *Dads on Dads: Needs and Expectations at Home and at Work*, London: Equal Opportunities Commission

Hattenstone, S. (2000) 'They Were Punished Enough by What They Did', *The Guardian*, 30.10.2000

Havighurst, R. J. (1972) *Developmental Tasks and Education*, New York: Addison-Wesley Longman Ltd

Hayes, N. (1994) *Foundations of Psychology: An Introductory Text*, London: Routledge

Hazan, C. and Shaver, P. (1987) 'Romantic Love Conceptualized as an Attachment Process', *Journal of Personality and Social Psychology*, 52: 511–24

Hazel, N., Ghate, D., Creighton, J., Fields, S. and Finch, J. (2003) 'Violence against Children: Thresholds of Acceptance for Physical Violence in a Normative Study of Parents, Children and Discipline', in E. Stanko (ed.), *The Meanings of Violence*, London: Routledge

Heath, H. (2002) 'Out in the Cold: Service Needs of Older Lesbians and Gay Men', 16(48): 18–19

Heelas, P., Lash, U., Scott, S. and Morris, P. (eds.) (1996) *Detraditionalisation*, Oxford: Blackwell

Helson, R. and Srivastava, S. (2002) 'Creative and Wise People: Similarities, Differences and How They Develop', *Personality and Social Psychology Bulletin*, 28(10): 1430–40

Hendry, L. B. and Kloep, M. (2002) *Lifespan Development: Sources, Challenges, Risks*, Oxford: Alden Press

Henriques, J., Hollway, W., Urwin, C. and Walkerdine, V. (1984) *Changing the Subject*, London: Methuen (2nd edition, 1998, Routledge)

Herbert, M. (2008) 'Adolescence', in M. Davies (ed.), *The Blackwell Companion to Social Work*, 3rd edition, Oxford: Blackwell

Herrnstein, R. J. and Murray, C. A. (1994) *The Bell Curve: Intelligence and Class Structure In American Life*, New York: Simon and Schuster

Hetherington, E. M. (2003) 'Social Support and the Adjustment of Children in Divorced and Remarried Families', *Childhood*, 10(2): 217–336

Heyl, V. and Schmitt, M. (2007) 'The Contribution of Adult Personality and Recalled Parent–Child Relations to Friendships in Middle and Old Age', *International Journal of Behavioral Development*, 31(1): 38–48

Heywood, C. (2001) *A History of Childhood*, Cambridge: Polity Press

Hill, A. (2007) 'Baby Boomers: Broke, Ailing and Anxious', *The Observer*, 10.06.2007

Hill, R., Foote, N., Alduous, J., Carlson, R. and Macdonald, R. (1970) *Family Development in Three Generations*, Cambridge, MA: Schenkman Books

Hillcoat-Nalletamby, S. and Dharmalingam, A. (2003) 'Mid-Life Parental Support for Adult Children in New Zealand', *Journal of Sociology*, 39(3): 271–90

Hilpern, K. (2008a) 'Umbilical Chords Just Got Longer', *The Guardian*, 10.09.2008, www.guardian.co.uk/education/2008/sep/10/parents.careerseducation, accessed 24.09.08

Hilpern, K. (2008b) 'Generation Game', *The Guardian*, 21.08.2008

Hinscliff, G. (2008) 'College Boom "Dividing Britain's Youth"', *The Guardian*, 21.12.2008

Hislop, J. and Arber, S. (2003) 'Sleepers Wake! The Gendered Nature of Sleep Disruption among Mid Life Women', *Sociology*, 37(4): 695–711

Hobbs, S. (2002) 'New Sociology and Old Psychology', in B. Goldson., M. Lavalette and J. McKechnie (eds.), *Children, Welfare and the State*, London: Sage

Hochschild, A. (1983) *The Managed Heart: Commercialization of Human Feeling*, Berkeley: University of California Press

Hockey, J. and James, A. (1993) *Growing Up and Growing Old*, London: Sage

Hockey, J. and James, A. (2003) *Social Identities across the Life Course*, Basingstoke: Palgrave Macmillan

Holdsworth, D. and Morgan, C. (2005) *Transitions in Context: Leaving Home, Independence and Adulthood*, Milton Keynes: Open University Press

Holland, J., Reynolds, T. and Weller, S. (2007) 'Transitions, Networks and Communities: The Significance of Social Capital in the Lives of Children and Young People', *Journal of Youth Studies*, 10(1): 97–116

Holloway, L. S. and Valentine, G. (2003) *Cyber Kids: Children in the Information Age*, London: RoutledgeFalmer

Holloway, M. (2007) *Negotiating Death in Contemporary Health and Social Care*, London: Policy Press

Holmes, M. (2006) 'Love Lives at a Distance: Distance Relationships over the Life Course', *Sociological Research Online*, 11(3), www.socresonline.org.uk/11/3/holmes.html

Holmwood, L. (2007) 'Moira Stuart Leaves BBC News amid Allegations of Ageism' *The Guardian*, 4.10.2007

Holstein, J. (1990) 'The Discourse of Age in Involuntary Commitment Proceedings', *Journal of Aging Studies*, 4: 111–20

Holstein, J. A. and Gubrium, J. F. (2007) 'Constructionist Perspectives on the Life Course', *Sociology Compass* 1(1): 335–52

Hood-Williams, P. (1990) 'Patriarchy for Children: On the Stability of Power Relations in Children's Lives', in L. Chisholm, P. Buchner, H. H. Kruger and P. Brown (eds.), *Childhood, Youth and Social Change*, London: Falmer

Horner, K. W., Rushton, J. P. and Vernon, P.A. (1986) 'Relation between Aging and Research Productivity of Academic Psychologists', *Psychology and Aging*, 1: 319–24

Horner, M. S. (1972) 'Towards an Understanding of Achievement-Related Conflicts in Women', *Journal of Social Issues*, 28: 157–76

Hostetler, A. J. and Cohl, B. J. (1997) 'Partnership, Singlehood and the Lesbian and Gay Life Course: A Research Agenda', *Journal of Gay, Lesbian and Bisexual Identity*, 2(3/4): 199–230

Howard, S. and Johnson, B. (2000) 'What Makes the Difference? Children and

Teachers Talk about Resilient Outcomes for Children "at Risk"', *Educational Studies*, 26(3): 321–37

Howe, D., Brandon, M., Hinings, D. and Schofield, G. (eds.) (1999) *Attachment Theory, Child Maltreatment and Family Support: A Practice and Assessment Model*, London: Macmillan

Hughes, J., Martin, P. and Sharrock, W. (1999) *Understanding Classical Sociology*, London: Sage

Humphry, D. (1999) 'Foreword', in J. Werth, Jr, *Contemporary Perspectives on Rational Suicide*, London: Bruner/Mazel

Hunt, S. (2005) *The Life Course: A Sociological Introduction*, Basingstoke: Palgrave

Hunt, K. (2002) 'A Generation Apart? Gender Related Experience and Health in Women in Early and Late Mid-Life', *Social Science and Medicine*, 54: 663–76

Hunter, S. and Sundel, M. (1989) *Midlife Myths: Issues, Findings and Practice Implications*, Newbury Park, CA: Sage

Hussain, Y. and Bagguley, P. (2005) 'Citizenship, Ethnicity and Identity: British Pakistanis after the 2001 "Riots"', *Sociology*, 39(3): 407–25

Huyck, M. H. (1999) 'Gender Roles and Gender Identity in Midlife', in S. L. Willis and J. D. Reid (eds.), *Life in the Middle: Psychosocial and Social Development in Middle Age*, San Diego, CA: Academic Press

Hyde, M. (2006) 'Disability', in G. Payne (ed.), *Social Divisions*, Basingstoke: Palgrave Macmillan

The Independent (2009) 'Model Moss Rapped for "Skinny Feels Good" Motto', Relax News, 20.11.2009, www.independent.co.uk, accessed 07.03.2010

Irwin, S. (2005) *Reshaping Social Life*, London: Routledge

Jack, G. (2000) 'Ecological Influences on Parenting and Child Development' *British Journal of Social Work*, 30: 703–20

Jackson, C. and Tinkler, P. (2007) '"Ladettes" and "Modern Girls": Troublesome Young Femininities', *The Sociological Review*, 55(2): 251–72

Jackson, S. and Scott, S. (2000) Childhood', in G. Payne (ed.), *Social Divisions*, Basingstoke: Macmillan

Jacobs, S. C., Kosten, T. R., Kasly, S.V., Ostfild, A. M., Berkman, L. and Charpentier, P. (1987–8) 'Attachment Theory and Multiple Dimensions of Grief', *Omega*, 18: 41–52

James, A. and James, A. L. (2004) *Constructing Childhood: Theory, Policy and Social Practice*, Basingstoke: Palgrave

James, A. and Prout, A. (eds.) (1997) *Constructing and Reconstructing Childhood*, 2nd edn, London: RoutledgeFalmer

James, A., Jenks, C. and Prout, A. (eds.) (1998) *Theorizing Childhood*, Cambridge: Polity

Jamieson, L., Anderson, M., McCrone, D., Bechofer, F., Stewart, R. and Li, Y. (2002) 'Cohabitation and Commitment: Partnership Plans of Young Men and Women', *The Sociological Review*, 50(3): 356–77

Jeffries, S. and Konnert, C. (2002) 'Regret and Psychological Wellbeing among Voluntarily and Involuntarily Childless Women', *International Journal of Aging and Human Development*, 54: 89–106

Jenkins, R. (1996) *Social Identities*, London: Routledge

Jenks, C. (1996) *Childhood*, London: Routledge

Jensen, A.R. (1969) *Environment, Heredity and Intelligence*, Cambridge, MA: Harvard Educational Review

Jimenez, A. (2003) 'Triple Jeopardy: Targeting Older Men of Color Who Have Sex with Men', *Journal of Acquired Immune Deficiency Syndromes*, 33: 222–5

John, O. P. and Gross, J. J. (2004) 'Healthy and Unhealthy Emotion Regulation: Personality Processes, Individual Differences and Life Span Development', *Journal of Personality*, 72(6): 1301–33

Johnson, A. (2007) 'Glastonbury Boss Woos a Younger Crowd as Middle-Aged Bands Top the Live Music Bill', *The Independent*, 9.09.2007

Johnson, M. (1999) 'Dependency and Interdependency', in J. Bond, P. Coleman and S. Peace (eds.), *Ageing in Society: An Introduction to Social Gerontology*, London: Sage

Johnston, O., Reilly, J. and Kremer, J. (2004) 'Women's Experiences of Appearance Concern and Body Control across the Lifespan: Challenging Accepted Wisdom', *Journal of Health Psychology*, 9(3): 397–410

Jones, A. (2008) 'Paramedics Arrested for Neglect of Dying Man', *The Guardian*, 31,12.08

Jones, M. (2004) 'Cosmetic Surgery and Postmodern Space', *Space and Culture*, 7(1): 90–101

Jordan, B. (2006) *Social Policy for the Twenty-First Century*, Cambridge: Polity

Joshi, H., Makepeace, G. and Dolton, P. (2007) 'More or Less Unequal? Evidence on the Pay of Men and Women from the British Birth Cohort Studies', *Gender, Work and Organization*, 14(1): 37–55

Jung, C. G. (1971) *The Portable Jung*, New York: Viking

Karasek, R., Gardell, B. and Lindell, J. (1987) 'Work and Non Work Correlates of Illness and Behaviour in Swedish Male and Female White Collar Workers', *Journal of Occupational Behaviour*, 8: 187–207

Kasi-Godley, J. E., Gatz, M. and Fiske, A. (1998) 'Depression and Depressive Symptoms in Old Age', in I. H. Nordhus, G. R. VandenBos, S. Berg and P. Fromholt (eds.), *Clinical Geropsychology*, Washington, DC: American Psychological Association

Kastenbaum, R. (1998) *Death, Society and Human Experience*, 6th edition, Boston: Allyn and Bacon

Katz, I. (1996) *The Construction of Racial Identity in Children of Mixed Parentage: Mixed Metaphors*, London: Jessica Kingsley

Kaufman, S. R. (1986) *The Ageless Self*, Madison, WI: Wisconsin Press

Kearney, P. M. and Griffin, T. (1991) 'Between Joy and Sorrow: Being a Parent of a Child with Developmental Disability', *Journal of Advanced Nursing*, 34(5): 582–92

Keats, D. M. (1982) 'Cultural Bases of Concepts of Intelligence: A Chinese versus Australian Comparison', in P. Sukontasarp, N. Yongsiri, P. Intasuwan, N. Joriban and C. Suvannathat (eds.), *Proceedings of the Second Asian Workshop on Child and Adolescent Development*, Bangkok: Burapasilpa Press

Keith, J. (1990) 'Age in Social and Cultural Context: Anthropological Perspectives', in R. H. Binstock and L. K. George (eds.), *Aging in the Social Sciences*, 3rd edition, San Diego, CA: Academic Press

Kelly, B. D. and McLoughlin, D. M. (2002) 'Euthanasia, Assisted Suicide and Psychiatry: A Pandora's Box', *British Journal of Psychiatry*, 181: 278

Kelly, P. (2003) 'Growing Up as Risky Business? Risks, Surveillance and the Institutionalised Mistrust of Youth', *Journal of Youth Studies*, 6(2): 165–80

Kessler, R. C., Chiu, W. T., Merikangas., K. W. and Walters, E. E. (2005) 'Prevalence, Severity and Comorbidity of Twelve Month DSM-IV Disorders in the National Comorbidity Survey Replication', *Archives of General Psychiatry*, 62(6): 617–26

Kiernan, K. (1988) 'Who Remains Celibate?' *Journal of Biosocial Science*, 20: 253–63

Kiernan, K. (2003) 'Unmarried Parenthood: Insights from the Millennium Cohort Study', *Population Trends*, 114: 26–33

Kirk, S., Glendinning, C. and Callery, P. (2005) 'Parent or Nurse? The Experience of Being the Parent of a Technology Dependent Child', *Journal of Advanced Nursing*, 51(5): 456–64

Kitzinger, J. (1997) 'Who Are You Kidding? Children, Power and the Struggle against Sexual Abuse', in A. James and A. Prout (eds.), *Constructing and Reconstructing Children*, London: RoutledgeFalmer

Kjolsrod, L. (2003) 'Adventure Revisited: On Structure and Metaphor in Specialized Play', *Sociology*, 37(3): 459–76

Klaczynski, P. (2001) 'Analytic and Heuristic Influences on Adolescent Reasoning and Decision Making', *Child Development*, 72: 844–61

Klass, D. and Goss, R. (1999) 'Spiritual Bonds to the Dead in Cross-Cultural and Historical Perspective: Comparative Religion and Modern Grief', *Death Studies*, 23(6): 547–67

Kleiber, D. A. (1999) *Leisure Experiences and Human Development*, New York: Basic Books

Klein, N. (2000) *No Logo*, London: HarperCollins Flamingo

Klein, W. (1996) 'Language Acquisition at Different Ages', in D. Magnusson (ed.), *The Lifespan Development of Individuals*, Cambridge: Cambridge University Press

Kleinman, A. (2004) 'Culture and Depression', *New England Journal of Medicine*, 31(10, September)

Kline, S. (2005) 'Is it Time to Rethink Media Panics?' in J. Qvortrup (ed.), *Studies in Modern Childhood: Society, Agency, Culture*, Basingstoke: Palgrave

Kluwer, E. S., Heesink, J. A. and van de Vliert, E. (2002) 'The Division of Labor across the Transition to Parenthood: A Justice Perspective', *Journal of Marriage and Family*, 64: 930–3

Kneen, J. (2007) 'Them and US', *The Guardian*, 18.09.07, Education Guardian Learn, P7

Kohlberg, L. (1976) 'Moral Stage and Moralization: The Cognitive Developmental Approach', in T. Lickona (ed.), *Moral Development and Behavior: Theory, Research and Social Issues*, New York: Holt, Rhinehart and Winston

Konstam, V. (2008) *Emerging and Young Adulthood: Multiple Perspectives, Diverse Narratives*, New York: Springer

Kotarba, J. (2005) 'Rock 'n' Roll Experiences in Middle Age', *American Behavioral Scientist*, 48(11): 1524–37

Kraut, R., Patterson, M., Landmark, V., Kiesler, S., Mukopadhyay, T. and Scherlis, W. (1998) 'Internet Paradox: A Social Technology that Reduces Social Involvement and Psychological Well-Being', *American Psychologist*, 53(9): 1011–31

Kubler Ross, E. (1969) *On Death and Dying*, New York: Macmillan

Kuhn, D. (2006) 'Do Cognitive Changes Accompany Developments in the Adolescent Brain?' *Perspectives on Psychological Science*, 1: 59–67

La Valle, I., Arthur, S., Millward, C., Scott, J. and Clayden, M. (2002) *Happy Families? Atypical Work and its Influence on Family Life*, Bristol: Policy Press

Labouvie-Vief, G. (1980) 'Beyond Formal Operations: Uses and Limits of Pre Logic in Life Span Development', *Human Development*, 23: 141–61

Labouvie-Vief, G. (1982) 'Dynamic Development and Mature Autonomy', *Human Development*, 25: 186–93

Labouvie-Vief, G. (1992) 'A Neo Piagetian Perspective on Adult Cognitive

Development', in R. J. Sternberg and C. A. Berg (eds.), *Intellectual Development*. New York: Cambridge University Press

Lachman, M. E. (2004) 'Development in Midlife', *Annual Review of Psychology*, 55: 305–31

Lachman, M. E., Lewkowicz, C., Marcus, A. and Peng, Y. (1994) 'Images of Midlife Development Among Young, Middle Aged and Older Adults', *Journal of Adult Development*, 1(4): 201–11

Ladd, K. (2007) 'Religiosity: The Need for Structure, Death Attitudes and Funeral Preferences', *Mental Health, Religion and Culture*, 10(5): 451–72

Laing, R. D. and Esterson, A. (1964) *Sanity, Madness and the Family*, Harmondsworth: Penguin

Lamblev. P. (1995) *The Middle Aged Rebel: Responding to the Challenges of Mid Life*, New York: Element Books

Lampard, R. and Peggs, K. (2007) *Identity and Repartnering*, Basingstoke: Palgrave

Lash, S. and Urry, J. (1987) *The End of Organised Capitalism*, Cambridge: Polity

Laslett, P. (1989) *A Fresh Map of Life: The Emergence of the Third Age*, London: George, Weidenfeld and Nicholson Ltd

Lavalette, M. (2005) '"In Defence of Childhood": Against the Neo Liberal Assault on Social Life', in J. Qvortrup (ed.), *Studies in Modern Childhood: Society, Agency, Culture*, Basingstoke: Palgrave

Lawler, S. (2008) *Identity: Sociological Perspectives*, Cambridge: Polity Press

Lawton, J. (1998) 'Contemporary Hospice Care: The Sequestration of the Unbounded Body and Dirty Dying', *Sociology of Health and Illness*, 20(2): 121–43

Lawton, M. P., Winter, L., Kleban, M. H. and Ruckdeschel, K. (1999) 'Affect and Quality of Life: Objective and Subjective', *Journal of Aging and Health*, 11: 16–198

Leach, E. (1967) *A Runaway World*, London: BBC Publications

Lee, N. (2001) *Childhood and Society: Growing Up in an Age of Uncertainty*, Buckingham: Open University Press

Lee, N. (2005) *Childhood and Human Value: Development, Separation and Separability*, Buckingham: Open University Press

Lees, S. (1993) *Sugar and Spice: Sexuality and Adolescent Girls*, London: Hutchinson

Leitner, N., Shapland, J. and Wiles, P. (1993) *Drug Usage and Prevention: The Views and Habits of the General Public*, London: HMSO

Levinson, D. J. (1978) *The Seasons of a Man's Life*, New York: Ballantine

Levinson, D. J. (1986) 'A Conception of Adult Development', *American Psychologist*, 41: 3–13

Levinson, D. J. (1996) *The Seasons of a Woman's Life*, New York: Knopf

Levy, B. (1996) 'Improving Memory in Old Age through Implicit Self Stereotyping', *Journal of Personality and Social Psychology*, 71: 1092–106

Levy, R., Ghisletta, P., Le Goff, J. M., Spini, D. and Widmer, E. (2005) 'Incitations for Interdisciplinarity in Life Course Research', *Advances in Life Course Research*, 10: 361–91

Levy, R. and the Pavie Team (2005) 'Why Look at Life Courses in an Interdisciplinary Research Perspective?' *Advances in Life Course Research*, 10: 3–32

Lewis, J. (2001) *The End of Marriage? Individualism and Intimate Relations*, Cheltenham: Edward Elgat

Lewis-Stempel, J. (2001) *Fatherhood: An Anthology*, London: Simon and Schuster

Lichtental, W., Cruess, D. G. and Prigerson, H. G. (2004) 'A Case for Establishing

Complicated Grief as a Distinct Mental Disorder under DSM IV', *Clinical Psychology Review*, 24(6): 637–62

Lindenberger, U. and Baltes, P. B. (1994) 'Sensory Functioning and Intelligence in Old Age: A Powerful Connection', *Psychology and Aging*, 9: 339–55

Lipsett, A. (2008) 'Government HE Target Unrealistic Say Tories', *The Guardian*, 28.03.2008, Guardian Education

Lipsett, A. (2009a) 'Record Numbers of Young Not in Work or Education', *The Guardian*, 20.04.09

Lipsett, A. (2009b) 'Rise in University Gender Pay Gap', *The Guardian*, 30.03.2009

Lister, R. (2003) 'Investing in Citizen-Workers of the Future: Transformation in Citizenship and the State under New Labour', *Social Policy and Administration*, 37(5): 427–43

Livingstone, S., Bober, M. and Helsper, E. (2005) *Inequalities and the Digital Divide in Children and Young People's Internet Use*, London: Children Go Online Project, www.children-go-online.net, accessed 10.12.2006

Lymberry, M. (2004) 'Managerialism and Care Management Practice with Older People', in M. Lymberry and S. Butler (eds.), *Social Work Ideals and Practice Realities*, Basingstoke: Palgrave Macmillan

Lyon, D. (2000) *Jesus in Disneyland: Religion in Postmodern Times*, Cambridge: Polity Press

Mac an Ghaill, M. (1994) *The Making of Men: Masculinities, Sexualities and Schooling*, Buckingham: Open University Press

Maccoby, E. E. (2000) 'Parenting and its Effects on Children: On Reading and Misreading Behavior Genetics', *Annual Review of Psychology*, 51: 1–21

Machin, L. (1998) 'Making Sense of Experience: Death and Old Age', *Journal of Social Work Practice*, 12(2): 217–26

Macionis, J. L. and Plummer, K. (2002) *Sociology: A Global Introduction*, Edinburgh: Pearson Education Limited.

Mackay, M. (2006) 'Many Are Turning to Plastic Surgery to Avoid Age Discrimination at Work', *The Independent*, 19.03.2006

Macleod, D. (2008) 'In They Swoop to Direct Their Children's Careers: The Helicopter Parents Have Landed', *The Guardian*, 03.01.08

Macmillan, R. (2005) 'The Structure of the Life Course: Classic Issues and Current Controversies', *Advances In Life Course Research*, 9: 3–24

Macunevich, D. J. (1999) 'The Fortune of One's Birth: Relative Cohort Size and Youth Labor in the United States', *Journal of Economics*, 12: 215–72

Macvarish, J. (2006) 'What Is "The Problem" of Singleness?' *Sociological Research Online*, 11(3), www.socresonline.org.uk/11/3/macvarish.html

Madge, N. (2005) *Children These Days*, Bristol: Policy Press

Maffesoli, M. (1996) *The Time of the Tribes: The Decline of Individualism in Mass Society*, London: Sage

Magee, B. (1973) *Popper*, London: Fontana

Mannheim, K. (1952) 'The Problem of Generations', in Mannheim, *Essays on the Sociology of Knowledge*, London: RKP

Marcia, J. (1966) 'Development and Validation of Ego Identity Status', *Journal of Personality and Social Psychology*, 3: 551–8

Marmot, M. (2004) *Status Syndrome*, London: Bloomsbury

Martin, T. and Doka, K. (2000) *Men Don't Cry . . . Women Do? Transcending Gender Stereotypes of Grief*, Philadelphia, PA: Taylor and Francis

Marx, K. (1844/1959) *Economic and Philosophical Manuscripts*, London: Lawrence and Wishart

Maslow, A. H. (1943) 'A Theory of Human Motivation', *Psychological Review*, 50(4): 370–96

Mason, D. (2006) 'Ethnicity', in G. Payne (ed.), *Social Divisions*, 2nd edition, Basingstoke: Palgrave

Masson, J. (1984) *The Assault on Truth: Freud's Suppression of the Seduction Theory*, New York: Farrar Strauss and Giroux

Mattheson, J. and Summerfield, J. (2001) *Social Focus on Men*, London: The Stationery Office

Matthews, S. (1979) *The Social World of Old Women*, Newbury Park, CA: Sage

Mayall, B. (2002) *Towards a Sociology for Childhood: Thinking from Children's Lives*, Buckingham: Open University Press

Mayer, J. D., Salovey, P. and Caruso, D. R. (2008) 'Emotional Intelligence: New Ability or Eclectic Traits?' *American Psychologist*, 63(6): 503–17

Mayer, K. U. (2003) 'The Sociology of the Life Course and Life Span Psychology: Diverging or Converging Pathways?' in U. M Staudinger and U. Lindenberger (eds.), *Understanding Human Development: Dialogues With the Life Span*, Yale: Yale Education

McAdam, D. (1989) 'The Biographical Consequences of Activism', *American Sociological Review*, 54: 744–60

McCrae, R. R. and Allik, J. (2002) *The Five Factor Model of Personality across Cultures*, New York: Kluwer

McElroy, L. P. (1992) 'Early Indicators of Pathological Dissociation in Sexually Abused Children', *Child Abuse And Neglect*, 18: 833–46

McGhee, P. (2001) *Thinking Psychologically*, Basingstoke: Palgrave Macmillan

McLafferty, I. and Morrison, F. (2004) 'Attitudes towards Hospitalised Older Adults', *Issues and Innovations in Nursing Education*, 47(4): 446–53

McNamara, B., Waddell, C. and Colcin, C. (1995) 'Threats to the Good Death: The Cultural Context of Stress and Coping amongst Hospice Nurses', *Sociology of Health and Illness*, 17(2): 223–44

McRobbie, A. (1978) 'Working Class Girls and the Culture of Femininity', in Women's Study Group, Centre for Contemporary Cultural Studies, *Women Take Issue: Aspects of Women's Subordination*, London: Hutchison

McRobbie, A. (1994) *Post Modernism and Modern Culture*, London: Routledge

McVeigh, K. (2007) '"A" Level Questions to Become More Difficult', *The Guardian*, 24.11.2007

Mead, G. (1927/1934) *Mind, Self and Society*, Chicago: University of Chicago Press

Measham, F. (2007) 'The Turning Tides of Intoxication: Young People's Drinking in Britain in the 2000s', *Health Education*, 108(3): 207–27

Mellor, P. and Shilling, C. (1993) 'Modernity, Self Identity and the Sequestration of Death', *Sociology*, 27(3): 411–31

Mellor, P. and Shilling, C. (1997) *Reforming the Body Religion: Community and Modernity*, London: Sage

Mikulincer, M., Florian, V. and Weller, A. (1993) 'Attachment Styles, Coping Strategies and Posttraumatic Psychological Distress: The Impact of the Gulf War in Israel', *Journal of Personality and Social Psychology*, 64: 817–26

Milburn, A. (2009) *Unleashing Aspiration: The Final Report of the Panel on Fair Access to the Professions*, www.cabinetoffice.gov.uk/media/227102/fair-access.pdf, accessed 01.09.09

Miles, S. (2000) *Youth Lifestyles in a Changing World*, Buckingham: Open University Press

Miller, L. S. and Lachman, M. E. (2000) 'Cognitive Performance and the Role of

Health and Control Beliefs in Midlife', *Aging and Neuropsychological Cognition*, 7: 69–85

Mills, C. Wright (1959) *The Sociological Imagination*, London: Penguin

Minichiello, V., Browne, J. and Kendig, H.(2000) 'Perceptions and Consequences of Agism: Views of Older People', *Ageing and Society*, 20(3): 253–78

Mintel (2003) *Teenage Shopping Habits*, www.reports.mintel.com/sinatra/reports

Mizen, P. (2004) *The Changing State of Youth*, Basingstoke: Palgrave

Moen, P. (1996) 'Gender, Age and the Life Course', in R. H. Binstock, L. K. George, V. W. Marshall, G. C. Merss and J. H Schulz (eds.), *Handbook of Aging and Social Sciences*, 4th edition, San Diego, CA: Academic Press

Moffit, T. (1993) 'Adolescent Limited and Life-Course Persistent Antisocial Behaviour: A Developmental Taxonomy', *Psychological Review* 100: 674–701

Montgomery, H. (2009) *An Introduction to Childhood: Anthropological Perspectives on Children's Lives*, Chichester: Wiley-Blackwell

Montgomery, H. and Burr, R. (2003) 'Children, Poverty and Social Inequality', in H. Montgomery, R. Burr and M. Woodhead (eds.), *Changing Childhoods: Global and Local*, Chichester: John Wiley

Morelli, G. A., Oppenheim, G., Rogoff, B. and Goldsmith, D. (1992) 'Cultural Variation in Children's Sleeping Arrangements – Questions of Independence', *Developmental Psychology*, 28: 604–13

Morgan, D. H. J. (1996) *Family Connections: An Introduction to Family Studies*, Cambridge: Polity Press

Morris, A. and Sloutsky, V. (1998) 'Understanding Logical Necessity: Developmental Antecedents and Cognitive Consequences', *Child Development*, 69: 721–41

Morrison, B. (2007) 'The Paternal Instinct', *The Guardian*, 16.06.2007, Family Supplement

Morss, J. R. (1996) *Growing Critical: Alternatives to Developmental Psychology*, London: Routledge

Morton, N. and Browne, K.D. (1998) 'Theory and Observation of Attachment and Maltreatment: A Review', *Child Abuse and Neglect*, 22(11): 1093–104

Moshman, D. (1999) *Adolescent Psychological Development: Rationality, Morality and Identity*, Mahwah, NJ: Erlbaum

Moss, P. and Petrie, P. (2002) *From Children's Services to Children's Spaces*, London: RoutledgeFalmer

Muncie, J. (2007) 'Youth Justice and the Governance of Young People', in S. Ventakesh and R. Kassimir (eds.), *Youth, Globalisation and the Law*, Stanford: Stanford University Press

Murphy, S. A., Johnson, L. C. and Weber, N. A. (2002) 'Coping Strategies Following a Child's Violent Death: How Parents Differ in Their Responses', *Journal of Death and Dying*, 45(2): 99–118

Myles, J. (2002) 'A New Social Contract For the Elderly', in G. Esping-Andersen, with D. Gallie and J. Myles (eds.), *Why We Need a New Welfare State*, Oxford: Oxford University Press

Naegel, G. and Walker, A. (2007) 'Social Protection, Incomes, Poverty and the Reform of the Pensions System', in J. Bond, S. Peace, F. Dittman-Kohli and G. Westerhof (eds.), *Ageing in Society*, 3rd edition, London: Sage

National Statistics Online (2008) 'Ageing', available at http://statistics.gov.uk, accessed 10.11.08

Nayak, A. (2006) 'Displaced Masculinities: Chavs, Youth and Class in the Post Industrial City', *Sociology*, 40: 813–31

Neugarten, B.L. (1968) 'Adult Personality: Towards a Psychology of the Lifecycle', in B. L. Neugarten (ed.), *Middle Age and Aging: A Reader in Social Psychology*, Chicago: University of Chicago Press

Neugarten, B. L. and Datan, N. (1974) *The Middle Years*, New York: Basic Books

Neugarten, B. L and Neugarten, D. L. (1986) 'Changing Meanings of Age in the Aging Society', in A. Pifer and P. Bronte (eds.), *Our Aging Society: Paradox and Promise*, New York: Norton

Newton, T. (2003) 'Truly Embodied Sociology: Marrying the Social and the Biological', *The Sociological Review*, 51(1): 20–42

Nie, N. H., Sunshine, H. and Erbring, L. (2002) 'Internet Use, Interpersonal Relations and Sociability: A Time Diary Study', in B. Wellman and C. Haythornwaite (eds.), *The Internet in Everyday Life*, Malden, MA: Blackwell

Nisbett, R. E., Kaiping, C., Incheol, and Norenzaan, Ara. (2001) 'Culture and Systems of Thought: Holistic versus Analytic Cognition', *Psychological Review*: 108: 291–310

Novak, T. (2002) 'Rich Children, Poor Children' in B. Goldson, M. Lavalette and J. McKechnie (eds.), *Children, Welfare and the State*, London: Sage

Nyiti, R. M. (1982) 'The Validity of Cultural Differences Explanations for Cross Cultural Variation in the Rate of Piagetian Development', in D. A. Wagner and H. W. Stevenson (eds.), *Cultural Perspectives on Child Development*, San Francisco: Freeman

O'Connor, K. and Chamberlain, K. (1996) 'Dimensions of Life Meaning: A Qualitative Investigation at Mid-Life', *British Journal of Psychology*, 87: 461–77

O'Connor, P. (1999) 'Women's Friendships in a Post Modern World', in R. G. Adams and G. Allan (eds.), *Placing Friendship in a Context*, Cambridge: Cambridge University Press

O'Gorman, S. (1998) 'Death and Dying in Contemporary Society: An Evaluation of Current Attitudes', *Journal of Advanced Nursing*, 27: 1127–35

O'Neill, C., Jamison, J., McCulloch, D. and Smith, D. (2001) 'Age Related Macular Degeneration: Cost of Illness Issues', *Drugs and Aging*, 18: 233–41

Office for National Statistics (2004) *Geographic Inequalities in Life Expectancy Persists across the United Kingdom* [pdf document], www.statististics.gov.uk/pdfdir/lifexp1003pdf, accessed 11.09.08

Office for National Statistics (2008) *Life Expectancy: Life Expectancy Continues to Rise*, available from www.statistics.gov.uk/cci/nugget.asp?Id=68, accessed 20.11.2008

Office for National Statistics (2009) *Population Estimates*, www.statistics.gov.uk/cci/nugget.asp?ID=6, accessed 24.11.2009

Oller, D.K. and Eilers, R. E. (1988) 'The Role of Audition in Infant Babbling', *Child Development*, 59: 441–9

Olliner, S. B. and Olliner, O. M. (1988) *The Altruistic Personality: Rescuers of Jews in Nazi Germany*, New York: Macmillan

Opie, I. and Opie, P. (1959) *The Language and Lore of Schoolchildren*, Oxford: Oxford University Press

Opie, I. and Opie, P. (1969) *Children's Games in Street and Playground*, Oxford: Oxford University Press

Orcutt, B.A. (1977) 'Stress in Family Interaction When a Member is Dying', in E. R. Prichard, J. Collard, B. Arcuth, A. Kutscher, I. Suland and H. Lefkoutz (eds.), *Social Work with the Dying Patient and Family*, London

Orrange, R. (2007) *Work, Family and Leisure: Uncertainty in A Risk Society*, Lanham, MD: Rowman and Littlefield

Osborne, H. (2008) 'Recession to Hit Young Adults Hardest', *The Guardian*, 20.10.2008

Osgerby, B. (2004) *Youth Media*, London: Routledge

Oswald, J. and Blanchflower, D. (2008) 'Is Well-Being U Shaped Over the Life Cycle?' *Social Science and Medicine*, 66(6): 1733–49

Owen, C. (2007) 'Statistics: The Mixed Category in Census 2001', in J. Mai Sims (ed.), *Mixed Heritage – Identity, Policy and Practice*, London: Runymede

Owen, D. (2006) 'Demographic Profile and Social Cohesion of Minority Ethnic Communities in England and Wales', *Journal of Community, Work and Family*, 9(3): 251–72

Owens, A. and Randhawa, G. (2004) '"It's Different from My Culture; They're Very Different": Providing Culturally Competent Palliative Care for South Asian People in the UK', *Health and Social Care in the Community*, 12(5): 414–21

Owusu-Bempah, J. and Howitt, D. (2000) *Psychology beyond Western Perspectives*, Leicester: BPS Books

Pahl, J. (1989) *Money and Marriage*, Basingstoke: Macmillan

Pahl, J. (2000) 'Our Changing Lives', in D. Dench (ed.), *Grandmothers of the Revolution*, London: HERA Trust with Institute of Community Studies

Pahl, R. and Pevalin, D. J. (2005) 'Between Family and Friends: A Longitudinal Analysis of Friendship Choice', *The British Journal of Sociology*, 56(3): 433–50

Pahl, R. and Spencer, L. (1996) 'The Politics of Friendship', *Renewal*, 5: 100–7

Pahl, R. and Spencer, L. (2004) 'Personal Communities: Not Simply Families of "Fate" or "Choice"', *Current Sociology,* 52(2): 199–221

Park, A., Curtice, J., Thomson, K., Jarvis, L. and Bromley, C. (2001) *British Social Attitudes: The 18th Report*, London: Sage

Parkes, C. M. (1972) *Bereavement: Studies of Grief in Adult Life*, London: Tavistock

Parkes, C. M. (1988) *Facing Death*, Cambridge: National Extension College

Parsons, T. (1942) 'Age and Sex in the Social Structure of the United States', *American Sociological Review*, 7(5): 604–16

Parsons, T. and Bales, R. (eds.) (1951) *Family, Socialization and the Interaction Process*, New York: Free Press

Partington, E., Partington, S., Fishwick, L. and Allin, L. (2005) 'Mid-Life Nuances and Negotiations: Narrative Maps and the Social Construction of Mid-Life in Sport and Physical Activity', *Sport, Education and Society*, 10(1): 85–99

Pavlov, I. P. (1927) *Conditioned Reflexes*, Oxford: Oxford University Press

Pearson, J. D., Morrell, C. H., Gordon-Salant, S., et al. (1995) 'Gender Differences in a Longitudinal Study of Age-Associated Hearing Loss', *Journal of the Acoustical Society of America*, 7: 1197–205

Peng, K. and Nisbett, E. (1999) 'Culture, Dialectics and Reasoning about Contradiction', *American Psychologist*, 54: 741–54

Penninx, B. W. J. H., van Tilburg, T., Boeke, A. J. P., Deeg, J. H., Kriegsman, D. M. W. and van Eijk, T. M. (1998) 'Effects of Social Support and Coping Resources on Depressive Symptoms: Different for Various Chronic Diseases', *Health Psychology*, 17: 51–558

Peters, A. and Liefbroer, A. C. (1997) 'Beyond Marital Status: Partner History and Wellbeing in Old Age', *Journal of Marriage and the Family*, 59: 687–99

Petitto, L. A. and Marentette, P. F. (1991) 'Babbling in the Manual Mode: Evidence for the Ontogeny of Language', *Science*, 251: 1483–96

Phillipson, C. (1997) 'Social Relationships in Later Life: A Review of the Research Literature', *International Journal of Geriatric Psychiatry*, 12: 505–12

Phillipson, C., Leach, R., Money, A. and Biggs, S. (2008) 'Social and Cultural Constructions of Ageing: The Case of the Baby Boomers', *Sociological Research Online*, 13(3), www.socresonline.org.uk/13/3/5/.html, accessed 14.04.09

Philp, I. (2008) 'Late Life Ageing', in M. Davies (ed.), *The Blackwell Companion to Social Work*, 3rd edition, Oxford: Blackwell

Piaget, J. (1926) The *Language and Thought of the Child*, New York: Harcourt, Brace and World

Piaget, J. (1932/1965) *The Moral Development of the Child*, New York: Free Press

Piaget, J. (1964) 'Development and Learning', in R. E. Ripple and V. N. Rockcastle (eds.), *Piaget Rediscovered: Conference in Cognitive Studies and Curriculum Development*, Ithaca, NY: Cornell University Press and University of California Press

Pilcher, J. (1994a) 'Mannheim's Sociology of Generations: An Undervalued Legacy', *The British Journal Of Sociology*, 45(3): 481–95

Pilcher, J. (1994b) *Age and Generation in Modern Britain*, Oxford: Oxford University Press

Pillemer, D. B., Ivcevic, Z. and Gooze, R. A. (2007) 'Self Esteem Memories: Feeling Good about Achievement Success, Feeling Bad about Relationship Distress', *Personality and Social Psychology Bulletin*, 33(9): 1292–305

Pinchbeck, I. and Hewitt, M. (1973) *Children in English Society, vol. II*, London: Panther

Pinker, S. (1994) *The Language Instinct: The New Science of Language and Mind*, Harmondsworth: Penguin

Platt, J. (1989) 'The Contribution of Social Science', in M. Loney (ed.), *The State or the Market: Politics and Welfare in Contemporary Britain*, London: Sage

Platt, L. (2007) 'Child Poverty, Employment and Ethnicity in the UK: The Role and Limitations of Policy', *European Societies*, 9(2): 175–99

Pollock, I. (2008) 'The State Pension Turns 100', *BBC News Online*, 31.07.2008

Pooley, C. J., Turnbull, J. and Adams, M. (2005) '" . . . Everywhere She Went I Had to Tag along Beside Her": Family, Life Course and Mobility in England since the 1940s', *History of the Family*, 10: 119–36

Postman, N. (1983) *The Disappearance of Childhood*, London: W. H. Allen

Prendergast, S. (1995) 'The Spaces of Childhood: Psyche, Soma and the Social Existence: Menstruation and Embodiment at Adolescence', in J. Brannen and M. O'Brien (eds.), *Childhood and Parenthood*, London: London Institute of Education

The President's Council on Bioethics (2005) *Taking Care: Ethical Caregiving in our Aging Society*, www.bioethics.gov, Sept. 2005

Press Association (2009) 'Life Meaningless for Young Adults', *The Guardian*, 05.01.2009

Price, D. (2006) 'The Poverty of Older People in the UK', *Journal of Social Work Practice*, 20(3): 251–66

Price, D. and Ginn, J. (2006) 'The Future of Inequalities in Retirement Income, in J. A. Vincent., C. R. Phillipson and M. Downs (eds.), *The Futures of Old Age*, London: Sage

Priestly, M. (2003) *Disability: A Life Course Approach*, Cambridge: Polity Press

Prigerson, H. G., Shear, M. K. and Jacobs, S. C. (1999) 'Consensus Criteria for Traumatic Grief: A Preliminary Empirical Test', *British Journal of Psychiatry*, 174: 67–74

Pullinger, J. and Summerfield, C. (eds.) (1997) *Social Focus on Families*, London: Office for National Statistics

Punch, S. (2005) 'The Generationing of Power: A Comparison of Child–Parent and Sibling Relations in Scotland', *Sociological Studies of Children and Youth*, 10:169–88

Putnam, R.D. (2000) *Bowling Alone: The Collapse and Revival of American Community*, New York: Simon and Schuster

Qvortrup, J. (1997) 'A Voice for Children in Statistical and Social Accounting: A Plea for Children to be Heard', in A. James and A. Prout (eds.), *Constructing and Reconstructing Children*, London: RoutledgeFalmer

Qvortrup, J. (2002) 'Sociology of Childhood: Conceptual Liberation of Children', in F. Mouritsen and J. Qvortrup (eds.), *Childhood and Children's Cultures*, Esbjerg, Denmark: University Press of Southern Denmark

Ramesh, R. (2010) 'Half of Black People Aged 16–24 Without a Job as Recession Hits Hard', *The Guardian*, 23.01.2010

Rando, T. A. (1986) *Parental Loss of a Child*, Champaign, IL: Research

Rani, A. (2007) *BBC Asian Network*, 8 January

Reay, D. (2005) 'Doing the Dirty Work of Social Class? Mothers' Work in Support of their Children's Schooling', in M. Glucksmann, L. Pettinger and J. West (eds.), *A New Sociology of Work*, Oxford: Blackwell

Reibstein, J. and Richards, M. (1992) *Sexual Arrangements: Marriage and Affairs*, London: Heinemann

Renold, E. (2002) 'Presumed Innocence: Hetero(sexual), Heterosexist and Homophobic Harassment amongst Primary School Boys and Girls', *Childhood*, 9: 415–34

Rest, J, R. (1979) *Development in Judging Moral Issues*, Minneapolis: University Of Minnesota Press

Rest, J. R., Narvaez, D. B., Murel, J. and Thoma, S. J. (1999) *Postconventional Moral Thinking: A Neo Kohlbergian Approach*, Mahwah, NJ: Erlbaum

Reynolds, J. (2006) 'Patterns in the Telling: Women's Intimate Relationships with Men', *Sociological Research Online*, 11(3), www.socresonline.org.uk/11/3/reynolds.htm

Rice, C. L. and Cunningham, D.A. (2002) 'Aging of the Neuromuscular System: Influences of Gender and Physical Activity', in R. J. Shephard (ed.), *Gender, Physical Activity and Aging*, Boca Raton, FL: CRC Press

Rich, B. (2003) 'Reflections on the Social Construction of Death', *Journal of Legal Medicine*, 24(2): 217–26

Richards, A., Acree, T. and Folkman, S. (1999) 'Spiritual Aspects of Loss amongst Partners of Men with AIDS: Post Bereavement Follow Up', *Death Studies*, 23: 10–207

Richards, M., Hardy, R. and Wadsworth, M.E. J. (2003) 'Does Active Leisure Protect Cognition? Evidence from a National Birth Cohort', *Social Science and Medicine*, 56: 785–982

Richardson, A. and Budd, T. (2003) *Alcohol, Crime and Disorder: A Study of Young Adults*, Home Office Research Study, 263, London: Home Office

Riches, G. and Dawson, P. (2000) *An Intimate Loneliness: Supporting Bereaved Parents and Siblings*, Buckingham: Open University Press

Risch, N., Herrell, R., Lehner, T. et al.(2009) 'Interaction between the Serotonin Transporter Gene (5–HTTLPR), Stressful Life Events and Risk of Depression: A Meta-Analysis', *JAMA*, 310(23): 2462–71

Roberts, K. (1996) 'Great Britain: Socioeconomic Polarisation and the Implications for Leisure', in C. Critcher, P. Bramham and A. Tomlinson (eds.), *Sociology of Leisure: A Reader*, London: E. and F. N. Spon

Roberts, K. (1997) 'Is There an Emerging British Underclass? The Evidence from Youth Research', in R. MacDonald (ed.), *Youth, The 'Underclass' and Social Exclusion*, London: Routledge

Roberts, P. and Newton, P. M. (1987) 'Levinsonian Studies of Women's Adult Development', *Psychology and Aging*, 2: 154–63

Robertson, R. (1992) *Globalization, Social Theory and Global Culture*, London: Sage

Robine, J. M., Michel, J. P. and Herrmann, F.R. (2007) 'Who Will Care for the Eldest People in our Society?' *British Medical Journal*, 334 (7593, March 2008): 570–1

Robinson, L. (2007) *Cross-Cultural Child Development for Social Workers: An Introduction*, Basingstoke: Palgrave

Roche, J., Tucker, S., Thomson, R. and Flynn, R. (eds.) (2004) *Youth in Society*, 2nd edition, London: Sage and Oxford University Press

Rokach, A., Matalon, R., Safaroz, A. and Bercovitch, M. (2007) 'The Loneliness Experience of the Dying and Those Who Care for Them', *Palliative and Supportive Care*, 5: 153–9

Rose, H., Rose, S. (and Jencks, C.) (eds.) (2000) *Alas Poor Darwin: Arguments against Evolutionary Psychology*, London: Jonathan Cape

Rose, M. (2003) 'Good Deal Bad Deal? Job Satisfaction in Occupations', *Work, Employment and Society*, 17(3): 503–30

Rose, N. (1991) *Governing the Soul*, London: Routledge

Roseneil, S. (2006) 'On Not Living with a Partner: Unpicking Coupledom and Cohabitation', *Sociological Research Online*, 11(3), www.socresonline.org.uk/11/3/roseneil.html

Rosier, K. B. and Kinney, D. A. (2005) 'Introduction to Volume 2: Historical and Contemporary Pressures on Children's Freedom', *Sociological Studies of Children and Youth*, 11: 1–20

Rosow, I. (1985) 'Status and Role Change through the Life Cycle', in R. H. Binstock and E. Shanas (eds.), *Handbook of Aging and the Social Sciences*, 2nd edition, New York: Van Nostrand

Rossi, A. S. and Rossi, P.H. (1990) *Of Human Bonding: Parent–Child Relations across the Life Course*, New York: de Gruyter

Rothaupt, W. and Becker, K. (2007) 'A Literature Review of Western Bereavement Theory: From Decathecting to Continuing Bonds', *The Family Journal: Counselling for Couples and Families*, 15(1): 6–15

Rutter, M. (1995) 'Clinical Implications of Attachment Concepts: Retrospect and Prospect', *Journal of Child Psychology and Psychiatry and Allied Disciplines*, 36(4): 549–71

Rutter, M. and the English and Romanian Adoptees Study Team (1988) 'Developmental Catch-Up and Deficit Following Adoption after Severe Early Global Privation', *Journal of Child Psychology and Psychiatry*, 39: 465–76

Rymer, R. (1994) *Genie: A Scientific Tragedy*, New York: HarperCollins

Sacker, A. and Cable, N. (2005) 'Do Adolescent Leisure-Time Activities Foster Health and Well-Being in Adulthood? Evidence from Two British Birth Cohorts', *European Journal of Public Health*, 16(3): 331–5

Salthouse, T. A. (1984) 'The Skill of Typing', *Scientific American*, 250: 128–35

Santrock, J. (2009) *Life Span Development*, 12th edition, Boston, MA: McGraw Hill

Sapolsky, R. M. (2000) 'The Trouble with Testosterone: Will Boys Just Be Boys?' in M. S. Kimmel (ed.), *The Gendered Society Reader*, Oxford: Oxford University Press

Savage, M. (2009) 'Baby Boom Drives British Population to Record High', *The Independent*, 28.08.09

Schaie, K. W. (1983a) 'What We Can Learn from the Longitudinal Study of Adult Psychological Development', in K. W. Schaie (ed.), *Longitudinal Studies of Adult Psychological Development*, New York: Guildford

Schaie, K. W. (1983b) 'The Seattle Longitudinal Study: A Twenty One Year Exploration of Psychometric Intelligence in Adulthood', in K.W. Schaie (ed.), *Longitudinal Studies of Adult Psychological Development*, New York: Guildford

Schaie, K. W. (1989) 'The Hazards of Cognitive Aging' *The Gerontologist*, 29: 484–93

Schaie, K. W. (1996) *Intellectual Development in Adulthood: The Seattle Longitudinal Study*, New York: Cambridge University Press

Schaie, K. W. and Willis, S. L. (2002) *Adult Development and Ageing*, 5th edition, New York: Prentice Hall

Scheper Hughes, N. (1992) *Death Without Weeping*, Berkeley: University of California Press

Schor, J. (2004) *Born to Buy*, New York: Scribners

Schwartz, B. (2004a) *The Paradox of Choice: Why More is Less*, New York: Harper Collins

Schwartz, B. (2004b) 'The Tyranny of Choice', *The Chronicle of Higher Education*, 50(2): B6, http://chronicle.com/weekly/v50/i20/20b00601.thm

Scott, N. R. (2000) 'Death of a Salesman, Japanese Style: The Social Epidemiology of Karoshi', paper presented at the American Sociological Association Conference, Washington, DC, 2000

Seale, C. (1990) 'Heroic Death', *Sociology*, 29(4): 597–693

Seale, C. (1998) *Constructing Death: The Sociology of Death and Dying*, Cambridge: Cambridge University Press

Segal, D. L., Coolidge, F. L. and Mizuno, H. (2007) 'Defence Mechanism Differences between Younger and Older Adults: A Cross-Sectional Investigation', *Aging and Mental Health*, 11(4): 415–22

Self, A. (ed.) (2008) *Social Trends No 38: Office for National Statistics*, Hampshire: Palgrave Macmillan

Seligman, M. (1975) *Helplessness: On Depression, Development and Death*, San Francisco: Freeman

Settersen, R. A. (2009) '"It Takes Two To Tango": The Uneasy Dance between Life-Course Sociology and Life Span Psychology', *Advances in Life Course Research*, 14(12): 74–81

Shepherd, J. (2009a) 'White Middle Class Families Dominate Top University Places', *The Guardian*, 03.02.09

Shepherd, J. (2009b) 'Universities Don't Like Common People Do They?' *The Guardian* 03.02.09

Shepherd, J. (2009c) 'Boom in Use of Private Tutors amongst State School Pupils', *The Guardian*, 11.06.2009

Shepherd, J. (2009d) 'The Grade Class: Private Pupils Widen Lead over State Schools', *The Guardian*, 21.08.09

Shildrick, T. (2003) 'Youth Culture, Subculture and the Importance of Neighbourhood', *Young: The Nordic Journal of Youth Research*, 14(1): 61–74

Shildrick, T. and MacDonald, R. (2006) 'In Defence of Subculture: Young People, Leisure and Social Divisions', *Journal of Youth Studies*, 9(2): 125–40

Shimamura, A. P., Berry, J. M., Mangels, J. A., Rusting, C. L. and Jurica, P. J. (1995) 'Memory and Cognitive Abilities in University Professors – Evidence for Successful Aging', *Psychological Science*, 6(5): 271–7

Shore, G. (1999) 'Soldiering On: An Exploration into Women's Perceptions and Experiences of Menopause', *Feminism and Psychology*, 9(2): 168–80

Siegal, M. (1991) *Knowing Children: Experiments in Conversation and Cognition*, Mahwah, NJ: Erlbaum

Siegel, J. M., Yancey, A. K., Aneshensel, C. S. and Schuler, R. (1999) 'Body Image, Perceived Pubertal Timing and Adolescent Mental Health', *Journal of Adolescent Health*, 25: 155–65

Siegler, R., Deloache, J. and Eisenberg, N. (2006) *How Children Develop*, 2nd edition, New York: Worth

Simonton, D. K. (1988) 'Career Paths and Creative Lives: A Theoretical Perspective on Late Life Potential', in C. E. Adams-Price (ed.), *Creativity and Successful Aging*, New York: Springer

Simonton, D. K. (1991) 'The Swan Song Phenomenon: Last Work Effects for 172 Classical Composers', *Psychology and Aging*, 4: 42–7

Simpson, R. (2006) 'The Intimate Relationships of Contemporary Spinsters', *Sociological Research Online*, 11(3), www.socresonline.org.uk/11/3/simpson.html

Sinclair, D. C. and Dangerfield, P. (1998) *Human Growth after Birth*, New York: Oxford University Press

Sinnott, J. D. (1998) *The Development of Logic in Adulthood: Postformal Thought and its Applications*, New York: Plenum Press

Sisk, C. and Zehr, J. (2005) 'Pubertal Hormones Organize the Adolescent Brain and Behaviour', *Frontiers in Neuroendocrinology*, 26: 163–74

Skinner, B. F. (1953) *Science and Human Behaviour*, New York: Macmillan

Small, S. and Solomos, J. (2007) 'Race, Immigration and Politics: Changing Policy Agendas and Conceptual Paradigms 1940s–2000s', *International Journal of Comparative Sociology*, 47(3–4): 35–257

Smart, C. (2007) 'Same Sex Couples and Marriage: Negotiating Relational Landscapes with Families and Friends', *The Sociological Review*, 55(4): 671–86

Smart, C., Neale, B. and Wade, A (2001) *The Changing Experience of Childhood: Families and Divorce*, Cambridge: Polity Press

Smetana, J. G., Campione-Barr, N. and Metzger, A. (2006) 'Adolescent Development in Interpersonal and Societal Contexts', *Annual Review of Psychology*, 52: 83–110

Smith, J. (1999) 'The Power of One', *The Guardian*, 26.04.1999

Smith, J. and Baltes, P. B. (1993) 'Differential Psychological Aging. Profiles of the Old and the Very Old', *Ageing and Society*, 13: 551–87

Snarey, C. (1995) 'Cross Cultural Universality of Social–Moral Development: A Critical Review of Kohlbergian Research', *Psychological Bulletin*, 97, 202–32

Sneed, J., Schwartz, S. and Cross, W. (2006) 'A Multicultural Critique of Identity Status Theory and Research: A Call for Integration', *Identity*, 6: 61–84

Social Trends [various years] *Social Trends*, London: HMSO, also available at www.Statistics.co.uk

Song, M. (2007) 'The Diversity of the Mixed Race Population in Britain', in J. Mai Sims (ed.), *Mixed Heritage: Identity, Policy and Practice*, London: Runnymede

Sonuga-Barke, E. (2010) 'Editorial: "It's The Environment Stupid": On Epigenetics, Programming and Plasticity in Child Mental Health', *Journal of Child Psychology and Psychiatry*, 51(2): 113–15

Sorce, J. F., Emde, R. N., Campos, J. and Klinnert, N. (1985) 'Maternal Emotional Signalling: Its Effect On the Visual Cliff Behaviour of One-Year-Olds', *Developmental Psychology*, 21(1): 195–200

Speece, M. W. and Brent, S.B. (1987) 'Irreversibility, Non Functionality and Universality: Children's Understandings of Three Components of a Death

Concept', in J. E. Showalter (ed.), *Children and Death: Perspectives from Birth through Adolescence*, New York: Praeger

Stack, N. and McKechnie, J. (2002) 'Working Children', in B. Goldson., M. Lavalette and J. McKechnie (eds.), *Children, Welfare and The State*, London: Sage

Stainton Rogers, W. (2001) 'Constructing Childhood, Constructing Child Concern', in P. Foley, J. Roche and S. Tucker (eds.), *Children in Society: Contemporary Theory, Policy and Practice*, Basingstoke: Palgrave / Open University Press

Stainton Rogers, W. and Stainton Rogers, R. (1992) *Stories of Childhood*, London: Harvester Wheatsheaf

Stainton Rogers, W., Stainton Rogers, R., Vyrost, J. and Lovas, L. (2004) 'World's Apart: Young People's Aspirations in a Changing Europe', in J. Roche, S. Tucker, R. Thomson and R. Flynn (eds.), *Youth in Society*, 2nd edition, London: Sage / Open University Press

Stanley, L. and Wise, S. (2000) 'What's Wrong with Socialisation?' in S. Jackson and S. Scott (eds.), *Gender: A Sociological Reader*, London: Routledge

Staudinger, U. M. and Bluck, S. (2001) 'A View on Midlife Development from a Life-Span Theory', in M. E. Lachman (ed.), *Handbook of Midlife Development*, New York: Wiley

Steele, H. and Steele, M. (1998) 'Attachment and Psychoanalysis: Time for A Reunion', *Social Development*, 7(1): 92–115

Steinberg, L. and Morris, A. (2001) 'Adolescent Development', *Annual Review of Psychology*, 52: 83–110

Stephen, D. E. and Squires, P. (2004) '"They're Still Children and Entitled to be Children": Problematising the Institutionalised Mistrust of Marginalised Youth', *Journal of Youth Studies*, 7(3): 351–69

Sternberg, R. J. (1986) 'A Triangular Theory of Love', *Psychological Review*, 93(2): 119–35

Sternberg, R. J. (2003) *Wisdom, Intelligence and Creativity Synthesised*, New York: Cambridge University Press

Stewart, A. J. and Ostrove, J. N. (1998) 'Women's Personality in Middle Age: Gender, History and Midcourse Corrections', *American Psychologist*, 53: 1185–94

Stewart, A. J. and Vandewater, E. (1999) '"If I Had to Do It Over Again . . .": Midlife Review, Midcourse Corrections and Women's Wellbeing in Midlife', *Journal of Personality and Social Psychology*, 76(2): 270–83

Stewart, S. (2008) 'Parents Defend Assisted Suicide of Paralysed Rugby Player', *The Guardian*, 17.01.2006

Stolley, K. S. and Hill, A. E. (1996) 'Presentations of the Elderly in Textbooks on Marriage and the Family', *Teaching Sociology*, 24(1): 34–45

Strachey, J. (ed.) (1940/1969) *The Standard Edition of the Complete Psychological Works of Sigmund Freud*, London: Hogarth Press

Strausbaugh, J. (2002) *Rock Till You Drop*, London: Verso

Strenger, C. (2009) 'Sosein: Active Self Acceptance in Midlife', *Journal of Humanistic Psychology*, 49(1): 46–65

Streufert, S. A., Pogash, R., Piasecki, M. and Post, G. M (1990) 'Age and Management Team Performance', *Psychology and Aging*, 5: 551–9

Stroebe, M. and Schut, S. (1999) 'The Dual Process for Coping with Bereavement: Rationale and Description', *Death Studies*, 23(3): 197–224

Stuart-Hamilton, I. (2006) *The Psychology of Ageing: An Introduction*, London: Jessica Kingsley

Subbotsky, E. (1993) *The Birth of Personality: The Development of Independent and Moral Behaviour in Preschool Children*, Hove: Harvester Wheatsheaf

Sudberry, J. (2009) *Human Growth and Development: An Introduction for Social Workers*, London: Routledge

Sudnow, D. (1967) *Passing On: The Social Organization of Dying*, Englewood Cliffs, NJ: Prentice Hall

Sugarman, L. (2001) *Life-Span Development Psychology: Frameworks, Accounts and Strategies*, Hove: Psychology Press

Sweeting, H. and Gilhooly, M. (1997) 'Dementia and the Phenomenon of the Social Death', *Sociology of Health and Illness*, 19(1): 93–117

Swensen, C. H., Eskew, R. W. and Kohlepp, K. A. (1981) 'Stage of Family Life Cycle, Ego Development and the Marriage Relationship', *Journal of Marriage and the Family*, 43: 841–85

Tanner, D. and Harris, J. (2006) *Working with Older People*, London: Routledge

Tanner, J. L. (2008) 'Book Review – Varda Konstam, "Emerging and Young Adulthood: Multiple Perspectives, Diverse Narratives", New York: Springer', *Journal of Youth and Adolescence*, 37: 888–91

Taylor, C. (2004) 'Underpinning Knowledge for Child Care Practice: Reconsidering Child Development Theory', *Child and Family Social Work*, 9: 225–35

The President's Council on Bioethics (CoB) (2005) 'Taking Care: Ethical Care Giving in our Aging Society', www.bioethics.gov

Thobaben, M. (2008) 'Elder Abuse Prevention', *Home Health Care Management and Practice*, 20 (Feb.): 194–6

Thompson, J. B. (1995) *The Media and Modernity: A Social Theory of the Media*, Stanford, CA: Stanford University Press

Thomson, T., Holland, R., McGrellis, S., Bell, R., Henderson, S. and Sharpe, S. (2004) 'Inventing Adulthoods: A Biographical Approach to Understanding Youth Citizenship', *The Sociological Review*, 52(2): 218–39

Thorne, B. (1993) *Gender Play*, New Jersey: Rutgers University Press

Thorne, B. (2007) 'Editorial: Crafting the Interdisciplinary Field of Childhood Studies', *Childhood*, 14(2): 14–152

Thornhill, R. and Palmer, C. T. (2000) *A Natural History of Rape: Biological Bases of Sexual Coercion*, Cambridge, MA: MIT Press

Thornton, S. (2002) *Growing Minds*, Basingstoke: Palgrave Macmillan

Thornton, S. (2008) *Understanding Human Development*, Basingstoke: Palgrave: Macmillan

Thurtle, V. (2005) 'Growth and Development', in J. Taylor and M. Woods (eds.), *Early Childhood Studies: An Holistic Introduction*, 2nd edition, London: Hodder Arnold

Timmermans, S. (1999) *Sudden Death and the Myth of CPR*, Philadelphia: Temple University Press

Timonen, V. (2008) *Ageing Societies: A Comparative Introduction*, Maidenhead: Open University Press

Tizard, B. and Phoenix, A. (1993) *Black, White or Mixed Race? Race and Racism in the Lives of Young People of Mixed Parentage*, London: Routledge

Tomlinson, S. (2005) *Education in a Post Welfare Society*, Buckingham: Open University Press

Tour, K (1989) *Ageing in Developing Countries*, Oxford: Oxford University Press

Townsend, P. (2006) 'Policies for the Aged in the 21st Century: More "Structured Dependency" or the Realisation of Human Rights?' *Ageing and Society*, 26(2): 161–79

Townsend, P. and Davidson, P. (1981) *Inequalities in Health: The Black Report*, Harmondsworth: Penguin

Trethewey, A. (2001) 'Reproducing and Resisting the Master Narrative of Decline', *Management Communication Quarterly*, 15(2): 183–226

Triandis, H.C. (1995) *Individualism and Collectivism*, Boulder: Westview Press

Troll, L., Miller, S. and Atchley, R. (1979) *Families in Later Life*, Belmont, CA: Wadsworth

Trotter, J. (2009) 'Ambiguities around Sexuality: An Approach to Understanding Harassment and Bullying of Young People in British Schools', *Journal of LGBT Youth*, 6(1): 7–23

Tulle, E. (2008) 'The Ageing Body and the Ontology of Ageing: Athletic Competence in Later Life', *Body and Society*, 14(3): 1–19

Turnbull, C. (1989) *The Mountain People*, London: Paladin

Uhlenberg, P. (1980) 'Death and the Family', *Journal of Family History*, 5: 313–20

Urry, J. (2000) *Sociology beyond Societies: Mobilities for the Twenty-First Century*, London: Routledge

Vaillant, G.E. (2002) *Aging Well*, Boston: Little Brown

Valentine, C. (2006) 'Academic Constructions of Bereavement', *Mortality*, 11(1): 57–78

Valentine, G. and Sporton, S. (2009) '"How Other People See You, It's Like There's Nothing Inside": The Impact of Processes of Disidentification and Disavowal on Young People's Subjectivities', *Sociology*, 43(4): 735–51

Van den Hoonaard, D. (2007) 'Editorial: Aging and Masculinity: A Topic Whose Time Has Come', *Journal of Aging Studies*, 21: 277–80

Veroff, J., Donovan, E. and Kulka, R.A. (1981) *The Inner American: A Self Portrait from 1957 to 1976*, New York: Basic Books

Victor, C. R. (2000) 'Health Services for Dying People and Their Carers', in D. Dickenson., M. Johnson and S. Katz (eds.), *Death, Dying and Bereavement*, 2nd edition, London: Sage

Vidal, J. (2009) 'Way We Eat Now: Later, Faster and Increasingly in Asian Restaurants', *The Guardian*, 05.01.2009

Vincent, J. (2003) *Old Age*, London: Routledge

Vincent, J. (2006) 'Age and Old Age', in G. Payne (eds.), *Social Divisions*, 2nd edition, Basingstoke: Palgrave

Vincent, J., Phillipson, C. R. and. Downs, M. (eds.) (2006) *The Futures of Old Age*, London: Sage

Vygotsky, L.S. (1978) *Mind in Society*, Cambridge, MA: Harvard University Press

Walker, A. and Foster, L. (2006) 'Ageing and Social Class: An Enduring Relationship', in J. Vincent, C. R. Phillipson and M. Downs (eds.), *The Futures of Old Age*, London: Sage

Walkerdine, V. (2004) 'Developmental Psychology and the Study of Childhood', in M. J. Kehily (ed.), *An Introduction to Childhood Studies*, Maidenhead: McGraw Hill / Open University Press

Walter, C. A. (2003) *Loss of a Life Partner: Narratives of the Bereaved*, New York: Columbia University Press

Walter, T. (1999) *The Revival of Death*, London: Routledge

Walter, T. (2008) 'The Sociology of Death', *Sociology Compass*, 2(1): 317–36

Walter, T., Littlewood, J. and Pickering, M. (1995) 'Death in the News: The Public Invigilation of Private Emotion', *Sociology*, 29(4): 579–96

Waltz, T. (2002) 'Crones, Dirty Old Men, Sex Seniors: Representations of the Sexuality of Older Persons', *Journal of Aging and Identity*, 7(2): 99–112

Ward, L. (2005) 'Flexible Work Rights Failing Middle-Aged Women', *The Guardian*, 19.02.05

Ward, L. (2007) 'Women Bosses Lose Out as Gender Pay Gap Widens in the Boardroom', *The Guardian*, 08.11.2009

Ware, L., Maconachie, M., Williams, M., Chandler, J. and Dodgeon, B. (2007) 'Gender Life Course Transitions from the Nuclear Family in England and Wales 1981–2001', *Sociological Research Online*, 12(4), www.socresonline.org.uk/12/4/6.html

Warner, M. (1994) *Managing Monsters: Six Myths of Our Time,* The Reith Lectures, 1994, London: Vintage

Waterman, A. S. (1985) 'Identity in the Context of Adolescent Psychology', in A. S. Waterman (ed.), *Identity in Adolescence: Progress and Contents,* New Directions for Child Development, 30, San Francisco: Jossey Bass

Watkins, S. (2007) 'The Medicalisation of the Male Menopause in America', *Social History of Medicine*, 20(2): 36–388

Watson, J. (1988/1924) *Behaviourism*, New Brunswick, NJ: Transaction

Watson, J. and Rayner R. (1920) 'Conditioned Emotional Reactions', *Journal of Experimental Psychology*, 3: 1–14

Waxman, B. F. (1991) 'Hatred: The Unacknowledged Dimension in Violence against Disabled People', *Sexuality and Disability*, 9(3): 185–99

Weber, M. (1930) *The Protestant Ethic and The Spirit of Capitalism*, London: Allen and Unwin

Webster, B. (2008) 'Full Throttle to a Dead End For the Middle-Aged on New Motorbikes', *The Times*, 01.01.2008

Webster, S., Simpson, D., MacDonald, R. et al.. (2004) *Poor Transitions: Social Exclusions and Young Adults*, Bristol: Policy Press

Weeks, J., Heaphy, B. and Donovan, C. (2001) *Same Sex Intimacies: Families of Choice and Other Life Experiments*, London: Routledge

Weg, R. B. (1987) 'Sexuality in the Menopause', in D. R. Mischel Jr (ed.), *Menopause: Physiology and Pharmacology*, Chicago: Year Book Medical Publishers

Wells, K. (2005) 'Strange Practices: Children's Discourses on Transgressive Unknowns in Urban Public Space', *Childhood*, 12(4): 495–506

Westerhof, G. J., Barrett, A. E. and Steverink, N. (2003) 'Forever Young: A Comparison of Age Identities in the United States and Germany', *Research on Aging*, 25(4): 367–83

Wetherall, M., Stiven, H. and Potter, J. (1987) 'Unequal Egalitarianism: A Preliminary Study of Discourses Concerning Gender and Employment Opportunities', *British Journal of Social Psychology*, 26: 59–71

Whitbourne, S. (2001) *The Aging Individual: Physical and Psychological Perspectives*, New York: Springer

Whitbourne, S., Neupert, S. D. and Lachman, M. E. (2008) 'Daily Physical Activity: Relation to Everyday Memory in Adulthood', *Journal of Applied Gerontology*, 27(3): 331–49

Widgery, D. (1993) 'Not Going Gently', in D. Dickenson and M. Johnson (eds.), *Death, Dying and Bereavement*, London: Sage

Williams, D. (2005) 'Degree of Compromise', *The Guardian*, 29.10.2005, Rise, P3

Williams, S. and Williams, L. (2005) 'Space Invaders: The Negotiation of Teenage Boundaries through the Mobile Phone', *The Sociological Review*, 53(2): 314–33

Williams, S. J. and Bendelow, G. A. (1998) 'Malignant Bodies: Children's Beliefs about Health, Cancer and Risk ', in S. Nettleton and J. Watson (eds.), *The Body in Everyday Life*, London: Routledge

Willis, P. (1977) *Learning to Labour: How Working Class Kids Get Working Class Jobs*, Farnborough: Saxon House

Willmott, H. (2000) 'Death. So What? Sociology, Sequestration and Emancipation', *The Sociological Review*, 48(4): 649–63

Wilson, A. R. (2007) 'With Friends Like These: The Liberalization of Queer Family Policy', *Critical Social Policy*, 27(1): 50–76

Wilson, G. (2000) *Understanding Old Age: Critical and Global Perspectives*, London: Sage

Wilson, R. (1966) *Forever Feminine*, New York: Pocket Books

Winnicott, D. (1953) 'Transitional Objects and Transitional Phenomena', *International Journal of Psychoanalysis*, 34: 89–97

Wober, M. (1975) *Psychology in Africa*, London: International African Institute

Woodhead, M. (1997) 'Psychology and the Cultural Construction of Children's Needs', in A. James and A. Prout (eds.), *Constructing and Reconstructing Children*, London: RoutledgeFalmer

Woodhead, M. (1999) 'Reconstructing Developmental Psychology – Some First Steps', *Children and Society*, 13: 3–19

Wolff, J. (2009) 'The Art and Science of Evidence About Drugs', *Education Guardian Higher*, 01.12.2009

Wolley, H. (2005) *Inclusion of Disabled Children in Primary School Playgrounds*, London: National Children's Bureau of the Joseph Rowntree Foundation

Worden, W. J. (1991) *Grief Counselling and Grief Therapy*, 2nd edition, London Routledge

Worden, W. J. (1996) *Children and Grief: When a Parent Dies*, New York: Guildford

Wortman, C.B. and Silver, R.C. (1990) 'Successful Mastery of Bereavement and Widowhood: A Life Course Perspective', in P. B. Baltes and M. M. Baltes (eds.), *Successful Ageing*, Cambridge: Cambridge University Press

Wray, S. (2003) 'Women Growing Older: Agency, Ethnicity and Culture', *Sociology*, 37(3): 511–27

Wray, S. (2007) 'Women Making Sense of Midlife: Ethnic and Cultural Diversity', *Journal of Aging Studies*, 21: 31–42

Wright, E. O., Shire, K., Hwang, S. L., Dolan, M. and Baxter, J. (1992) 'The Non-effects of Class in the Gender Division of Labor in the Home: A Comparative Study of Sweden and the United States', *Gender and Society*, 6: 252–82

Wrong, D. (1961) 'The Oversocialized Concept of Man in Modern Sociology', *American Sociological Review*, 26: 183–93

Wyn, J. and Woodman, D. (2007) 'Researching Youth in a Context of Social Change: A Reply to Roberts', *Journal of Youth Studies*, 10(3): 373–81

Wyness, M. (2006) *Childhood and Society: An Introduction to the Sociology of Childhood*, Basingstoke: Palgrave

Yeoman, F. (2006) 'Carers Sought for Baby Charlotte as Parents Part', *The Times*, 17.10.2006

Young, A., Green, L. and Rogers, K. (2008) 'Resilience and Deaf Children: A Literature Review', *Deafness and Education International*, 10(1): 40–55

Zarrit, S H. (1996) 'Continuities and Discontinuities in Very Late Life', in V. l. Bengston (ed.), *Adulthood and Aging: Research on Continuities and Discontinuities*, New York: Springer

Zebrowitz, L. A. and Montepare, J. A. (2000) 'Too Young, Too Old: Stigmatising Adolescents and the Elderly', in T. Heatherton, R. Kleck, J. G. Hull and M. Hebi (eds.), *Stigma*, New York: Guildford Publications

Zeelenberg, M. and Peters, R. (2007) 'A Theory of Regret Regulation 1.0', *Journal of Consumer Psychology*, 17: 3–16

Zelizer, V. (1985) *Pricing the Priceless Child: Changing the Social Value of Children*, New York: Basic Books

Zhao, S. (2006) 'The Internet and the Transformation of the Reality of Everyday Life: Toward a New Analytic Stance in Sociology', *Sociological Inquiry*, 6(4): 458–74

Zinnecker, J. (2001) 'Children in Young and Aging Societies: The Order of Generations and Models of Childhood in Comparative Perspective', in S. L. Hofferth and T. J. Owens (eds.), *Children at The Millennium: Where Have We Come From, Where Are We Going?* Amsterdam and London: Elsevier Science Ltd

Index